The History of the Epic

Palgrave Histories of Literature

Titles include:

Adeline Johns-Putra
THE HISTORY OF THE EPIC

Adam Roberts
THE HISTORY OF SCIENCE FICTION

Forthcoming titles in the series:

Andrew Pepper
THE HISTORY OF CRIME WRITING

Palgrave Histories of Literature
Series Standing Order ISBN 1–4039–1196–7 (hardback)   1-4039-1212-2 **(paperback)**
(*outside North America only*)

You can receive future titles in this series as they are published by placing a standing order. Please contact your bookseller or, in case of difficulty, write to us at the address below with your name and address, the title of the series and the ISBN quoted above.

The History of the Epic

Adeline Johns-Putra

First published 2006 by
PALGRAVE MACMILLAN
Houndmills, Basingstoke, Hampshire RG21 6XS and
175 Fifth Avenue, New York, N.Y. 10010
Companies and representatives throughout the world

PALGRAVE MACMILLAN is the global academic imprint of the Palgrave
Macmillan division of St. Martin's Press, LLC and of Palgrave Macmillan Ltd.
Macmillan® is a registered trademark in the United States, United Kingdom
and other countries. Palgrave is a registered trademark in the European
Union and other countries.

ISBN-13: 978–1–4039–1212–1 hardback
ISBN-10: 1–4039–1212–2 hardback

This book is printed on paper suitable for recycling and made from fully
managed and sustained forest sources.

A catalogue record for this book is available from the British Library.

Library of Congress Cataloging-in-Publication Data
Johns-Putra, Adeline, 1973–
   The history of the epic / Adeline Johns-Putra.
      p.   cm. — (Palgrave histories of literature)
   Includes bibliographical references and index.
   ISBN 1–4039–1212–2 (cloth)
   1. Epic literature—History and criticism.   I. Title.   II. Series.
   PN56.E65J65 2006
   809—dc22   2005056730

10   9   8   7   6   5   4   3   2   1
15   14   13   12   11   10   09   08   07   06

Transferred to Digital Printing 2007

For my mother,
with love and gratitude

Contents

Acknowledgements

The original idea for this book came from a suggestion by Claire Colebrook, who has been an inspirational example. A great deal of this book was written during study leave in 2003–4, which was provided by the University of Exeter and made possible by a grant from the Arts and Humanities Research Board. A version of the Introduction was presented at the Poetics and Linguistics Association in Istanbul in June 2003, travel to which was enabled by the British Academy. A version of Chapter 4 was presented at the British Association for Romantic Studies in Warwick in July 2003, travel to which was enabled by the School of English, University of Exeter.

I have been encouraged and supported throughout by my colleagues at Exeter. Robert Mack read and commented on several chapter drafts; his advice and friendship have been indispensable. I am grateful too to Rick Rylance and Richard Seaford, for their very helpful detailed comments; and to Regenia Gagnier, Bob Lawson-Peebles and Helen Taylor, as well as to Simon Dentith of the University of Gloucestershire and Jacqueline Labbe of the University of Warwick, for help and advice along the way. My colleagues in Cornwall – Marion Gibson and Ella Westland – have been particularly supportive. Thanks too to the students of my Modern Epic module at the University of Exeter in Cornwall in the spring of 2005, whose insights allowed me to make some final revisions and clarifications. However, despite the best efforts and advice of so many who helped me with this book, faults remain, and are entirely my own.

My deepest thanks are expressed in the dedication, but I would also like to record my thanks to my sisters for their support, to Charlie Nicholls for her constant and abiding friendship, and to Nicole Smith, Elizabeth Bartrum, Sandy Mak, Stephanie Ning and Maree Martin for some much-needed time-out.

Introduction: What is the Epic?

This book seeks to describe the history of the epic in Western culture, ending with evocations of the epic in literature and film in the English-speaking world. In order to do so, it must first ask the obvious question: What is the epic? Unfortunately, however, there is no equally obvious answer. Ours is an age in which 'epic' describes not just the likes of the *Odyssey* and *Paradise Lost*, but a bewildering range of texts, in the loosest sense of the word. The label 'epic' is applied today to contemporary novels, Hollywood blockbusters and rock songs, as well as 'real-life' events: sporting contests, corporate takeovers, political elections, court cases.[1] At the beginning of the twenty-first century, the epic, or at least the label 'epic', is ubiquitous. How, then, do we deal with this ubiquity? We could presume that the label has become useless in its frequency, merely an overexposed and imprecise adjective suggesting size and significance. Or, intrigued by the polysemy of the word, we could look more closely at it, for it reveals two things. It suggests a modern or, more accurately, postmodern fascination with the epic, and a need to invoke it in all kinds of texts and situations. It also suggests an accumulation of definitions, a piling on, as it were, of different meanings from different points in the epic's history. Thus, the epic's efflorescence today is, first, an intriguing moment in its development and, second, a reflection of that development; that is, a reflection of past moments. Perhaps the best way to answer the question is to investigate fully the plurality of responses, both past and present. In other words, rather than searching for a single definition of the epic, it is more fruitful to move beyond definitions. Instead of throwing up our hands in despair over the epic's apparent indeterminacy, we could attempt to engage with that very indeterminacy.

It is easy to think that the problems of defining the epic lie primarily with the epic itself. After all, a simple definition of the epic would have to account

1

for the endless variations displayed by all the texts currently considered epic, even if we restrict ourselves to the literary canon. Yet, to attempt a detailed definition, adding as many features as possible to the list, is to render it unwieldy and, what is more, potentially self-contradictory. For example, the simple definition of the epic as a long heroic and nationalistic poem would include Virgil's *Aeneid* but exclude Dante's *Divina Commedia*, while the reference to heroism would subsume the Homeric epics but might create problems for *Paradise Lost*. Inversely, to scale down the definition and to work with just one or two prerequisites is to cease to have a definition at all. For example, to define the epic simply as a long poem is to rely on a single and therefore useless criterion, since length is a feature of many works of literature not considered to be epics. The fact is that so many of the characteristics we associate with epic – great length, awe-inspiring heroism, nationalism – are traits that the form has displayed at some times but not at others. The fact is that epic itself is changeful and indeterminate.

To understand fully the indeterminacy of the epic, we must look beyond the epic, to the issue of genre. This is because the question of what the epic is, and indeed the very validity of that question, is based on larger problems about genre and how it functions. The difficulties faced in defining the epic are not peculiar to the epic at all, but are to be faced in defining any genre, and in defining genre itself.

Genre has long been conceived as a hierarchical system, a taxonomy of categories, a collection of boxes to be filled with texts. Such a view is based – very loosely, as Gérard Genette has shown – on the writings of Plato and Aristotle.[2] Plato stipulated that a work of art can be represented in one of just three ways, while Aristotle's *Poetics* discusses literature according to whether it is epic or tragic. When genre theory arose in earnest in the Renaissance critics, first in Italy and then in France and England, these ideas enabled a tripartite scheme of literary divisions – epic, tragedy and comic – with the possibility of various subdivisions.[3] More significantly, they facilitated the interpretation of genres as fixed and separate literary forms, which prevailed at least until the end of the neoclassical age. With the onset of Romanticism, though, generic rules, with their implications of generic purity and uniformity, were largely rejected. Yet even the Romantics, who challenged so many of the hierarchies and taxonomies of their predecessors, retained a pseudo-Platonic-Aristotelian sense of generic intrinsicality, the idea that a genre could be distilled to its essence.[4] As Jean-Marie Schaeffer has shown, this meant that the Romantics preserved the notion of fixed and timeless definitions for given genres, as well as maintained a simplistic model of texts 'belonging to' these ideal genres.[5]

These two closely related assumptions – that a given genre is a fixed entity and that it offers a set of criteria for texts – have, as we have seen, their share of inconsistencies. For one thing, those criteria are not as easily applied in practice. More worrying than the issue of applicability, however, is the question of authority. The existence of unchangeable generic criteria smacks of prescriptivism, of the suffocation of authorial (or textual) autonomy and the penalisation of originality. Generic criteria would seem, in other words, to be inimical to literature itself. To conceive of genre as fixed criteria is to do the notion of genre itself a disservice, opening it up to charges of pernicious narrow-mindedness. And such charges have indeed been made, most recently by Jacques Derrida, who describes what he calls the 'law of genre' thus: 'as soon as genre announces **itself**, one must respect a norm, one must not cross a line of demarcation, one must not risk impurity, anomaly or monstrosity'.[6] For Derrida, genre imposes limits, but literature necessarily takes place just outside these limits; thus genre 'put[s] to death the very thing that it engenders'.[7]

Derrida's criticism, however, is a little late in coming, as it fails to consider that the idea of genres as fixed criteria became increasingly outmoded in the twentieth century. At the beginning of the twenty-first century, it is no longer possible, or desirable, in conducting a genre-based analysis such as this to ignore developments in genre studies of the last half of the previous century. Such recent developments have their basis in the writings of European formalists and structuralists in the early twentieth century. Though distinct in many ways, formalist and structuralist attitudes to genre are properly discussed together, since, as David Duff helpfully notes, 'the distinction between the two methodologies is especially hard to preserve in the area of genre theory, which almost by definition partakes of both'.[8]

One important conceptual breakthrough owed to formalism and structuralism is the application of Saussurean linguistics to genre studies. Saussure's notion of *langue* and *parole* – *langue* referring to the system of language and *parole* to the individual utterance – is easily adaptable to the relationship between genre and text. Structuralist genre studies, such as the work of Tzvetan Todorov, foreground the way an agreed system of signs enables communication to take place.[9] It reminds us, in other words, that genre provides a shared set of rules to facilitate both the production and the interpretation of a given text, just as an agreed linguistic system of signs enables communication to take place. Another significant development in this direction is the work of E. D. Hirsch, which presents genre as a kind of middle term between *langue* and *parole*. For Hirsch, language contains numerous types of utterances; genre is a type of utterance and is therefore

contained by *langue* but governs the interpretation of *parole*.[10] The difference
between Hirsch and Todorov is not a profoundly conceptual one – Hirsch
simply preserves the idea of *langue* as an overriding language system rather
than using it as a convenient analogy for genre. What both approaches
share are the emphasis on genre as an aid to communication and the
reminder that there can be no understanding of a text without generic
expectations to serve as a foundation for that understanding. In other
words, genre, rather than establishing a set of rules, provides a theory of
what a text is, for both authors and readers, which forms the basis for a
contract between them.

Another important contribution made by Russian formalism to the study
of genre is the notion of the evolutionary or, more accurately, revolutionary
nature of literature and hence of genre. It must be noted, however, that it
was the European Romantics who first emphasised the importance of historicity to studies of genre – it was Hegel, for example, who pointed out that
literature, and genres with it, was capable of evolution. Yet, Hegel's theory
of generic evolution is also a theory of generic organicism; it is about texts
becoming, developing into, achieving generic fulfilment.[11] It therefore
preserves generic intrinsicality. Generic revolution, on the other hand, foregrounds change as fundamental to genre and precludes generic intrinsicality. In the twentieth century, historicist theories of genre have vacillated
between these evolutionist (or organicist) and revolutionist concepts of
genre. To the former belongs Northrop Frye's highly stylised paradigm of
generic development as a complex cycle of stages.[12] Also evolutionist,
though less extreme, is Alastair Fowler's hypothesis that genres live and
decay over a brief period of time, which presupposes relatively coherent and
stable genres – after all, for Fowler, incoherence and instability are what
bring about generic death.[13] More flexible and revolutionist are the recent
writings of Hans Robert Jauss and Ralph Cohen, who describe genres as
open, unpredictable and constantly changing. For Jauss, 'the conflict
between the authoritative generic norm and the immanent poetics [of a text]
can become precisely the motive force that keeps the historical process of
the genre moving'.[14] In other words, generic change is propelled by the
disparity between conservative canonical forces and a radical text, and is thus
a matter of revolution rather than evolution. According to Cohen:

> [Classifications] are historical assumptions constructed by authors, audi-
> ences, and critics in order to serve communicative and aesthetic purposes.
> Such groupings are always in terms of distinctions and interrelations, and
> they form a system or community of genres. The purposes they serve are

social and aesthetic. Groupings arise at particular historical moments, and as they include more and more members, they are subject to repeated redefinitions or abandonment.[15]

Significantly, this is not so very different from Derrida's insistence that literature and genre occur at the very moment of the collapse of generic boundaries – what Derrida labels 'degenerescence'.[16] What is important is that this historicist and revolutionist genre theory, instead of forbidding experimentation as inimical to genre, recognises it as central to genre. In other words, the approaches taken by Jauss and Cohen enable the idea that genre, far from being fixed, is itself a *process*.

These conceptions of genre – as *contract* and as *process* – challenge the idea that genre and text relate to each other simply as whole and part. To think of genre as theory, for example, is to think of the utterance or text (*parole*) as received and understood by referring to past utterances or texts of that type or genre (*langue*). Each of these utterances or texts does not necessarily possess identical characteristics to every other; they simply resemble each other in a chain. The analogy most usefully invoked, then, is that of Wittgenstein's 'family resemblances', according to which members of a group can display any number of a given set of features.[17] The idea of genre as process, as temporally determined, reiterates this. The 'whole' and its 'parts' are unstable. Certain textual characteristics may meaningfully contribute to a genre in one epoch but not in another. They are tangentially, not intricately, linked. In Jean-Marie Schaeffer's words:

> The different texts that we integrate into a genre are often linked by simple 'family resemblances' in Wittgenstein's sense: they do not all necessarily share the same recurrent characteristic or characteristics, but a given text shares some characteristics with some of its 'congeners', some other characteristics with other 'congeners'. Thus a text p shares the bundle of traits A with texts q and r; q in turn shares traits B (different from A) with s, which, furthermore, shares part of traits A with q and r; r in turn, in addition to the A traits that it shares with p, shares other traits C with it and with s, etc. In other words, a genre is far from forming a univocal class; it is formed of several networks of partial resemblances that, through a process of overlapping, form the literary genre in its historical variability.[18]

The idea of genre as both process and contract may appear to be self-contradictory, however, if we consider that a contract must be temporally stable in order to be binding. The contradiction is especially acute if we focus on the author's (or text's) generic intentions rather than the reader's generic expectations. In other words, if we imagine that the author's (or text's) meaning can be truly appreciated only if a certain kind of interpretation is made, regardless of the reader's historical position, then the contract can never change or evolve. Certainly, this is inherent in Hirsch's formulation of genre as theory, specifically of genre as contract. Hirsch insists on the existence of fixed, 'intrinsic' genres, positing these as the only way to ensure textual determinacy and hence interpretative validity. Yet, there is a way to resolve the contradiction. We could imagine a contract that can change, by focusing on the reader's, rather than the author's, side of the equation. This is what Jauss does with his approach of 'rezeption Aesthetik', that is, the aesthetics of reception. For Jauss, the contract that is genre is shaped by the reader's expectations. This suggests that there is more than one contract, not as many as there are readers, but certainly as many as there are groups of readers. And this suggests that the contract can and will change over time. For Jauss, indeed, genre's historicity and its contractual nature are causally linked – genre evolves because of its social dimension.[19]

What, then, of an analysis of epic as a genre? If genre is a shared set of expectations and if that set itself changes over time, then a discussion of the epic should ask the following questions: What were the expectations – both productive and interpretative – at the time of writing of a certain text? What major changes have taken place on the interpretative side of that equation, as new texts appear? To ask these questions is not to seek a single definition of the epic, but to understand it, and indeed to understand any genre, as a totality that exists both across time and between textual producers and interpreters.

For all this, though, it must be borne in mind that this totality of genre is being understood and analysed from the critic's vantage point, that is, from the present time, from our place at the beginning of the twenty-first century. In other words, this study is primarily concerned with what we understand the epic to be at this point in time, and how that understanding has been shaped by productive and interpretative moments in past time. The epic, as far as there is such a thing, is the accumulation of texts and of ideas over time, with some ideas maintained and others shed. Thus, we must take into account the authorial intentions as well as the critical receptions of specific texts, which constitute the contract that is genre. But because the generic contract is subject to change, we must keep track of the nature of that change, comparing any contractual moment with the moments that have come before. The ultimate aim is a comparative analysis of generic development, almost a series of snapshots, in the belief that this is all that can be said about what the epic has been and therefore is.

Our discussion of the epic will begin with the earliest known epic – the epic of *Gilgamesh*. Dating in its oral form to 2000 BC, *Gilgamesh* contains that element that we perhaps most closely connect to epic – heroism. For *Gilgamesh* sets out, as so many subsequent epics do, a narrative of great and courageous deeds against the backdrop of watershed historical and even prehistorical events. Though considerably little is known about the precise connection between the literature of the ancient Near East and the ancient Greeks, it is possible to acknowledge *Gilgamesh* as a forerunner to Homer's *Iliad* and *Odyssey*, and therefore to see how epic heroism becomes consolidated in the classical Greek tradition. The Homeric poems precede the very concept of the epic, and hence define it. Such is the case with the earliest epic theory, inaugurated by Aristotle's *Poetics*. It is only with Virgil's attempts to emulate Homer in the *Aeneid*, and thus to translate the Homeric poems into a Roman context, that the epic tradition begins in earnest.

Virgil casts a long shadow over the Middle Ages and Renaissance. Crucially, however, the pre-eminence he enjoyed in the Renaissance (something very like the pre-eminence enjoyed by Homer among the ancient Greeks and Romans) is tempered by an anxiety over his pre-Christian, even unchristian, provenance. The Homeric conventions consolidated by Virgil, particularly the heroism displayed by Aeneas, find themselves modulated to a Christian sensibility. The search for a Christianised form of heroism is what motivates, for example, the spiritual and autobiographical tendencies of Dante's *Divina Commedia*. But, more importantly, the pagan origins of epic come face-to-face, in the Renaissance, with the Christianised form that is the medieval romance. The ensuing battle between epic and romance manifests itself in Ariosto's *Orlando Furioso*, Tasso's *Gerusalemme Liberata* and Spenser's *Faerie Queene*. The result is the allegorising of the epic form, as it seeks to accommodate romance elements and Christian mores within existing epic conventions. Thus, the knightly quest of romance comes to provide an alibi for narrating the Christian soul's progress towards heaven. The allegorical romance-epic of the Renaissance is soon overturned, however, by the direct Christianising impulse of Milton's *Paradise Lost*. Eschewing the indirectness of allegory, Milton turns the epic into a vehicle for nothing less than divine truth.

Where epic is concerned, however, *Paradise Lost* is not the only watershed event to take place towards the end of the Renaissance. Cervantes' *Don Quixote*, often deemed the first novel, constitutes an important moment in the history of the epic, not least because of its determinedly anti-epic drive.

It is a direct ancestor of the 'comic epics' of the eighteenth century, most notably Henry Fielding's *Tom Jones* and *Joseph Andrews*, and hence of the modern novel. It is, in other words, an important instigator of the split between epic and novel that takes place at the start of the eighteenth century.

If *Don Quixote* heralds one path taken by epic – the innovatory impulse that eventually turns into the novel – then *Paradise Lost* signals another, more conservative trajectory. Milton exerts a strong influence, both positively and negatively, over epic attempts in the eighteenth and nineteenth centuries. As if paralysed by Milton's formidable transformation of the epic into the prophetic, the majority of epic activity in the eighteenth century takes the form of translation and parody, and, although it produces landmark epic translations and mock-epics by the likes of John Dryden and Alexander Pope, it could be argued that it results in very little real innovation.

It is in the nineteenth century that Milton's prophetic example provides the inspiration for a distinctly Romantic form of truth-telling, that of self-development. A need for an everyday anti-epic heroism, a heroism of the self, that had manifested itself in Fielding's Cervantine novels, now emerges in the Romantic epics of Wordsworth, Keats and Byron, with their emphasis on the poet-hero and his quest for poetic power. The question of selfhood – more specifically, the question of how self-development occurs in tandem with social demands – becomes the focus for Victorian epics. Although Elizabeth Barrett Browning purports to reconcile self and society in *Aurora Leigh*, the tension between the two, and indeed the instability that inheres in selfhood, haunts a range of late nineteenth-century works in the epic tradition, from Tolstoy's *War and Peace* to Tennyson's *Idylls of the King* and Browning's *The Ring and the Book*.

Such an awareness of the polyvalence of subjectivity is, in the twentieth century, the defining characteristic of epic. Modernist poets invested in an interpretation of epic – derived from a perhaps misplaced nostalgia for the classical – as a comprehensive expression of an age. The epic becomes, in the early twentieth century, a vehicle for conveying the increasing confusion, fragmentation and slippages in perception that constitute the Modernist ethos. The Modernist epic may be the expression of the age, but that age is construed as lacking in unity and coherence, and, potentially, lacking in heroism. This new form of epic has persisted throughout the twentieth century, emerging in recent works such as Derek Walcott's *Omeros* and Tom Paulin's *Invasion Handbook*.

Finally, in the twentieth century, the name of epic occurs in conjunction with another art form – film. The final chapter in this history considers the development of what is the distinct but related genre of epic film. The form undergoes its own generic trajectory from early historical film to increasingly extravagant demonstrations of spectacle and special effects first in the mid-twentieth century and then at the beginning of the twenty-first. None the less, the links between literary epic and epic film are evident in a shared concern with heroism and grandeur of scale. The epic film, this book argues, is a manifestation of the epic impulse in contemporary culture whose significance cannot be ignored.

The study of any genre, then, is a study of generic change; in the case of epic, it is necessarily a survey and analysis of the innovations and imitations that have gone into the creation of a long line of influence. In its stated aims, this book therefore differs substantially from long-standing pillars of epic scholarship, such as C. M. Bowra's *Heroic Poetry* and E. M. W. Tillyard's *The English Epic and Its Background*, which demonstrate an anxiousness to establish strict boundaries between epic and non-epic texts.[20] Such traditional studies have given rise to some simple commonplaces of epic criticism, whose usefulness, in the face of the complexity of generic behaviour, is sometimes limited. One such commonplace is the insistence that the epic has ceased to be a relevant art form, given the increasingly sophisticated and individualist worldview that comes about in the modern era. Tillyard, for example, suggests that the epic tradition 'expired at the end of the eighteenth century', to be replaced by the novel.[21] Such a view is also found in the theories of the novel of the Marxist critic Georg Lukács and the Russian Formalist Mikhail Bakhtin.[22] Certainly, it recognises the impact of historical shifts in thought on the epic, but is unfortunate in its refusal to pursue the relationship between modern works and the epic tradition that precedes them, even when they show every intention of participating in that tradition.

Another standard of traditional epic criticism – one that this book does not challenge implicitly – is the concept of primary versus secondary epic, the former defined as oral or primitive and the latter as literary. Such a distinction is a valid one, for it allows us to differentiate between the many vast oral narratives that have occurred in cultures around the world and the tradition made up of mostly literary texts that we tend to call 'epic' in the Western world. It is, however, a simple distinction that makes it easy to gloss over the complexity of the genre of epic. Furthermore, while distinguishing between the two types of epic, this assumption can have the opposite effect of grouping a vast number of quite varied texts under the umbrella term of 'epic'. It therefore fails to take account of the importance of influence and reception in the formation of genre. Such forces are the primary objects of study in this book; for this reason, a certain tradition of epic – largely literary – will be the focus here.

This study is the logical culmination of relatively recent studies of epic, which are concerned not with prescribing but with describing, specifically with exploring some of the inter-textual influences and changes that have gone into making the epic what it is. That epic persists into the modern era – a possibility pointedly denied by Tillyard's and Bowra's surveys – was amply demonstrated by such works as Thomas M. Greene's *The Descent from Heaven* and Thomas Vogler's *Preludes to Vision: The Epic Venture in Blake, Wordsworth, Keats and Hart Crane*.[23] Of late, epic scholarship has also shown the changes at work in epic from antiquity onwards. David Quint's *Epic and Empire: Politics and Generic Form from Virgil to Milton* and Colin Burrow's *Epic Romance: Homer to Milton* are two fine examples of this, which examine shifts in emphasis in the epic from antiquity to the Renaissance.[24] Quint traces the influence of Virgil's construction of imperial ideology while Burrow examines the changing emotional make-up of the epic hero. Some scholars have usefully reminded us, moreover, that polysemy lies at the very heart of classical epic: Susanne Lindgren Wofford has demonstrated how epic texts such as Homeric epics and Virgil's *Aeneid* set up possibilities for interrogating the epic's heroic code even as they help to construct it, and D. C. Feeney's exhaustive account of classical epic after Homer shows the richness and variety of epic constructions of gods and mortals in antiquity.[25] It must be pointed out, however, that I know of no single study that contemplates a range of generic changes in the epic from antiquity to modernity, ending with a contemporary medium such as cinema. None the less, two books must be mentioned as important landmarks in epic scholarship: John Newman's *The Classical Epic Tradition* chronicles the epic tradition from Homer to film within the strict parameters of the influence of the classical Greek critic Callimachus, while Paul Merchant's *The Epic* is an excellent – though now somewhat outdated – introduction.[26]

The premise of our examination of epic, that it is essential to explore the terrain rather than stake out its boundaries, presents a final problem. The selection of texts implies criteria for selection, and the existence of criteria implies a definition of the epic, but this study rests on the notion that there is no fixed definition of epic. It must be conceded here that a selection of texts will always precede a full-length discussion of genre, and, to some extent, a set of criteria will precede that selection.[27] These criteria exist *a priori* to the analysis and, in this case, consist only of the contemporary critical consensus about what texts are to be labelled epics.

This does enable, however, another tautology. This study aims to shed light on our current understanding of the epic by examining a series of texts, but that series will have to be selected based on our current understanding of epic. The sticking point is the misperception that the aim of this study is a definition, an explanation, a revelation, of the epic. It is therefore possible to refute any charges of inconsistency and tautology by refusing to think of genre and text – the idea of the epic and the epics in question, or the epic as we understand it now and the epics of the past – as two sides of an equation and therefore two components in an unbreakable circuit. That is, the objective here is mere description of texts and textual relationships, with no ensuing discovery of the genre in question. This neutralises the problem that there has existed *a priori* to this analysis enough of an idea of what that genre is in order to select those texts.

In outlining the rationale for the selection of epic texts discussed here, a word must be said about the choice of editions and/or translations. All non-English texts are quoted in English, from easily accessible, but reliably accurate translations. This policy has the advantage of simplicity and consistency, as the texts discussed come from a wide range of languages and cultures. Similarly, all texts are cited from relatively up-to-date, scholarly editions, whose details are made explicit in the notes.

To sum up, this study will not seek to explain or to reveal or to discover the essential epic at all; nor will it attempt to catalogue comprehensively all the texts that have come to be designated as 'epic'. But it will analyse a certain complex network marked by plurality and indeterminacy. That is what the epic is. That is as close as we can get to asking, and answering, that vexed question, 'What is the epic?'

1
The Classical Age: Beginnings

By predicating the epic on the notion of influence and inter-textual dynamics, we can trace the genre along a retrospect of influence to the eighth century BC – that is, to the *Iliad* and the *Odyssey* of Homer. Even then, it must be borne in mind that these Greek epics, which we attribute to Homer, were not composed in a vacuum. They were the result of an oral tradition of narratives telling of the creation of the world and of significant events in early human history. They are comparable – indeed, intimately related – to a body of stories circulating in the neighbouring Near East, among them a narrative often thought of as the earliest recorded epic: the epic of *Gilgamesh*. We begin our history of the epic, then, with *Gilgamesh*, before addressing Homer's *Iliad* and *Odyssey*. Homeric influence would of course extend well beyond later classical Greek literature and thought into the age of the Roman Empire, when Homer's monumental achievements inspire, primarily, Virgil's *Aeneid*. Virgil's conscious and often meticulous imitation of Homer is the generic genuflection that establishes the epic as a living genre in the first place. Further innovation follows, and would comprise works such as Lucan's *Bellum Civile* and Ovid's *Metamorphoses*.

To trace the epic to Homer, and tentatively to *Gilgamesh* beyond it, is to discover that the epic begins as a narrative of heroic action played out against a backdrop of divine intervention. The tendency to treat 'epic' as synonymous with 'heroic poetry', therefore, has an historical justification. As Walter Ong points out in his influential discussion of orality, heroic action is central to oral expression in its function as history, precisely because it facilitates the retention of this history:

> Oral memory works effectively with 'heavy' characters, persons whose deeds are monumental, memorable and commonly public...not for

romantic reasons or reflectively didactic reasons but for much more basic reasons: to organize experience in some sort of permanently memorable form. Colorless personalities do not survive oral mnemonics.[1]

The heroic element of epic poetry is perhaps its primary defining characteristic. As the epic evolves, however, this feature becomes subject to generic change. Indeed, as more and more secondary characteristics and tropes begin to gather around the genre, they affect its heroic core. The heroism of epic, then, remains in some respects essential to the genre, but the manner in which that same heroism is defined and represented is naturally subject to change. Therefore, in addition to discussing the simple evolution of the epic genre in the classical age – the composition and reception of early epic texts – this chapter will also chronicle the development of the genre's central feature: the epic hero.

The epic of *Gilgamesh*

The story of *Gilgamesh* originates in the Near East region of Mesopotamia, in present-day Iraq. Versions of *Gilgamesh* circulated over two millennia, from 2200 BC to about 200 BC.[2] They first occur orally and are eventually committed to writing, in both Sumerian and Akkadian, the two languages of the region. If an historical Gilgamesh existed at all, he lived around the time of the early Sumerian city-states, that is, roughly about 2800 BC. Sumerian oral poems heroicising him were probably sung as court entertainments from 2200 to 2000 BC. Sumerian writing dates from at least 2600 BC and Akkadian writing from at least 2300 BC. There is evidence that the Sumerian songs of *Gilgamesh* were written down by 2000 BC. By the eighteenth century BC, there existed a single integrated *Gilgamesh* narrative written in Akkadian. The standard text now published and read as the epic of *Gilgamesh* is an Akkadian text dating from about 1100 BC, by which time it had been augmented with a prologue. Discovered in the royal libraries in the citadel of Nineveh, it is termed the Nineveh text (the civilisations at both Sumer and Akkad having been subsumed under the Babylonian Empire since the eighteenth century BC, it is alternatively referred to as the Standard Babylonian Text). Unlike other versions of the tale, this standard text has a name attached to it – *Sîn-liqe-unninni* – which identifies the author as a priest, and presumably a scholar and scribe who revised and redacted an earlier version of the narrative as he wrote it down. Based on eleven tablets of cuneiform Akkadian, the fragmentary standard text is necessarily informed by much editorial guesswork. A twelfth tablet, based on one of the earlier

Sumerian Gilgamesh poems, but relation of which to the main body of the poem is in doubt, is usually appended to modern editions.³ Versions of *Gilgamesh* occur somewhat later in several other languages of adjacent civilisations, such as the Hittite and Ugrit. Such wide circulation attests to its widespread popularity in the Near East.

The *Gilgamesh* stories, and hence the integrated narrative of *Gilgamesh*, are part of a cycle of creationist stories, set within a wider context of what Johannes Haubold terms 'an Akkadian history of the world'.⁴ These stories include *Enuma eliš*, which details an Akkadian cosmogony, and hence chronicles an early part of this history, and *Atrahasis*, the narrative of which relates the story of a deluge involving the Noah-like figure Uta-napishti. The gods instruct Uta-napishti to build a boat and put in it every living thing. All these stories are predicated on, and must be read in the context of, a coherent mythological vision of creation and early humanity.⁵ *Gilgamesh*, then, offers the story of an heroic individual whose exploits take place within this established cosmological paradigm.

The poem tells how Gilgamesh's tyranny over his people prompts them to pray to the gods for salvation. The gods respond by creating the wild man Enkidu to challenge Gilgamesh. The pair ultimately become companions, however, and engage in several heroic adventures, including a perilous journey to the Forest of Cedar to kill the monster Humbaba (or Huwawa) and the slaying of the Bull of Heaven. The Bull had been sent in punishment by the goddess Ishtar, whose proposal of marriage Gilgamesh had rejected. In this last adventure, however, Enkidu is killed. A distraught Gilgamesh sets off again, this time to the edge of the world to discover the secret of immortality. Here he encounters Uta-napishti who, as the only mortal to survive the divine deluge, has alone been able to discover the secret. Gilgamesh, however, does not attain the knowledge himself. Instead Uta-napishti's words seem to imply a criticism of Gilgamesh's lack of appreciation of his status and would appear likewise to chide him for neglect of his kingly duties:

> Said Uta-napishti to him, to [Gilgamesh:]
>   'Why, Gilgamesh, do you ever [chase] sorrow?
> You, who are [built] from gods' flesh and human,
>   whom the [gods did fashion] like your father and mother!
>
> '[Did *you*] ever, Gilgamesh [*compare your lot*] with the fool?
>   They placed a throne in the assembly, and [*told you,*] '*Sit!*'
> The fool gets left-over yeast instead of fresh ghee,
>   bran and grist instead of [*best flour.*]

'He is clad in a rag, instead of [*fine garments,*]
   instead of a belt, *he is girt* [*with old rope.*]
Because he has no *advisers* [*to guide him,*]
   His affairs lack counsel . . . .

'Have thought for him, Gilgamesh . . .,
   [*who is*] their master, as many as . . .?

$$(X.266-79)^6$$

More importantly, in a passage that anticipates a truly Homeric apprehension of the transitory nature of our own existence, Uta-napishti's words insist on the inevitability and inscrutability of death:

'No one at all sees Death,
   no one at all sees the face [of Death,]
no one at all [hears] the voice of Death,
   Death so savage, who hacks men down.

'Ever do we build our households,
   ever do we make our nests,
ever do brothers divide their inheritance,
   ever do feuds arise in *the land*.

'Ever the river has risen and brought us the flood,
   the mayfly floating on the water.
On the face of the sun its countenance gazes,
   then all of a sudden nothing is there!

'The abducted and the dead, how alike is their lot!
   But never was drawn the likeness of Death,
never in the land did the dead greet a man.

'The Anunnaki, the great gods, held an assembly,
   Mammitum, maker of destiny, fixed fates with them:
both Death and Life they have established,
   but the day of Death they do no disclose.'

$$(X.304-22)$$

Uta-napishti then challenges Gilgamesh to remain awake for seven days, a trial that Gilgamesh fails almost immediately. Before he leaves, Uta-napishti ensures that Gilgamesh is ritually cleansed and dressed, and tells him of a plant of eternal youth growing under the sea. Gilgamesh attempts to obtain this but fails. Still distraught, Gilgamesh returns to his kingdom and the poem ends.

The death of Enkidu, and the subsequent solitary journey of Gilgamesh, arguably render the epic much more appealing to many modern readers – readers who look to define the ethic of heroism within the context of individual achievement, judgement and physical prowess. Yet, the text does not make explicit just how much of a resolution these events and the conclusion represent, for life after Gilgamesh's return is not depicted. Certainly, the significance of Gilgamesh's quest has been foreshadowed by the poem's Introduction, which tells us that the hero of the poem 'learnt of everything the sum of wisdom. / He saw what was secret, discovered what was hidden, / he brought back a tale from before the Deluge' (I.6–8). Yet, the precise nature of the lessons Gilgamesh learned remains unclear. Gilgamesh's one action after his return and just before the poem's conclusion is to give Uta-napishti's boatman, Ur-shanabi, a detailed description of his city's foundations. That these words are a repetition of an earlier description of Uruk which occurs in the Introduction seems to lend them some undefined significance, but hardly present a summative conclusion, though they raise tantalising questions. Why, for example, are they repeated as precisely and as clearly as they are? Is their repetition simply formulaic or are they meant to be understood as a crucial demarcation of the degree of knowledge – or lack thereof – attained by the hero? Only the apocryphal twelfth tablet, a version of an earlier Sumerian tale of 'Gilgamesh, Enkidu and the Netherworld', brings an uneasy closure to the text. This story, in which Gilgamesh converses with Enkidu after Enkidu's death and discusses his experiences in the netherworld, allows a vague dénouement by including a reunion of sorts between Gilgamesh and Enkidu, as well as by demonstrating Gilgamesh's attainment of secrets of the afterlife and therefore underlining the knowledge he has gained from his adventures.[7]

The nature of Gilgamesh's 'sum of wisdom' is a puzzle indeed. It is tempting to read the text teleologically, paying special attention to the lesson finally learned by Gilgamesh. Thus the insistence by various scholars of the text that the point of the poem lies in its conclusion and that it narrates a growing acceptance of mortality. Donald Mills, for example, suggests of Gilgamesh that 'First he defies [death] in true heroic fashion when he confronts Huwawa, then he denies it both in his excessive grief for Enkidu and the journey to Utnapishtim. Finally, by accepting its inevitability, he recognizes that it is an inseparable part of life.'[8] For Mills, such a trajectory represents 'the beginnings of a new kind of heroism, one based on an awareness of mortality'.[9] Unfortunately, the burden of a socially aware and socially responsible heroism sits somewhat uncomfortably on the ambiguous *Gilgamesh*. As Benjamin Ray's reading suggests, the poem's conclusion is so obscure and indefinite as to be almost perfunctory, and the real meaning behind Gilgamesh's 'sum of wisdom' lies in his obtaining of it.[10] The poem ends simply with Gilgamesh's realisation that his constant questioning and questing must end. What appears to have been of real importance is that he has engaged in such questioning and questing in the first place. Indeed, the Prologue to the standard text calls on its reader to approach the tablet-box in which the text is presumably kept and to 'read out / the travails of Gilgamesh, all that he went through' (I.27–8). As with Akkadian wisdom literature in general, Ray suggests, *Gilgamesh* calls on its audience to 'question conventional wisdom and think for themselves'.[11] I would argue, however, that the Prologue is not as heavily didactic as Ray insists, and not as easily read as Gilgamesh's message to future generations. What is evident is the text's insistence on means rather than ends – on extraordinary and courageous action rather than simple quest and attainment as the true measure of its 'tall, magnificent, and terrible' (I.37) hero.

Teleological interpretations of *Gilgamesh* are difficult to avoid, thanks to, as Haubold puts it, 'the unlikely resemblance it bears to Greek epic and its European-looking preoccupation with death and the human condition'.[12] This same perceived resemblance brings us to the question of the link between *Gilgamesh* and the Homeric epics. It is eminently sensible, no doubt, to draw lines of cultural influence from the Near East of the second millennium BC to ancient Greece in the first millennium. Archaeological evidence supports the notion of commercial and cultural exchange, and there are various possible intermediaries, such as the Phoenicians, who straddled the Near East and the Mediterranean in terms of both their position as seafaring traders and their geographical position in what is present-day Lebanon.[13]

None the less, a direct link between the Akkadian and the Greek narratives is still an area of much speculation. In further support, many scholars point to a number of thematic, structural and narrative parallels between the texts, such as the friendship between Gilgamesh and Enkidu and that between Achilleus and Patroklos, or the power dynamics that underlie Ishtar's attempted seduction of Gilgamesh and Kalypso's and Circe's relationships with Odysseus.[14] Yet, Haubold rightly warns against 'parallel-hunting' for its own sake.[15] Such an activity is particularly dangerous when it leads to fanciful impositions of Greek-style techniques of plotting and characterisation on to a stubbornly inconclusive text such as *Gilgamesh*, such as when Sarah Morris suggests that Gilgamesh 'acquir[es] wisdom and self-knowledge through trials and travels' as Odysseus does, or 'progress[es] from heroic to tragic' in much the same manner as Achilleus.[16] In the absence of concrete proof of a genetic link between *Gilgamesh* and Homer's epics, the caution that Haubold urges must also be exercised when applying the label epic to *Gilgamesh*. If, after all, we allow that the label pertains not merely to lengthy heroic poems, but to texts that participate in the generic game of influence and innovation, the only way to contextualise *Gilgamesh* within the epic genre is to assign it an originary and primal, formative position. Such a position, it must finally be conceded, cannot be so easily allocated.

None the less, as Haubold demonstrates, there is room in which to discuss the link between Akkadian and Greek heroic narrative, for each finds its place within a 'history of the world'. That is, *Gilgamesh* on the one hand and the Homeric epics on the other belong to a broader collection of stories presenting Akkadian and Greek versions of, respectively, how the universe was created and how humanity was established. It is the way in which a cosmological myth system informs heroic narrative in each case that is of particular interest here. Both the Akkadian and Greek 'histories of the world' imagine a moment between the creation of the world and the present time of the audience when courageous deeds of superhuman ability could be carried out, when heroic men played out their actions in the company of gods. It would seem that if any link is to be established between *Gilgamesh* and the Homeric poems, it is in the way that the cycle of creationist narratives found in the Near East forms part of a broad base of influence for the Greek cosmogony that underpins Greek epic and its celebration of a heroic age of extraordinary action.

Homer

The Homeric epics emerge from a corpus of Greek heroic poetry, what the Greeks themselves called 'song', a collection of narratives composed orally by anonymous singers over centuries.[17] It is this body of song that corresponds to Haubold's notion of a 'history of the world', consisting as it does of a cosmogony as well as a cycle of stories around the watershed historical event of the invasion of Troy, asserted by later Greeks themselves – and tentatively by modern archaeology – to have taken place in 1200 BC. The Greek cosmogony was outlined by the Homeric contemporary Hesiod in his *Theogony* and *Catalogue of Women*, while Trojan stories materialised not only in the *Iliad* and the *Odyssey*, but in the so-called *Epic Cycle* of lost epics also attributed to Homer, which includes the *Nostoi* – the homecomings from Troy of all the major Greek warriors. We can therefore imagine the Homeric epics to be a selection and refinement of existing heroic song into more or less integrated narratives. As Andrew Ford's analysis shows, the Homeric poet – or, more accurately, poets – conceived of this epic material as emerging from a 'larger realm of interconnected stories'.[18] Ford suggests that the poet would have imagined his epic subjects spatially and, moreover, would have arranged these spaces sequentially.[19] This sequence of epic themes comprehends, chronologically, the creation of the world and gods, the creation of men and the heroic deeds of godlike men, ending well before the present day of its audience. According to Ford:

> The paths of song are very extensive, but they do not go on forever: the continuum of stories pulls up at a time somewhat short of the present. ... The epic poet, then, is essentially a poet of the past, not a poet of heroes or gods in particular. For his past he may turn, as Homer does, to the noble heroes who fought beside gods at Troy, four dark centuries before his day; or he may move further back in time, to even earlier themes, to the women who, mating with gods, founded the great royal lines, as Hesiod does, in a *Catalogue of Women*.[20]

It must be borne in mind that the realm of stories from which the epics were composed was a body of oral narrative. The Homeric poems too were essentially oral. The content of the Homeric poems themselves, as well as that of Hesiod's work, suggests that such narratives would have been recited by an *aiodos*, a singer. The examples of the bards Phemios and Demodokos (who appear in Books I and XIII, respectively, in the *Odyssey*) imply that the *aiodos* would have performed at feasts, where, ideally, he would have received an attentive audience.[21] Indeed, who can forget that much of the *Odyssey* is recited by Odysseus himself at the court of the Phaiakans? Achilles too is present at one point in the *Iliad* as a kind of bard. These self-reflexive descriptions of bards refer us to an itinerant Homeric poet, whose skills result in the rewards and company of noblemen – an artisan who would have occupied a special place in society. Indeed, this space exists somehow outside society, for while the bard's invited participation in the noble ritual of gift-exchange sets him apart from ordinary craftsmen, the restriction of his role to recipient rather than donor places him well beneath noblemen.[22]

However, the question of the orality of the Homeric poems is complicated by the coincidence of their composition and the invention of writing in Greece. The Greeks of the fifth century thought of Hesiod and Homer as close contemporaries; we know that Hesiod lived around 700 BC and that the linguistic style of Homer shows archaisms that pre-date Hesiod by a generation or two. The invention of writing in Greece also occurs around 700 BC. We can suppose, then, that the composition of the relatively integrated Homeric epics based on sections of the early mythical and heroic material was followed relatively quickly by their written composition. The most interesting evidence of the contemporaneity of the existence of writing and the composition of the Homeric poems is the acknowledgement of writing in the *Iliad* itself. In Book 6, when Glaukos recounts his genealogy to Diomedes, he tells the story of his ancestor, Bellerophontes, who refused the overtures of Anteia, wife of Protos, King of Ephyre. In revenge, Anteia accused Bellerophontes of attempting to seduce her, and her husband punished Bellerophontes by sending him to Anteia's father with a folded tablet inscribed with 'murderous symbols' (VI.168) that would incriminate him. Yet, scholarly attempts to transform this episode into proof of a Homeric poet's ability to write remain unconvincing. For one thing, the knowledge of the existence of writing does not equate with knowing how to write. In addition, as Barry Powell shows, the story is likely to be derived from a tale from the Near East and therefore refers to cuneiform writing on clay tablets, such as Sumerian and Akkadian, which, as we have seen, pre-date Greek writing by so many centuries.[23] Moreover, Powell demonstrates that a comparison of this reference to another Homeric reference to written signs indicates that the poet possessed little understanding of the physical items, the materials and the practical mechanics that constitute writing. In Book 7, the Achaian warriors draw lots to determine who will meet Hektor in one-to-one combat. Their lots consist of stones on which each warrior has made a 'mark' (VII.178), clearly an illiterate one, since it has to be identified by the warrior who made it. Yet, these marks are described with the same word, *sēmata*, as the symbols that comprise the clearly literate form of communication in the story of Bellerophontes. Perhaps if the Homeric poet played a role at all in the writing of his poems, it was in dictation to a scribe.

There are, however, other reasons to believe in the basic orality of the Homeric epics. The very nature of the texts indicates the compositional techniques of a pre-literate age. The psychological and therefore social and cultural differences between oral and literate communities have been famously discussed by Ong.[24] The inherent orality of the Homeric poems was first demonstrated by Milman Parry in the 1920s, evidenced by what he described as 'formulae'. Parry defined the Homeric 'formula' as 'a group of words which is regularly employed under the same metrical conditions to express a given essential idea'.[25] Thus, the oft-repeated Homeric combination of epithet and noun, as in 'grey-eyed Athene', 'circumspect Penelope', and 'wine-dark sea', occur by demand not so much of plot or character but of metre. As Ong puts it, 'Odysseus is *polymētis* (clever) not just because he is this kind of character but also because without the epithet *polymētis* he could not be readily worked into the meter'.[26] Achilles is described as 'swift-footed' even when he is sitting down. The requirements of the metre used in the Homeric epics (the dactylic hexameter, composed of five units of long and short syllables ending with two short syllables) are very precise, demanding the use of a range of formulae. Depending on the length and metrical shape of a noun such as 'Achilleus' or 'the sea', the right epithet could be employed to 'finish off' the phrase. Most importantly, what Parry demonstrated is that such formulae are not the result of individual poetic choice, but had been determined by tradition, which provides a storehouse of words and phrases from which a poet could choose. This is why they are repeated throughout the Homeric poems – by one reckoning, as much as one third of the *Iliad* and the *Odyssey* is made up of repeated lines, or fragments of lines.[27]

Exactly how the Homeric poet or poets would have viewed the poet's position vis-à-vis this tradition is also of interest, for it gives rise to several other conventions that we now associate with epic. The most significant of these is the poet's close relationship with the muses. As Ford reminds us, this concept of goddesses who act as guardians of higher knowledge is a uniquely Greek one.[28] Ford demonstrates how the Homeric poems imply that the poet possesses special power, based on privileged access to the muses.[29] The muses safeguard knowledge of the 'history of the world' which provides material for epic. Through the muses, the poet can access this special knowledge and convey it to his audience. The epics are thus peppered, and crucially begin, with invocations to the muse: 'Sing, goddess...' (*Iliad* I.1) and 'Tell me, Muse...' (*Odyssey* I.1). Similarly, before embarking on the famous 'catalogue of ships', which constitutes the Achaian forces in the *Iliad*, the poet pauses in order to obtain a special boost of inspiration from the muses in order that he might do justice to this lengthy list:

Tell me now, you Muses who have your homes on Olympos.
For you, who are goddesses, are there, and you know all things,
and we have heard only the rumour of it and know nothing.
Who then of those were the chief men and the lords of the Danaans?
I could not tell over the multitude of them nor name them,
not if I had ten tongues and ten mouths, not if I had
a voice never to be broken and a heart of bronze within me,
not unless the Muses of Olympia, daughters

of Zeus of the aegis, remembered all those who came beneath Ilion.
I will tell the lords of the ships, and the ships' numbers.

(II.484–92)

Here, the poet seems to concede the limits of his own mortal memory, for
he is unable to recall the list of warriors in its entirety – the 'multitude' of
men. However, he does subtly advertise the privilege of his position, for he
is able to tell not what he remembers but what the muses remember, and is
therefore able to recite at least the ships and their captains. He proceeds to
relay, in other words, a crucial slice of history thanks to the muses, who are
eyewitnesses to that history. Essentially, the poet is not a creator of art, but a
conveyer of history. He is, after all, 'a singer rather than a maker, an *aiodos*
rather than *poiētēs*, because he is the voice and the vehicle of an ancient
wisdom'.[30] The Homeric poet's own self-construction therefore chimes with
the workings of the oral tradition as described by Parry and Ong, among
others. He is not so much the originator of his matter, but the shaper, quite
literally, the maker – *poiētēs*, or poet, deriving from *poiein*, to make.

The muses are evidently an essential part of the oral tradition that underpins the Homeric poems. Rather less clear to many modern readers,
however, is the rationale behind another significant Homeric characteristic,
the so-called epic simile. These lengthy similes, slightly more frequent in
the *Iliad* than in the *Odyssey*, can run to as much as ten lines. A clue to their
possible provenance is found in Ong, who describes the tendency of oral
expression to amplification: 'In oral delivery, though a pause may be
effective, hesitation is always disabling. Hence it is better to repeat something, artfully if possible, rather than simply to stop speaking while fishing
for the next idea.'[31] However, this does not necessarily mean that the
Homeric epic similes were part of the poems' earliest stages of composition,
for, as Charles Rowan Beye points out, the cultural world described in many
of the similes belongs to a period near the end of the epic tradition. At some
point, then, Beye suggests, these similes crept into the poems, perhaps
thanks to the habits of poets over time as they recited the narratives.[32]

If the Homeric epics emerge out of a 'tradition' that we define as an accre-
tion of storytelling techniques over centuries, the question arises as to
whether we can attribute the Homeric epics to a single poet, whether we can
indeed speak of a poet called 'Homer'. According to Parry:

the character of [the language of the *Iliad* and the *Odyssey*] reveals that it
is a work beyond the powers of a single man, or even of a single generation

of poets; consequently we know that we are in the presence of a stylistic element which is the product of a tradition and which every bard of Homer's time must have used.[33]

Such thinking, however, must take account of the impression of artistic unity given by the Homeric epics. Some Homeric scholars therefore prefer to think of a single poet, at least for each epic, responsible for the final refinement of the pre-existing body of song into integrated narratives. As Beye notes, 'the absolute control of the plot and the well-developed point of view consistently maintained throughout the story suggest that the traditional material has been impressed by one vision'.[34] The poet thus referred to as Homer in such readings would be, in a manner of speaking, the final Homer, the last poet to handle this material, who did so with a relative degree of poetic vision and who might even have overseen their transcription.

Perhaps the best solution is that offered by Gregory Nagy, who suggests that the artistic unity of the Homeric epics is itself a result of tradition. Nagy urges a reading of the poems as the product of many poets over a great period of time, eschewing any mention of a single Homer. 'The key' to the works' success, that is to say, 'is not so much the genius of Homer but the genius of the overall poetic tradition that culminated in our *Iliad* and *Odyssey*'.[35] Whatever we decide about the extent of poetic agency in composing the Homeric epics, one certainty is that the notion of an historical Homer as a blind bard, possibly from the island of Chios and conjectured to have been a well-travelled man, is mere fancy, the product of a Homeric biography that emerged from the fifth century BC onwards.[36] At the very least, such a close to hagiographic tradition bestowed on the Homeric poems an even greater authority than they might otherwise – for all their intrinsic value – ever have possessed.

Any assumptions about a single Homer inevitably lead to the question of whether the same poet was responsible for both poems. It could be argued that the subject matter of the *Odyssey* places it after the *Iliad*, perhaps even in the shadow of a poem that had achieved some fame and that had motivated an appetite among listeners for more of the same.[37] The *Odyssey* could, in modern terms, be thought of as a kind of 'sequel'. But the fact that the poet of the *Odyssey* refers to the events of the *Iliad* is much more likely to be a function of their emergence from a common oral tradition. In the final analysis, as Nagy suggests, the discussion becomes a comparison of parallel traditions, an Iliadic tradition and an Odyssean one, each referring to a collection of themes and audience expectations that may or may not play off each other.[38] Finally, to acknowledge the Homeric epics as emerging out of a cumulative oral tradition is to appreciate that their inauguration of the epic genre is a spontaneous outcome of this tradition rather than an individually artistic act.

How, then, do we define the genre of Homeric epic? We can have no certain recourse to the word *epos*, which is applied specifically to the Homeric poems relatively late, in the fifth century BC. It is the acceptance of the existence of *epos* as genre that allows Aristotle to juxtapose 'epic' with 'tragedy' in his *Poetics*, as we shall see later. *Epos* can quite literally mean that which is spoken; in Homeric poetry, *epos* signifies merely 'word', 'speech', 'counsel' or 'command'. It also connotes a tale or song, a proverb or a maxim; it is, at some point, in the plural *epea* used to signify poetry in heroic verse, e.g. epic poetry, as opposed to *melos*, or lyric poetry. But what, in its own age, set Homeric epic off from other forms of lyric expression? Some scholars, such as William Thalmann, point to the epic's metre as a generic marker, aligning the epics with all poetry in Greek dactylic hexameter.[39] Yet, as Ford suggests, the Homeric poems can be even more specifically defined. The absence of singing *per se* and of dancing from Homeric self-descriptions of poetic performance distinguishes the poems from the melodic song that is *melos*, but the presence of the poet's lyre suggests at least a rhythmic accompaniment.[40] More importantly, the privileged relationship enjoyed by the poet with the muses, particularly as it results in the poet's ability to recite sections of a mythic history, is an important part of what Ford calls the poems' 'ethos'.[41] This ethos aligns the poems, for example, with Hesiod's poems, which similarly offer such slices of history. However, Homer's poems can be further set off when we consider that a work such as Hesiod's *Works and Days* depends on a specific relationship between poet and listener, specifically, an exhortative one. In contrast, the Homeric epics (and Hesiod's extended narratives) do not give specific instructions as to precisely how the poetic content is to serve as a lesson for the audience.[42] As Ford ultimately defines it, archaic Greek epic is:

> a long, solo song performed in a rhythmical recitative; it narrated on the authority of the Muses the deeds of gods and early heroes. The themes epic treated, the 'paths' it could take, were extensive but firmly circumscribed by a mythic conception of a long-lost golden age. The stories were presented dramatically and without explicit cues for how to apply them to their auditors' lives.[43]

More than just heroic narrative in a specific metrical form, the Homeric epics would have stood out for their audience as a specially marked mode, a poetic 'kind' that presented a lost glorious age of divine and near-divine achievement.

At the heart of Homeric epic, then, is its heroic function. This function is captured in the phrase *klea* – 'glorious deeds'. As Nagy states, the word *kleos*, or 'fame' (literally, 'that which is heard'), refers not simply to the fame that is achieved by the hero who is sung, but is also 'the formal word which the Singer himself (*aiodos*) used to designate the songs which he sang in praise of gods and men, or, by extension, the songs which people learned to sing from him'.[44] Thus, the heroic deeds are inseparable from the song that immortalises them. Indeed, '*kleos* is fundamental as a measure of one's value to others and to oneself'.[45] Underpinning *kleos*, then, is the notion that glory is about reputation, heroism about public honour. The Homeric poems do not simply demonstrate this heroic code, they rigorously interrogate it, exploring and exposing its limits. It is to this close to ironic nature of Homeric verse – its doubleness or self-awareness of its own inherent contradictions – that we shall turn our attention.

Homer's *Iliad*

The hero and subject of the *Iliad* is set out in its very first line, 'the anger of Peleus' son Achilleus / and its devastation' (I.1). Achilleus is famously defined by his wrath (*mēnis*), which will have crippling effects on both his people and on their enemy (for, as the poem's first lines surprisingly point out, Achilleus' wrath 'put pains thousandfold' [I.2] not on the Trojans alone but on his own side – the Achaians – as well). The poem opens with the cause of Achilleus' wrath, which is a quarrel with the Achaian leader Agamemnon and, like the abduction of Helen by Paris, yet another jealous squabble about the possession of women. This quarrel precipitates Achilleus' desertion from battle and thus the Achaians' near defeat. It is, however, the root of Achilleus' wrath that is at stake here. For his wrath is based on Achilleus' special position within the heroic code. The heroic code is essentially a warrior code. A warrior is defined by his proximity to death, both in the risk he takes of being killed and his own role as killer.

Routinely described as 'the best of the Achaians' (I.244, 412; XVI.271), Achilleus is set into special focus as a warrior because he has known all his life that he is destined to die in battle. The fate of Achilleus as a warrior destined for death is a recurring one. We learn of it the very first time in the poem that Achilleus addresses his immortal mother Thetis: 'my mother, you bore me to be a man with a short life' (I.352). His mother's words echo her son's acknowledgement, with her lament to him that 'Your birth was bitterness' (I.414) for 'indeed your lifetime is to be short, of no length' (I.416). Thetis' immortality further accentuates Achilleus' mortality, not simply because it sets him apart from his semi-divine parentage but also because it emphasises her divine foreknowledge of his death, her privileged knowledge of his fate as 'short-lived' (I.505), as when she explicitly informs Achilleus that 'it is decreed your death must come soon after Hektor's' (XVIII.96). Moreover, Thetis' status underscores a painful tension in Achilleus between mortality and – if not immortality – then divinity.[46] Having been born of a sea-nymph, Achilleus is loved by the gods, but because of her marriage to a mortal – Peleus – he is inevitably mortal. The text draws on, although it does not explicitly mention, the mythical prophecy that had warned Thetis, leader of the sea nymphs, that she would give birth to a son who would eventually usurp his father, a prophecy that led to her rejection as a potential partner by both Zeus and Poseidon and her necessary marriage to a mortal. Achilleus is, in an odd way, the product of a consummation that could, and should, have taken place between immortals. Thetis' immortality, the apparent birthright of her son, gives Achilleus' mortality the appearance of an anomaly, a flaw in his otherwise godlike brilliance. He is quite literally marked by his own birth as a kind of walking oxymoron – at once a god and yet a man – a being destined finally to feel at home in the world of neither.

It could be argued, however, that the divine prophecy that Achilleus will be killed – and killed while yet a young man – enhances his own capacity to kill. It is because he is both touched by divinity and aware of his early death that he possesses the powerful combination of inherent martial ability and thirst for glory. His very armour serves as an emblem of his stature, recalling simultaneously his prowess as a warrior, his status as the son of an immortal, and his own mortal existence, since it was a wedding present from the gods to his father, 'the day they drove [Thetis] to the marriage bed of a mortal' (XVIII.85). Furthermore, in the comprehensive and universally symbolic depiction that Hephaestos places on his armour, Achilleus quite literally bears the weight of the world on his shoulders.

Achilleus' awareness of his inevitable early death, combined with his prowess as a warrior, means that he invests heavily in the heroic code of honour, of *kleos*. For if a long, quiet life is not available to him, then he will at least live a short and glorious one. Achilleus knows that his is a choice between the two irreconcilable extremes:

> For my mother Thetis the goddess of the silver feet tells me
> I carry two sorts of destiny toward the day of my death. Either,

> if I stay here and fight beside the city of the Trojans,
> my return home is gone, but my glory shall be everlasting;
> but if I return home to the beloved land of my fathers,
> the excellence of my glory is gone...

(IX.409–14)

Kleos, the immortality of fame, is therefore Achilleus' 'eternal consolation', as Nagy puts it, for the loss of *nostos*, of homecoming.[47] So completely does Achilleus commit to the system of *kleos* that a perceived lack of commitment to this heroic code by others brings about his terrible – and incommensurate – wrath. The wrath that Achilleus displays is unique to him, for the word *mēnis* is applied to no other character in the *Iliad*. It is the extreme expression of an extreme warrior. When Agamemnon withholds Briseis, the girl Achilleus has been awarded as his prize in battle, the code of hospitality, gift-giving and social procedure, has, in Achilleus' eyes, been breached to an unacceptable degree. That Agamemnon's own prize, Chryseis, has to be returned is a decree of the gods, for the Achaians must appease Apollo, of whom the girl's father is priest. But Agamemnon's petulant decision to snatch Briseis in place of Chryseis is an unsanctioned violation of the system of *kleos*. The booty of war – which in this world includes women taken in battle – is an integral part of the system of *kleos*, a system based on clearly visible rewards for martial prowess. That this indeed is the case is made clear in Sarpedon's words to Glaukos as they prepare to fight:

> 'Glaukos, why is it you and I are honoured before others
> with pride of place, the choice meats and the filled wine cups
> in Lykia, and all men look on us as if we were immortals,
> and we are appointed a great piece of land by the banks of Xanthos,
> good land, orchard and vineyard, and ploughland for the planting of
>   wheat?
> Therefore it is our duty in the forefront of Lykians
> to take our stand, and bear our part of the blazing of battle,
> so that a man of the close-armoured Lykians may say of us:
> 'Indeed, these are no ignoble men who are lords of Lykia,
> these kings of ours, who feed upon the fat sheep appointed
> and drink the exquisite sweet wine, since indeed there is strength
> of valour in them, since they fight in the forefront of the Lykians.'

(XII.311–21)

Seth Schein notes of the word *timē*, or 'honour', that it refers to:

> 'price' or 'value' in a tangible sense. The word can be used of a woman
> like Briseis, who was a *geras* or special 'gift of honor' from the army to
> Achilles, as well as of the seat of honor, full wine goblets, meats, and
> fertile land mentioned by Sarpedon as rewards for prowess in battle and
> reasons for continued bravery and achievement. Those who win such
> tangible honors also receive honor conceived abstractly; from this comes
> *kleos*, 'glory and reputation', what is said about them near and far, even
> when they are dead.[48]

As Schein suggests, the logic for a warrior such as Sarpedon is a simple one.
He gains material comfort as the well-earned reward for valour in battle.
What is immediately understood is that such a reward is merely the due
compensation for the risk of death the warrior faces. Achilleus too abides
by the ethos wherein honour in the material sense – *timē* – is complemented
by honour in the abstract sense – *kleos*. Agamemnon's selfish actions are
incompatible with, indeed incomprehensible to, Achilleus' value system:
'this thought comes as a bitter sorrow to my heart and my spirit / when a
man tries to foul one who is his equal, to take back / a prize of honour,
because he goes in greater authority' (XVII.52–4). According to the logic of
the heroic code, if Achilleus has been denied his prize, he has no real
reason for fighting at all. But because he is the 'best of the Achaians', his
reaction constitutes a tactical disaster for the troops assembled against
Troy. Unfortunately for the Achaians, a breakdown in the equation that is
the heroic code leads potentially to ultimate defeat when one of the sides
in that equation happens to be the supreme warrior of the force. Achilleus
and the code by which he abides quite literally form the glue that holds the
army together.

It is well worth noting that – although it appears to be an act of close to
childish selfishness – Achilleus' withdrawal from battle is actually a sign of
his unconditional commitment to the warrior code. It is easy to forget that,
in the pre-nationalist world that shaped the Homeric epics, this code took
precedence over loyalty to state or leader. As Richard Seaford suggests, the
Homeric code of honour is based on communal consensus, not imposed by
state. It is therefore to be preserved by reciprocity and ritual, by such rites as
the exchange of gifts and the pursuit of just and righteous vengeance.[49] It
could be argued, then, that the rationale for war against Troy is one of justifiable revenge for the abduction of Helen (good guests do not, after all,
abduct the wives of their hosts), but is superseded for Achilleus by the need

for personal revenge against Agamemnon. The idea that Achilleus must bow to the demands of his acknowledged overlord as a matter of Achaian solidarity is never countenanced. We further remember that, unlike the other warriors assembled in the expedition against Troy, Achilleus – too young to have been a party to the request to defend Helen – was never even obliged to fight in the first place.

In the course of his sustained withdrawal from the field of battle, however, Achilleus himself comes to question the equation that underlies the heroic code. His very prowess as a warrior places him beyond the normal limits of the heroic code. Not only does he invest so much in terms of martial prowess that the possibility of sufficient reward is diminished, the certainty of his death removes the element of risk and nullifies the compensatory effect of *timē* in the material sense. All he is left with is *kleos* (which, by virtue of the poem's continued existence, the reader can be reassured he will receive). Achilleus' example therefore reduces the issue of *kleos* to its essence. Through him, we are compelled to question the value of *kleos* as compensation for death. We are forced to question the values that equate a warrior's death with fame and then assert that some fame will lead to immortality.

Achilleus first expresses doubts over the idea of *kleos* when he is confronted by the poem's central episode – the Embassy of Odysseus, Aiax and Phoinix, bearing both gifts and apology from Agamemnon and, therefore, a kind of belated *timē*. Initially, however, Achilleus seems to be obsessed with Agamemnon's earlier withholding of *timē*. He returns incessantly to the question of having been cheated of his rightful prize:

> Neither
> do I think the son of Atreus, Agamemnon, will persuade me,
> nor the rest of the Danaans, since there was no gratitude given
> for fighting incessantly forever against your enemies.

> (IX.314–17)

Similarly, he complains some lines later of Agamemnon that 'All the other prizes of honour he gave the great men and the princes / are held fast by them, but from me alone of all the Achaians / he has taken and keeps the bride of my heart' (IX.334–6). As much as he dwells on the fact that his prize has been unjustly taken from him, however, Achilleus questions the value of material reward in death: 'A man dies still if he has nothing, as one who has done much. / Nothing is won for me, now that my heart has gone through its afflictions / in forever setting my life on the hazard of battle' (IX.318–22). Eventually, as Achilleus works through his argument, he puts aside any interest in the gifts of *timē* and concentrates on the question of whether there can be any adequate recompense for a warrior's death:

> Of possessions
> cattle and fat sheep are things to be had for the lifting,
> and tripods can be won, and the tawny high heads of horses,
> but a man's life cannot come back again, it cannot be lifted
> nor captured again by force, once it has cross the teeth's barrier.
>
> (IX.405–9)

It is at this point that Achilleus ponders the choice between *kleos* and *nostos*, between 'everlasting' (IX.413) glory and a 'beloved' (IX.414) home, between a brief life yielding immortality through fame and a long life ending in peace. His argument comes to rest inevitably on the recognition that a return home will mean that 'there will be a long life / left for me, and my end in death will not come to me quickly' (IX.414–15). If the value of glory is being questioned, that of peace and familial affection is correspondingly upheld.

This attitude prefigures Achilleus' full rejection of *kleos* when he learns of Patroklos' death. This rejection is implicit in his decision to return to battle, a decision motivated not by a thirst for glory but by bereavement. Yet this is also the moment of Achilleus' *aristeia*, or excellence as a warrior. It is worth noting, then, that Achilleus gives the outward appearance of investing in *kleos* even as he has inwardly turned away from it, for he enters the final, climactic phase of the poem resembling a warrior but differing essentially from one. His reason for fighting is not to seek fame but to assuage loss. Indeed, in Schein's terms, he is defined now by *philia*, or love, rather than *mēnis*, or wrath.[50] I would suggest, however, that Achilleus is here experiencing a second wave of wrath defined by a rejection of *kleos* as much as the first wave of wrath was underscored by an investment in it.

The killing of Patroklos is the pivot on which Achilleus' rejection of *kleos* rests because it prefigures Achilleus' own death. As Nagy puts it, Patroklos functions as a *therápōn*, a 'ritual substitute', for Achilleus.[51] Patroklos' life is now put on a par with that of Achilleus, for Achilleus describes Patroklos as 'loved beyond all other companions, / as well as my own life' (XVIII.81–2). Thetis' reaction to Patroklos' death is thus really a lamentation for Achilleus; indeed, it could be a borrowed description of Achilleus' death from another source.[52] Thetis' words bear recourse to the now-familiar juxtaposition of Achilleus' near-divinity with his doomed mortality:

> Ah me, my sorrow, the bitterness in this best of child-bearing,
> since I gave birth to a son who was without fault and powerful,
> conspicuous among heroes...
>   ...but I shall never again receive him
> won home again to his country and into the house of Peleus.
>
> (XVIII.54–6; 59–60)

Achilleus too responds to Patroklos' death with a new awareness of his own impending end. He frames his return to the role of warrior with thoughts not of *kleos* or *timē* but of death (XVIII.114–16). He makes the merest mention of the glory he will gain, only to place it in the context of the grief of the Trojans and, by implication, that of his mother (for him) and of himself (for Patroklos):

> Now I must win excellent glory,
> and drive some one of the women of Troy, or some deep-girdled
> Dardanian woman, lifting up to her soft cheeks both hands
> to wipe away the close bursts of tears in lamentation,
> and learn that I stayed too long out of the fighting.
>
> (XVIII.121–5)

Again, the glory gained from war and its killing is a hollow one when set against the suffering of family and friends, against the loss of peace and happiness. In his most definitive rejection of *kleos*, Achilleus even denounces war, regretting not just his own wrath but all bellicosity: 'why, I wish that strife would vanish away from among gods and mortals' (XVIII.107).

Yet, such an expression of hatred for martiality does not deter Achilleus from expressing his own excessively violent desecration as he first kills Hektor and then defiles the body, all the while sorrowing for Patroklos. This act is the final manifestation of Achilleus' disillusionment with the heroic code. He is no more the warrior of glory and honour who could pay due respect to his victims, as in Andromache's description of how he killed her father, 'but did not strip his armour, for his heart respected the dead man, / but burned the body in all its elaborate war-gear / and piled a grave mound over it' (VI.417–19).[53] It is only when Achilleus meets Priam, who raises in him 'a passion for grieving for his own father' (XXIV.507–8), and he returns

Hektor's body out of a sense of compassion, that he performs anything like a recovery of his old warrior self. Importantly, however, the text does not allow him to regain an investment in *kleos*, and maintains its tone of mourning, for the loss of Patroklos as well as Hektor, for the inevitable death of Achilleus, and, it would seem, for the suffering inherent in all war. Strikingly, the heroic code that provides the very basis for action in the *Iliad* has, by the time the poem reaches its end, begun to be questioned and even undermined.

Homer's *Odyssey*

Just as the *Iliad* bases its story on the crucial issue of Achilleus' wrath, the *Odyssey* is centred on Odysseus' cunning. The first line establishes Odysseus' wiliness as key to his character: 'Tell me, Muse, of the man of many ways, who was driven / far journeys, after he had sacked Troy's sacred citadel' (I.1–2). It is further suggested by Odysseus' epithet – close to untranslatable but usually rendered as 'resourceful' (e.g. IV.203, 214). Although such epithets are generally determined by formula, Odysseus' is important as an unusually apt description of his fundamental personality. Nor is Odysseus the only one to display such cunning, for his wife Penelope is routinely described as 'circumspect' and his son Telemachus as 'thoughtful'. And the goddess Athene, who looks on Odysseus as a favourite, sees such cunning as the characteristic trait that connects them as unassailable allies in a world of gullible mortals. The goddess's affectionate address to Odysseus underlines this bond:

> 'It would be a sharp one, and a stealthy one, who would ever get past you
> in any contriving; even if it were a god against you.
> You wretch, so devious, never weary of tricks, then you would not
> even in your own country give over your ways of deceiving
> and your thievish tales. They are near to you in your very nature.
>   ...you are far the best of all mortal
> men for counsel and stories, and I among all the divinities
> am famous for wit and sharpness...
>
> (XIII.291–5, 297–9)

Odysseus is as much defined by his *mētis*, or cunning, as Achilleus by his *bíē*, or violent force of strength. As Nagy suggests, the opposition between Odysseus' artifice and Achilleus' rather less intellectual prowess is already well developed in the *Iliad*, in which Odysseus' powers of persuasion are criticised by Achilleus: 'For, as I detest the doorways of Death, I detest that man, who / hides one thing in the depths of his heart, and speaks forth another' (*Iliad* IX.312–13).[54]

For all such seeming contradictions, though, the two epics in fact present complementary perspectives on heroism and the warrior code at the heart of it. Both poems place their heroes outside the heroic code, spatially and psychologically, and view them from a vantage point that questions its values. While Achilleus in the *Iliad* actively questions the demands placed on him as a warrior, Odysseus in the *Odyssey* engages in a quest to return home that implies a critique of the sacrifices required by war. His first adventure against the Kikonians (allies of the Trojans) only emphasises the pathetic futility of martial conflict. After all, his weeping on Kalypso's island as he looks across the sea longing for home is a proleptic anticipation of the tears he sheds on hearing Demodokos sing about the Trojan War, which are in turn compared to the tears of a woman weeping for her warrior husband:

> . . . Odysseus
> melted, and from under his eyes the tears ran down, drenching
> his cheeks. As a woman weeps, lying over the body
> of her dear husband, who fell fighting for her city and people
> as he tried to beat off the pitiless day from city and children . . .
>
> (XIII.521–5)

In order to complete this long-awaited homecoming, Odysseus must exercise all his cunning, and his success in doing so establishes a heroism based not on physical strength but on guile. On his adventures, he learns the necessity of dissimulation, deception and the risks of undisguised truth or even sincerity if he is to achieve a homecoming at last. Part of his victory over the Cyclops Polyphemos lies in the trick he plays in identifying himself as 'Nobody'. Significantly, he undermines his own success (and endangers the lives of his crew) by then revealing his name in an inappropriate taunting and allowing Poseidon to take revenge for his son's injuries and so prolong his wanderings. After this mistake, he is careful to withhold his identity and to use this concealment to his advantage. For example, he gains information from the Phaiakians about the effects of his absence and, on his return to Ithaca, he tests his family and friends to ensure their loyalty. Most importantly, by holding back from announcing his return, he is able to ambush and defeat the suitors who have besieged his wife Penelope.

However, his cunning and justified (if brutal) elimination of the suitors means that he also manages to achieve his *aristeia*. Like Achilleus, then, he presents as a supreme warrior while allowing the warrior code to be questioned. The first four books of the poem – the Telemachy – have the effect of preparing the reader or auditor for Odysseus' return as an heroic achievement, by demonstrating the dire consequences of his absence. They set Odysseus' *aristeia* in even greater light. They also establish Telemachus' position as the heir to his heroic father. When Odysseus and Telemachus fight alongside each other against the suitors, the warrior code is pictured as a rite of initiation – a necessary component of masculine maturity.

The patriarchal basis to the heroic code is none the less offset by the almost feminised nature of Odysseus' alternative heroism of cunning. It is telling that Odysseus' mental agility is a trait shared not simply with Athene (who, as an immortal capable of assuming various forms and gender, is not a fully feminised figure) but with Penelope. For the success of Odysseus' homecoming would be marred if his wife had not practised her own brand of deceit on her suitors, for example, in promising to accept a proposal of marriage after completing a shroud for her father-in-law, which she spends her nights unweaving. That Odysseus and Penelope are united in their pragmatism and canniness is suggested early on by Odysseus' description of marital happiness as 'sweet agreement / in all things' (VI.181–2). Penelope's circumspection as proof of her rightful place with her husband is further emphasised when set in relief against the faithless and unreliable Clytemnestra and Helen. Strikingly, Penelope too deserves *kleos* – the only woman in the Homeric epics to do so – when her husband remarks that her 'fame goes up into the wide heaven' (XIX.108).

Thus, where Achilleus has to choose between a life of peace and glory in war, that is, between *nostos* and *kleos*, Odysseus seems to achieve both.[55] His is a double heroism of careful circumspection and martial courage. It demonstrates that a warrior's prowess can only be complemented by thoughtfulness (of which a woman, too, is capable). Odysseus' heroism is therefore a combination of brawn and brain, masculine and feminine, public and personal. It is paralleled by the poem's insistence that war must be balanced with, and indeed superseded by, peace.

The *Iliad* and the *Odyssey* simultaneously construct and deconstruct a heroic warrior code. This code, suggests Susanne Wofford, is at the heart of epic ideology.[56] Though questioned at the very moment of its inception, it remains the crux of the epic tradition as it takes shape. In the critical reception of the Homeric epics from the fifth century BC onwards and, more obviously, in the taking up of the epic by Roman poets, the question of exactly what constitutes epic heroism remains central to the form.

Before taking up the subject of the reception of the Homeric epics, it is worth looking briefly at the role played by divine authority in the construction of epic heroism. Though Homer's gods operate as overseers of human action, in particular as guardians of fate, they do not carry any specific moral function. Although, in the *Odyssey*, Athene seems to assist Odysseus in what appears to be a moral victory over Penelope's suitors, her motivation has more to do with her special affection for him than for any inherent rightness that his quest may hold. So it is that the gods are divided over the outcome of the Trojan War in the *Iliad*, and their loyalties are determined by simple favouritism. Their lack of moral authority is most apparent in Book 20, in which the gods join in the battle with almost comic consequences. The struggle is ended only when Zeus decides in the Achaians' favour, a victory determined not by objective moral criteria but by the scales of fate. The gods rarely, if ever, act as moral agents in either poem, although there are some suggestions that we are moving towards such a universe. Thus, the paradox of Homeric heroism, for future generations of epic poets and critics, is that the gods, though present, are never central to the mores of the heroic code.

The beginning of epic theory

By the fifth century BC, the Homeric epics enjoyed a position of immense influence in Greek society, not simply as great poems but as a means of understanding the world, representing what Eric Havelock as called 'the Homeric encyclopaedia'.[57] Homer was perceived as a pan-Hellenic teacher, his works offering lessons on various modes of behaviour, from warfare to leadership, codes of honour to modes of familial interaction. As we have seen, Ong explains how poetry in an oral society comes to carry much more than it does in a literate one, its metrical regularity aiding memorisation and thus enabling the conservation of history.[58] In a newly literate society, the Homeric poems formed the basis for a school curriculum, and were read and recited in elementary Greek classrooms.

The Homeric epics were, moreover, in demand as performance pieces. In a cultural shift that is not fully understood, the old figure of the *aiodos*, or singer, who appears in the Homeric poems as a divinely inspired bard who creates his poems in conjunction with the muses (or, from our perspective, with an oral tradition) had given way to the *rhapsode*, a reciter of a relatively fixed, received text.[59] The typical *rhapsode* is immortalised, and indeed derided, by Plato in his dialogue *Ion*, and viewed with some disdain as being mere 'stitchers of words' rather than composers. None the less, they were instrumental in elevating Homer and the Homeric epics to near-mythical status in Greek society from the fifth century onwards.[60] Rhapsodic societies such as the Homeridae, or the sons of Homer, certainly played a role in preserving and disseminating the Homeric texts and in venerating the poet believed to be responsible for them.[61] Their contributions helped shape the manuscripts that finally would be stabilised around the second century BC as a source for the Homeric poems.[62]

The use of Homer as a supremely didactic text did not, however, go unchallenged. The question of the moral suitability of Homer, particularly of his gods, was raised, for example, by the philosopher-poet Xenophones, who remarked that 'Homer and Hesiod attributed to the gods all things that bring shame and censure to men: theft, adultery and deception'.[63] This 'quarrel between poetry and philosophy' was most famously added to by Plato who, in his *Republic* in the fifth century BC, banished poets from his ideal state on a primarily moral argument, specifically poetry's over-reliance on the emotions and, more dangerously, for its *mimesis*, or imitation, of reality. Plato, for whom truth is an ideal form that is removed from what we know of reality, held that poets, in creating representations of this reality, were dangerously off the mark, indeed were twice removed from truth.[64]

When Aristotle wrote his *Poetics* in the fourth century BC, he did so partly as a response to – and partly in continuation of – Plato's distrust of poetry. Much of what survives of the *Poetics*, it must be noted, is a commentary on tragedy, which for Aristotle represented an improvement on epic; ultimately, indeed, Aristotle seems to conclude that epic is a much inferior genre to tragedy. Therefore, Aristotelian epic theory is really an elaboration of Aristotelian thought on tragedy. None the less, as we will see in subsequent chapters, his ideas would form the basis for much epic theory in the Renaissance and beyond, particularly with the appearance of Alessandro Pazzi's revised Latin edition of the *Poetics* in 1536.[65]

For Aristotle, the epic may be assumed to share with tragedy the core elements of plot, character and diction, but differs with regard to metricality and length:

> Epic poetry corresponds to tragedy in so far as it is an imitation in verse of admirable people. But they differ in that epic uses one verse-form alone, and is narrative. They also differ in length, since tragedy tries so far as possible to keep within a single day, or not to exceed it by much, whereas epic is unrestricted in time . . .[66]

The first significant idea for succeeding epic theorists is Aristotle's insistence on 'unity of plot' (or 'unity of action') for tragedy and hence for epic. The text, according to Aristotle, should relate a single action, not all the actions of a single person. For Aristotle, Homer is the case in point, for his texts possess unity of plot in that they are constructed of a chain of events that lead logically from one to another, that lend each other either necessity or probability:

> Just as Homer excels in other respects, he seems to have seen this point clearly as well, whether through art or instinct. When he composed the *Odyssey* he did not include everything which happened to Odysseus (e.g. the wounding on Parnassus and the pretence of madness during the mobilization: the occurrence of both these events did not make the occurrence of the other necessary or probable); instead, he constructed the *Odyssey* about a single action of the kind we are discussing. The same is true of the *Iliad*.

Unlike tragedy, epic, due to its length, must embellish this single action through the use of episodes. According to Aristotle, 'In plays the episodes are concise, but in epic poetry they are used to increase the length'.[67] This Aristotelian description of epic as made up of a single, unified plot, expanded through a number of episodes, has been an enduring one, and one of the most frequently mentioned in later epic theory.

Other important Aristotelian ideas emerge in a brief section on epic towards the end of the *Poetics*, particularly on the two characteristics of length and metre identified earlier as distinguishing epic from tragedy. Aristotle discusses, for example, the question of length in the epic as compared to the tragedy. The epic is allowed to be longer than tragedy because one is narrative, the other performative:

> In tragedy it is not possible to imitate many parts of the action being carried on simultaneously, but only the one on stage involving the actors. But in epic, because it is narrative, it is possible to treat many parts being carried on simultaneously; and there (provided they are germane) make the poem more impressive.

The significant phrase here – 'provided they are germane' – seems to have decided succeeding interpretations of this statement as one about 'unity of time'; that is, that the epic action is allowed to take place over a greater period of time as long as it is relevant and unified. When it comes to metre,

Aristotle advocates the use of 'heroic verse', that is, the dactylic hexameter of Homer, because it is the 'most stately and grandiose'.[68] Epic theorists and poets have since struggled with the notion that epic requires an appropriately stately metre, or elevated language, since any epic written in the vernacular is obviously unable to retain the Greek hexameter. Thus, as we shall see in subsequent chapters, the choice of metre in epic has become a serious question, carrying with it the potential for controversy.

A final important notion for future epic theorists is that of the function of astonishment and the irrational, captured in Aristotle's famous statement that, in epic, 'Probable impossibilities are preferable to implausible possibilities'.[69] The narrative nature of epic allows for the depiction of actions that would seem outrageous on stage. The epic poet, for Aristotle, succeeds with these by capturing the right balance between the pleasurably interesting and the manifestly absurd. As we shall see, Aristotle's remarks on the probable and improbable evolve, in Renaissance epic theory, into detailed discussions on the nature of the supernatural and the marvellous in epic, and how far these can be allowed before offending either reason or religion. We shall see in subsequent chapters that all the Aristotelian ideas discussed here – unity of plot or action, unity of time, suitable length, appropriate heroic metre, and the probable or improbable – resonate through epic theory into the Renaissance.

An important corollary of Aristotle's thought for discussions of Homeric epic in particular stems from his analysis of tragedy vis-à-vis comedy, although his observations on comedy are infrequent or lost. His distinction between the two forms is often simplified as one whereby tragedy often (though not always) results in a shift from good fortune to bad, while comedy presents the reverse. Yet, Aristotle, elsewhere in the *Poetics*, suggests the possibility of a type of tragedy that results in good fortune. The result is a lack of certainty over what constitutes tragic – and therefore epic – dénouement and the extent of the distinction between tragedy and epic on the one hand and comedy on the other. As Stephen Halliwell points out, this indecision often arises in analyses of the *Odyssey*, and there has been some debate over whether it qualifies in Aristotle's terms as comedy.[70] It would seem that Aristotle's discussion of comedy facilitates an identification of the *Odyssey* as less tragic and therefore less epic than the *Iliad*, paving the way, with the popularity of romance as a genre in the Middle Ages and Renaissance, for the two texts to be placed at the head of the two divergent forms, with the *Iliad* read as inaugural epic and the *Odyssey* as inaugural romance. This is so if one juxtaposes the fantastical storytelling of the *Odyssey* to the *Iliad*'s arguably tighter focus on 'real' history.

Certainly, the many adventures that make up the *Odyssey* are suggestive of the endless postponement of resolution that marks romance, whereas the *Iliad* is relatively driven in terms of plot. Such an approach, however, ignores the fact that the *Odyssey* does ultimately harness its episodes to the demands of teleology, and Odysseus' quest, long and varied as it is, is eventually attained, which is not always the case with medieval and Renaissance romance.

It is worth noting also that the differing natures of the two epics and their respective heroes created a tendency from the outset to contrast the *Odyssey* unfavourably with the *Iliad*. The brilliant and beautiful Achilleus has traditionally come off better when compared with the crafty and cunning Odysseus.[71] Aristotle's latent preference for the *Iliad* may indeed have been inherited from Plato, who notes Socrates' observation: 'I have heard your father say that the *Iliad* is a finer poem than the *Odyssey* by as much as Achilleus is a better man than Odysseus.'[72] The legacy of such a judgement is best articulated in *Treatise on the Sublime*, dated to around the first century AD and often dubiously ascribed to Longinus, which takes the question further and suggests that the *Odyssey* is the product of an old man's waning abilities:

> In the *Odyssey* Homer may be likened to a sinking sun, whose grandeur remains without its intensity. He does not in the *Odyssey* maintain so high a pitch as in those poems of Ilium. ... there is not the same profusion of accumulated passions, nor the supple and oratorical style, packed with images drawn from real life. You seem to see ... the ebb and flow of greatness, and a fancy roving in the fabulous and incredible ...[73]

The question of the relative merits of the two Homeric epics should not, however, detract us from what is most important about the classical reception of Homer, which is the unassailable centrality with which Homer occupies Greek thought on epic and on literature. For both Aristotle and Plato, indeed, epic in general is synonymous with Homeric epic in particular. Moreover, Aristotle posits that both tragedy and comedy ultimately derive from Homer, for the former is a species of the epic in the style of the *Iliad* and the *Odyssey* and the latter may be traced to a lost Homeric mock-epic, the *Margites*. The critiques of Plato and Aristotle serve only to confirm the pre-eminence of Homer's position. Their writings represent a broader critical mood, one that enabled the recognition of a genre called epic, and, more importantly, the essential distillation of this genre to just two key texts: the *Iliad* and the *Odyssey*.

Virgil's *Aeneid*

Between Virgil and Homer, there lie two significant groups of epics, one in Greek and the other in Latin. These are those of the Hellenistic age of the fifth century BC onwards, such as Apollonius' *Argonautica* (of about the end of the third century BC) and the Roman historical epics of the first century BC, such as Naevius' *Bellum Poenicum* ('The Punic War') and Quintus Ennius' *Annales* ('Annals'). Their significance for us lies in their significance for Virgil, for whom these poems stood alongside the Homeric texts as additional possible models for his own entry into the genre. The *Argonautica*, which recounts the story of Jason and the Argonauts' search for the Golden Fleece, is a curiously flaccid narrative in so far as Jason is demonstrably unheroic – as Hainsworth puts it, he is 'a weak and colourless figure, at best a supple diplomat, overshadowed by Medea'.[74] As such, it represents a potential departure from the Homeric model for the epic tradition. The second group consists of texts of which very little survives.[75] When we consider the profound admiration the Romans held for the literature of the Greeks, it is to be expected that they accepted epic as a peculiarly Greek form. Yet, they did eventually seek to Latinise this form. The first known example of Roman epic is Naevius' verse chronicle of the Punic War, of which little is known. More influential was the *Annales* by Ennius, which purports to recount Roman history from the foundation of the Empire to contemporary events. Significantly, both Naevius and Ennius, in reacting to the Homeric epics' narration of important milestones in the Greek 'history of the world', supplied the Romans with specifically Roman epics. In doing so, they helped to establish an important feature of epic – its nationalism. In this respect, Ennius was an especially important influence on Virgil. His great contribution to classical epic convention was the transformation of Homer's dactylic hexameter into Latin.[76] He therefore demonstrated the possibilities of transforming epic, previously confined to its Greek, and especially its Homeric, forebears, into an expression of Romanness. Specifically, he showed that this was to be done by retaining much of the shape and character of the Homeric poems, which would serve to throw into relief the Latin medium and the Roman historical content.

When Virgil set out to write the *Aeneid* in about 29 BC, he had before him, chiefly, Homer's epics, but also the epics of Apollonius and Ennius. Specifically, he chose to emulate the Homeric epics, and followed Ennius's example in doing so. As Richard Heinze states, 'A heroic epic written in anything other than Homeric metre and style was inconceivable, and Homeric style in Latin that was independent of Ennius was equally inconceivable'.[77] Virgil therefore adopted the dactylic hexameter of Ennius and Homer before him, as well as the lengthy 'epic similes' first found in Homer. More than this, a range of features characteristic of Homer was worked into the narrative by Virgil: 'Gods were inescapable, and funeral games, descents to Hades, catalogs of tribes and heroes, ornamented shields, night raids, *aristeai*, and duels were hardly less so'.[78] Added to these was the opening *in medias res*, that is, 'in the midst of things', a characteristic method of beginning that Virgil's contemporary Horace ascribed to Homer in his *Ars Poetica*. In other words, Virgil effectively put into place a full range of features that would come to be conventions for the epic for succeeding generations of poets.

Virgil self-consciously adapted the plots of the two Homeric epics. The *Aeneid* tells the story of the foundation of the Roman Empire by the Trojan warrior Aeneas, son of Venus. The Emperor Augustus, ostensibly the patron of the poem, traced his lineage through his adopted father Julius Caesar back to Aeneas, who had supposedly come to Italy after fleeing Troy. After a period of trials at sea imposed by Juno out of hatred for Troy, Aeneas is wooed by, but rejects, the Carthaginian queen, Dido. When he finally lands in Italy, he makes a tentative peace with the king of Latium, Latinus. Latinus, in accordance with oracular decrees that his daughter marry a foreign prince, decides to offer Aeneas his daughter, Lavinia. The plan is shattered by Lavinia's betrothed Turnus and war ensues, but ends in triumph for Aeneas. The *Aeneid* is therefore neatly divided into two – the Odyssean and Iliadic halves – a pattern identified by commentators since Virgil's best known classical critic, Servius, wrote of this in the fourth century AD.[79] Aeneas' quest to find a new home to replace the ruins of Troy corresponds to the lengthy and difficult *nostos* experienced by Odysseus in the *Odyssey*. Meanwhile his challenge to Turnus in gaining the hand of Lavinia and settlement of Latium echoes the Achaians' invasion of Troy, and allows Aeneas to display his *aristeia* and achieve *kleos*.

Thus, Aeneas would seem to be simultaneously returner and invader. More than this, he is both conscious of the need for domestic peace and devoted to his role as conquering hero. Yet, the two roles are not easy to combine. Aeneas possesses something of a dual personality, displaying a desire for domestic ties while acknowledging fully, though sometimes wearily, the urgency of his mission to found an empire. Clashes are inevitable. Aeneas' search for personal, particularly romantic, happiness is sacrificed to the imperialist project when he abandons Dido at the behest of Jupiter. The effort that this costs him is made abundantly clear as Dido confronts him: 'Aeneas, mindful of Jove's words, kept his eyes / Unyielding, and with a great effort repressed his feeling for her' (IV.331–2).[80] The poem ends in another spectacular conflict between the compassionate Aeneas and his bellicose persona. When Aeneas kills Turnus (who has slain his ally Evander's son Pallas) he fulfils his Achillean destiny, which is to effect an invader's victory and avenge the death of a comrade. Yet, the claims of domestic peace almost nullify those of martial imperialism. As Turnus gives up Lavinia – 'Lavinia is yours to wed. / Don't carry hatred further' (XII.937–8) – Aeneas almost falters:

> Aeneas stood over him, poised
> On the edge of the stroke, but his eyes were restless, he did not strike.
> And now what Turnus had said was taking effect, was making him
> More and more indecisive . . .

> (XII.938–41)

Eventually, however, he espies the baldric stripped off Pallas by Turnus, kills his enemy and claims his version of *kleos*.

Specifically, the *Aeneid* combine the two drives of Homeric epic, *kleos* and *nostos*, by reconciling these distinct motives of Achilleus and Odysseus under the aegis of Aeneas' own special characteristic – *pietas*. If the Homeric poems are about Achilleus' wrath and Odysseus' wiles, Virgil's epic is about Aeneas' innate piety; he is, from the start of the poem, identified as 'a man / Renowned for piety' (I.9–10). Importantly, *pietas* in the context in which Virgil composed his poem was uniquely fitted to subsuming the ostensibly contrary interests of public and the private that mark Homeric *kleos* and *nostos*. For, as Colin Burrow reminds us, the word *pietas* resonated in the Roman world as a commitment to both nation and family.[81] Cicero, for example, acknowledged both demands on one's *pietas*, and instructed Romans to 'cultivate justice and *pietas*, which is great towards parents and relations, but greatest in relation to one's country'.[82] As Burrow remarks, the two aspects of *pietas* mark the two parts of the *Aeneid* respectively, for, as the poem progresses, 'Pietas gradually loses its familial warmth and acquires more and more of what might be called a "deontic" force: it becomes cold obligation'.[83] *Pietas* allows Aeneas to be both compassionate and bellicose. Hainsworth, citing the commentaries of Servius, spells out this paradox as it relates to the final episode of the *Aeneid*:

> When Turnus lay wounded at his feet, it crossed Aeneas' mind to spare him. That, said the ancient commentator Servius, showed his *pietas*, his humanity. But Aeneas' eyes then fell on the trophy Turnus had torn from

the body of Pallas, and in vengeance he drove home the sword. That too, said the commentator, showed *pietas*.[84]

The *Aeneid* increasingly emphasises, and therefore privileges, the nationalistic side of *pietas*. In placing this patriotic form of *pietas*, ultimately, at the heart of Aeneas' heroism, it transforms the basis of epic heroism from individual to nationalistic glory-seeking. As David Quint suggests:

> Aeneas is not allowed to transfer affective ties except to a collective Roman future; he is asked to give up the ties that constitute individual personality and will. The result is the lackluster, depersonalized hero for which readers have praised and (mostly) blamed Virgil, a hero stolid to the point of passivity – especially when Aeneas is compared to his Homeric prototypes, the passionate and willful characters of Odysseus and Achilles. ...The *Aeneid* thus redefines the epic hero, whose heroic virtue now consists in the sacrifice of his own independent will – a will independent from his national mission.[85]

Pietas – as correlative to duty – reveals a streak of coldness and sternness in Aeneas' character. Its obverse, seen in Dido and Turnus and most obviously in Juno, is *furor*, fury or irrationality. That Juno, an immortal, displays such fury carries with it a significance that is not lost in the text's opening lines: 'What grievance made the queen of heaven so harry a man / Renowned for piety, through such toils, such a cycle of calamity? / Can a divine being so persevere in anger' (I.9–11). Juno's *furor* and Aeneas' *pietas* are juxtaposed from the outset, for she becomes the primary antagonist to the fulfilment of his quest. The divine origins of Juno's *furor* only emphasise the centrality of this characteristic as a foil to *pietas*. Meanwhile, the displays of *furor* seen in Dido and Turnus show us that its opposite, *pietas*, is primarily about a reconciliation of the demands of peace and war. Dido's lovesick ravings are set against Aeneas' cool ability to put aside marriage for duty. He knows when and how to choose between the opposing demands of *pietas*, and will not succumb to the demands of mere love. Yet, he will not display simple martial bloodlust, as Turnus does. His one display of anger in battle when he slays Turnus is explicitly an act of imperialist *pietas*, for it leads to victory. It defines Aeneas as a leader of his people rather than just a brilliant warrior.

The extent to which *pietas* could be equated with patriotic duty is to be seen in its relationship to the notion of *pax deorum*, the idea of a compact between the Roman Empire and the gods or fates, which decreed and ensured Rome's imperialist supremacy. *Pietas*, as described by Livy, was a respect for religion and for religious behaviour that guaranteed that this pact endured. Aeneas' *pietas*, then, exemplifies the *pietas* required of all Romans. His respect for the gods is actually a prerequisite for Roman imperial glory, since his obeisance to Jupiter's decrees, not to mention the behests of his mother, Venus, lead directly to his founding an empire in Italy. In positing *pietas* – the cornerstone of the *pax deorum* – as the defining characteristic of epic heroism, Virgil's *Aeneid* oversees the epic's evolution from ancient Greece to imperialist Rome as a transition from a mythical narrative of a 'history of the world' to a vehicle for nationalist ideology. The gods may be an unquestioned part of the fabric of history for Homer, but they are active guarantors of Rome's position as a superpower for Virgil. The *Aeneid*, then, represents the inauguration of what would become a commonplace in theory (though not necessarily, as we shall see, a mainstay of practice): the use of the epic form to embody nationalist ideology.

It is difficult, then, not to detect an element of propaganda in the *Aeneid*. Certainly, as we have noted, Virgil wrote his epic in response to a request from his emperor, Augustus. Augustus had united Rome after generations of civil war and, at the time of Virgil's writing, required a poem in celebration of Rome's newly established nationhood. Yet, it must be remembered that the imperialist enthusiasm evident in the *Aeneid* is simply part of an established Roman belief in the moral rightness of Rome's position as conqueror and civiliser of others.

The unease caused by the *Aeneid*'s imperialist statements can be seen in its critical reception, particularly in the proliferation of opposing 'pessimistic' and 'optimistic' stances. No doubt it is possible to read the *Aeneid* optimistically, for the subjectivity which marks Virgil's technique of characterisation means that differing viewpoints seem to proliferate in the text. Most obviously, the sympathy with which we respond, and are surely asked to respond, to Dido's tragic end unavoidably challenges the primacy of Aeneas' quest. Even Turnus is no cardboard villain, and his sufferings as a result of Aeneas' imperialist programme are not easily accounted for. It is possible, then, as an 'optimist' critic such as Gian Biagio Conte suggests, that Virgil fully intended to interrogate the ideology of *pietas* and thus of empire by adopting what Conte calls a 'polycentric' viewpoint.[86] Above all else, what is certain is that the connection between the epic form and the question of nationhood so forged by Virgil was to prove a lasting one.

The *Aeneid* was accepted as a Latinised version of Homer soon after its composition and dissemination. Indeed, it could be said that Virgil was being celebrated as a second Homer even before his epic had been completed; the poet Propertius apparently saying of it that 'something greater than the

Iliad is being born'.[87] This is significant, considering the pride of place accorded to Homer's epics by both Greek and Roman audiences. It would seem that, already widely read and taught before producing the *Aeneid*, Virgil's place as a national poet was cemented by the patriotic, imperially sanctioned subject matter of his epic. Soon after its composition, the accumulation of commentary on the *Aeneid* came to rival that of Homer's epics. With this, Virgil had inaugurated the epic tradition.

Coda: Ovid's *Metamorphoses* and Lucan's *Bellum Civile*

Thanks to Virgil, the epic was now tightly bound to notions of patriotic achievement and the sacrifice of individual will to the national good. Moreover, it had been definitively crytallised, perhaps even fossilised as far as Roman literature was concerned. When Ovid and Lucan approached the genre, they each responded directly to Virgil, but in very different ways. Lucan wrote in the mode of historical epic and Ovid created what could almost be called mock-epic. However, by writing against Virgil, paradoxically, they affirmed Virgil's standing and influence.

It would be easy to discount Ovid's *Metamorphoses* from a discussion of epic on the grounds that it is not a continuous narrative, being a collection of various mythological tales of metamorphosis, such as that of Narcissus' transformation into a flower and Arachne's into a spider. Yet, Ovid deserves at least a brief mention in this history of the epic by virtue of his implied intentions to write a very different kind of epic.

Ovid's epic claim is made from the outset. Not only is the poem in the by now standard epic metre of hexameters, but Ovid makes a bold statement in his brief proem:

> Of bodies changed to other forms I tell;
> You Gods, who have yourselves wrought every change,
> Inspire my enterprise and lead my lay
> In one continuous song from nature's first
> Remote beginnings to our modern times.
>
> (I.1–5)[88]

The poet's insistence that his text is a continuous one is especially significant if we consider the twin allusions at play here. In the invocation to the gods to 'lead [his] lay', he adopts the same language used by the respected Greek poet Callimachus in his *Aitia*, in which Callimachus explicitly describes his poem as led, or finely spun, by the gods, and therefore as a delicately woven and resolutely unepic long poem.[89] Yet, the simultaneous reference to continuity contradicts this, for it aligns the poem with unified narrative, that is, with epic. Ovid, then, is suggesting a different kind of epic, one that is digressive yet, in its digressiveness, is focused on the question of change. It is as if Ovid is pointing out the impossibility of unity in life – the only certainty being uncertainty – and therefore the futility of writing an insistently teleological epic. In order to emphasise this, Ovid sometimes forces the links between his tales, which serve to consolidate his poem into a 'continuous song'. They highlight the delusory nature of order, even pointing to the epic poet's role in maintaining this delusion. Without his epic claim, then, Ovid's poem would hark back to the didactic cosmogonies of Hesiod. In the light of his playful allusion to epic, however, it becomes a way of retelling life as narrated by Homer and especially Virgil. It becomes, in short, a sort of anti-epic.

Lucan's incomplete epic, entitled *De bello civili* ('On the Civil War') and variously called the *Pharsalia* (in reference to its central battle of Pharsalus) or *Bellum Civile* ('The Civil War'), narrates the events of the Roman civil war of 49–45 BC, in which Julius Caesar defeated Pompey to gain absolute power over Rome before his assassination in 44 BC. Lucan was the grandson of Seneca the elder, the rhetorician, and nephew of Seneca the younger, the Stoic philosopher. Lucan was himself very much a Stoic, believing generally in the exercise of reason over human urges to gain power, wealth and pleasure. His epic, therefore, inveighs against the excesses of civil war, not simply depicting the barbarism of war in general but reflecting on the senselessness of such barbarism when acted out between countrymen. The villain of Lucan's poem is Caesar, whose bloodlust takes him to such obscene measures as refusing legitimate burials to his enemies and the desecration of sacred lands. There is no clear hero. The most obvious candidate, Pompey, is a weak general, though a compassionate husband. There is, however, the philosopher Cato, who decries the bloodshed and places his nation before himself at all times, thus displaying all the virtues of Stoicism. Yet not only is Cato a stern and one-dimensional character, he is absent for a great deal of the poem. The combination of explicit condemnation of war with a lack of heroic action results, as we shall see, in a sustained critique of the epic form.

Lucan's epic has tended to be read as a criticism of the autocratic imperialism of his own day, and a typically Stoic call for a return to republicanism. Indeed, Lucan's troubled relationship with his emperor, Nero, would lend credence to a view of his *Bellum Civile* as an anti-establishment piece. As Susan Braund reminds us, however, Lucan began as a favourite of Nero's, before a falling-out led him to join a conspiracy to overthrow the emperor, all of which resulted in the censorship of his poetry and his own punishment by death.[90] Indeed, in the *Bellum Civile*, Lucan makes special attempts to flatter Nero, through grandiose prefatory remarks and a positive portrayal of Nero's ancestor Domitius. None of this aligns Nero explicitly with Caesar and demonises imperialism *qua* imperialism. It would seem that Lucan's concerns are not so much with the evils of imperialist rule in itself as with the callous, megalomaniacal version of it that Caesar practises.

As an insistent critique of imperialist and martial excesses, the *Bellum Civile* runs headlong into the conventions and concerns of epic as established by Virgil. Epic heroism as the attainment of Homeric *kleos* under the aegis of Virgillian *pietas* is untenable in a world in which warfare primarily causes suffering. Tellingly, the single display of *aristeia* in the poem belongs to Scaeva, a solider of Caesar. His moment of glory, though, is only another instance of evil in the cause of megalomania: 'he did not know / how great a crime is valour in a civil war' (VI.147–8).[91] No wonder, then, that there are no heroes in Lucan's epic, for there can be no heroes, indeed no triumphs, in the ugliness of civil strife. Other epic conventions passed down by Virgil are omitted or pressed into the service of Lucan's overriding message of the tyranny of civil war. The machinery of gods is conspicuously absent. Not only does Lucan's Stoic rationality discountenance the active roles of divinities, but the senseless struggles he depicts are impossible to reconcile with the existence of a supreme, perhaps benign, creator. Even the journey to the underworld becomes, in Lucan's text, an opportunity to align civil war with the black arts, as Pompey's son Sextus descends to hell to consult with the necromancing witch Erichtho. All Lucan allows is the existence of *fatum* and *fortuna* – fate and fortune – that determines men's destinies in often inexplicable fashion. Finally, Virgil's flexible, fluid use of hexameter is passed over in favour of a heavy-handed treatment, and any ornamentation kept to a minimum. Lucan, showing his training in rhetoric, enjoys instead the use of *sententiae*, ponderous maxims that help to hammer his message home.

Lucan's decision to write an epic on the horrors of war perpetrated by the Roman Empire in the shadow of an epic extolling the foundation of that empire *through* war can only be seen as an overtly un-Virgilian gesture. It is therefore possible, as Quint does, to read Lucan as well as Ovid as a writer of anti-epic.[92] Significantly, Lucan's text was not forgotten in the reception of Roman epic that followed – Dante apparently ranked him alongside Homer, Virgil, Horace and Ovid. Yet, as Quint points out, Lucan helps to consolidate the conventions and ideologies of Virgilian epic by negative example.

As the next chapter will suggest, the direction taken by the form in succeeding centuries was not in the footsteps of either Lucan's Stoical resistance to war or Ovid's playful challenge to teleology. The resolute heroism of Virgil's *Aeneid*, in which martial valour is married to the milder claims of conscience, eclipsed both, as well as effectively transforming the heroic code of individualistic glory that was its forerunner. Finally, this analysis of the early epic has explored its origins in a pre-history of great men and their deeds, which developed into an impulse that would come to be marshalled under a nationalistic credo.

Fleeting mention must be made, then, of the equally impressive mythological narratives of other traditions. Works such as the Judaeo-Christian Old Testament, the Hindu *Mahabhrata* and *Ramayana* and the Slavic songs of return are all possibly relatable to *Gilgamesh* and thus to Homer in various yet unknown ways. Even now, they occupy a space between religion and myth and literature, depending on the context of their readership. Though these no doubt fulfilled (and, for some, may continue to fulfil) a social role similar to that assumed by the Homeric epics, these are outside the scope of this discussion, outside the generic play and counter-play set off by the poet or poets we now know as Homer. It is epic as a game of inter-textuality that we will continue to consider, as we proceed to the Middle Ages and the Renaissance.

2
The Middle Ages and Renaissance: Epic in the Christian Era

From the Middle Ages and into the Renaissance, the epic tradition resonates with the influence of the *Aeneid*. Yet Virgil's long shadow falls across a territory marked by Christianity. Both epic poets and their commentators, writing in a Christianised age, felt the need to account for the pagan origins of epic heroism, which, whether as the wrath of Achilles or the unforgiving patriotism of Aeneas, could be perceived as cruel and unchristian. These needed to be reconciled with the demands of a Christian moral system, with its attendant emphases on compassion and kindness.

The encounter between what was perceived as a pagan – and possibly barbaric – code of honour on the one hand and Christian mercy on the other coincides with a clash between epic and romance. It is no accident that the epic legacy handed down from the classical age is distracted in the late Middle Ages and Renaissance by the possibilities offered by the intervening genre of chivalric romance, specifically, the *chansons de geste* ('heroic songs') of the tenth to twelfth centuries. The romance is fundamentally a Christianised genre, telling of the battle between chivalric good-heartedness and pagan wickedness. Such good-heartedness differs from the cool conduct exemplified by Aeneas, particularly in his killing of Turnus at the end of the *Aeneid* in the name of Roman victory. The history of epic in the Renaissance is the story of conflict between these two differing modes of heroic conduct, one premised on patriotism, the other on love and compassion, extremes emblematised by Aeneas in his desertion of Dido, and the knight of romance fighting for both honour and chastity.

In addition, the form of romance is given to allegory, with heroic action becoming a parable for the universal conflict between good and evil that, for Christians, is supposedly constant and ubiquitous until the end of time. The allegorical tendencies of the Middle Ages reveal themselves not just in the detailed symbolism of the medieval romance, but in the tendency, too, to read classical epic as allegorical, in order to account for the sometimes inexplicable ways of pagan honour.

But the trappings of romance are not always easily integrated into epic, and the tight teleological focus of Virgilian epic does not give way lightly to the digressions of romance. The tension between the two is often expressed in Renaissance epics as a distraction from heroic quests, such as the fulfilment of honour, by the attractions of love and sex. Moreover, ultimately, the digressions of chivalric romance are not always easily accommodated to a Christian vision, and the history of Renaissance epic is the story of romance first embraced and then rejected in the search for a way to Christianise the epic.

The problems faced by the epic in the Middle Ages and Renaissance, writ large as the conflict between epic and romance, are discernible in the body of epic theory that accumulates in this period. Medieval epic theory as we know it today is piecemeal, consisting of descriptions of heroic poetry and commentaries on Virgil; yet, these – particularly the latter – do demonstrate that the question of Christianity and the epic was beginning to emerge. As we shall see, in Renaissance Italy the introduction of Aristotle's *Poetics* allows the matter to be raised with greater force, particularly in debates about the importance and nature of the divine and marvellous in epic, as well as implicitly in the question of whether romance could be combined with epic.

The rise of classical knowledge, accompanied by an increasing moral anxiety, is a trajectory not just in epic theory but in epic poetry of the period. Once the concerns of epic theory have been outlined, this chapter will deal with a Christianised heroic narrative composed without the explicit knowledge of Virgilian epic (and, as an oral or 'primary' epic, situated outside the generic line of 'secondary' epics that takes us from the classical to the Renaissance epics). This is *Beowulf*, composed some time between the eighth and tenth centuries. A subsequent look at epics in the later Middle Ages clarifies the moral dilemmas faced by those Christian poets who knew of the classical epic form and who were aware of Virgil if not of Homer. The problem of understanding this inherited pagan epic heroism through Christian mores is first tackled by Dante in his *Divina Commedia* ('The Divine Comedy'), written at the end of the thirteenth century. The possibility of romance as a way of dealing with this problem emerges in subsequent epics. Looking back briefly at the medieval romance, exemplified by the twelfth-century *Chanson de Roland* ('Song of Roland'), in order to understand better its later influence on epic as a way of introducing Christian morality to heroic narrative, this chapter will then explore how romance sensibilities are integrated into epic. First, they are wholly embraced by Ludovico Ariosto in *Orlando Furioso* (1532), which was written not just as a version of *Roland* but as a sequel to Matteomaria Boiardo's *Orlando Innamorato* (1487). We find, subsequently, a strenuous effort to combine epic and romance, in terms of both heroic conduct and narrative direction, first in Torquato Tasso's *Gerusalemme Liberata* ('Jerusalem Delivered') (1580), then in Edmund Spenser's *The Faerie Queene* (1590–6). The question of how to Christianise the genre, and the role of romance in this process, come to a head in an even more ambitious epic statement – John Milton's *Paradise Lost* (1667). Milton employs allegory in an altogether different mode, and employs Christian morality not as context but as text. The conflict between good and evil is, for Milton, to be presented as central action. Romance's fights between Christian knights and pagan wickedness yield here to the allegedly original story of good versus evil. With that, the simple exempla provided by the fictitious plot and action of heroic poetry give way to the pretensions at truth-telling that necessarily accompany creationist narrative. The problems for subsequent epic poets in the shadow of Milton's definitive attempt have become a critical commonplace – that is, the 'anxiety of influence' and the supposed death of the epic as we know it.

In a coda, however, this chapter deals with a text that eventually becomes a watershed in the epic tradition to rival *Paradise Lost*, though it may not in itself be classifiable as epic. *Don Quixote* (1605–15) by Miguel des Cervantes gives rise to alternative visions of heroism in the eighteenth century and beyond, and for that reason earns its place in this history of the epic.

Medieval and Renaissance epic theory

Discussions of the epic from the Middle Ages to the Renaissance are more concerned with Virgil than with Homer. For one thing, Homer may have been known, but was certainly not read, in Western Europe until the gradual introduction of Greek language and literature from Byzantium to Italy in the fourteenth century, the first printed edition of Homer's epics appearing in Florence in 1488. Even after this, Renaissance critics consistently showed a preference for Virgil, reading him as the more knowledgeable, accomplished and morally appropriate poet.[1]

Crucially, medieval commentary on Virgil is not the same thing as medieval commentary on the epic. Relatively little is known about criticism on the epic in the Middle Ages, when, as Hans Robert Jauss suggests, set generic categories were coming into being but were not a prominent feature of literary commentary, which showed instead a preference for discussing style, discourse and subject matter. There is some evidence, according to Jauss, that the *chanson de geste* was a recognisable genre, but that it was not identified as heroic poetry in the vein of the *Aeneid*.[2] However, while medieval epic criticism in itself is sparse, medieval commentary on Virgil is relatively plentiful, and we find that Aeneas is well known in the Middle Ages. The story of Aeneas' flight from Troy became a small part of a greater legend about the fall of Troy and the foundation of Rome, known as far afield as medieval England, to where it had been exported from Italy.[3] Moreover, Virgil's reputation, not just as a great poet but as a great teacher, had been consolidated over a period of intense Virgilian criticism from the first to fourth centuries AD, which culminated in Servius' well-known and detailed commentary.[4] Lines of Virgilian poetry were fragmented and adapted into centos (literally, poetic 'patchworks' of quotations), which held great cultural authority from the early Christian centuries into the Middle Ages. Importantly, these centos adapt Virgil's poetry to Christian sentiments.[5] Significantly, by what we could call the beginning of the Middle Ages, we find a sixth-century commentary by Fulgentius, which presents an allegorical reading of the *Aeneid*, interpreting its various books 'as stages in the spiritual life of man'.[6] Fulgentius' interpretation was taken up by subsequent medieval commentators and became the basis for what Christopher Baswell terms the 'allegorizing' treatment of Virgil in the Middle Ages.[7]

A second, not unconnected, medieval approach to Virgil was to retell the *Aeneid* as romance. This approach, which Baswell labels the 'romance' vision, manifests itself in such vernacular versions of the *Aeneid* as the *Roman d'Eneas* of the mid-twelfth century, itself an important influence on Geoffrey Chaucer's version of the *Aeneid* in *House of Fame* of the 1370s.[8] Such romance retellings tend to emphasise Aeneas' relationships with women, particularly, of course, with Dido. Telling the Aeneas and Dido story in isolation from the story of the founding of imperial Rome allows Aeneas to appear as more romantic lover than epic warrior.

Both approaches, as Baswell notes, demonstrate an attempt to inject a streak of compassion – both Christian and chivalric – into Virgil's epic heroism:

These two Virgillianisms – one learned and recondite, the other more popular and accessible – may seem very different. But they have in common a will to make Virgillian authority more immediately accessible and relevant to their contemporary world, be it spiritual or secular, moral or imperial.[9]

This moral unease over Aeneas' brand of heroism is crystallised by the medieval treatment of his defining characteristic – *pietas*.[10] As Aeneas entered the medieval vernacular, so did *pietas*. More specifically, Roman *pietas* was translated into Romance *pieta* and *pité*, and thus was transposed from that alloy of familial love and patriotic duty at the base of the *pax romana* into pity in the modern sense – that is, simple compassion and sympathy for others. The influential Renaissance critic Julius Caesar Scaliger's notation on the word *pietas* in his *Poetics* of 1561 is instructive:

> *Pietas* comes into play either with regard to affections, or in relation to obligations, and it flows from human minds either towards the gods, or towards one's country, or towards parents, wife, children, neighbours, friends . . . . *Pietas* also from time to time means 'pity'.[11]

Such an extrapolation of compassion from the more complex amalgam of familial love and patriotic duty of Roman *pietas* is emblematic of the way in which classical epic heroism was being reconsidered from the Middle Ages onwards.

With the rediscovery of Aristotle's *Poetics* in the early Renaissance – in particular, Alessandro Pazzi's influential Italian translation of 1536 – detailed study of epic began in earnest.[12] The Italian Renaissance saw the development of a formidable body of epic conventions, whose elaborations on Aristotelian ideas could sometimes take the form of fussy prescriptions and proscriptions. Thus, for example, Minturno's ideas on 'unity of time', and therefore on the proper length or duration of epic action, culminate in his arbitrary pronouncement that epic action should span no longer than a year.[13] The epic conventions established in the classical Roman continuation of ancient Greek epic tradition, such as the beginning *in medias res*, the descent of the hero to the underworld and the invocation of a muse, came to be widely recognised as such, and therefore became easy markers of the form.

Importantly, the Aristotelian convention of 'unity of action' gives rise to a romance versus epic debate, specifically whether romance, with its subplots and digressions, could qualify as epic. As Daniel Javitch suggests, much Renaissance genre theory is written in reaction to contemporary generic forms such as the romance rather than as a simple celebration of classical epic theory and practice.[14] It must be remembered that such romance-inspired works as Boiardo's *Orlando Innamorato* and Ariosto's *Orlando Furioso* had been composed in ignorance of the *Poetics*. As Aristotle's remarks on epic became wider knowledge, the question arose of whether such contemporary heroic narratives were indeed epic. At the heart of the debate was the Aristotelian dictum that the epic must be unified in its narration of one action, rather than, as in the case of romance, a narration of one man. Thus, for example, Trissino, who wrote the epic *Italia Liberata* in faithful exemplification of Aristotle's rules, discounted both Boiardo's and Ariosto's texts as epic, for the reason that if they were unified at all, it was by a single hero. On the other hand, Geraldi Cinthio exemplifies the liberal position, with his defiance of Aristotle's original statement in his insistence on the possibility of a 'biographical epic', and his consequent readiness to embrace Italian romances as new forms of epic.[15] This debate about the merits of romance's digressive tendencies over the teleology of epic is therefore also a clash between the digressive amorous exploits of the romance knight and the purpose-driven action of the Virgilian epic hero. The rise of Aristotelian theory, in other words, injects fresh vigour into the conflict between *pietas* and pity.

In addition, Aristotle's ideas on the marvellous, and his remarks on 'probable impossibilities' and 'possible improbabilities', mean that the small matter of supernatural and divine machinery – sidestepped, as Baswell suggests, in the Middle Ages – could no longer be ignored.[16] The religious basis of epic came under intense scrutiny. In this, Swedenberg notes, 'it was Tasso's opinion that became the commonplace in later critical writing on the subject'.[17] In weighing up the question of what subject matter would suit epic best, Tasso remarks in his *Discourses on the Heroic Poem*:

> the argument of the best epic should be based on history. But history involves a religion either false or true. Now I do not think the actions of the pagans offer the fittest subject for the epic poem, since in such poems either we do or we do not wish to have recourse to the gods worshipped by the pagans. If we do not, we lose the marvellous; and if we do resort to the gods invoked by the ancients, in that part we lost the verisimilar and credible, or get it by virtue not of the fable or imitation, but of the verse and other ornaments.[18]

For Tasso, the only way to solve this dilemma – that is, to invoke the marvellousness of the supernatural while adhering to the verisimilitude of 'true' religion – is to place the supernatural within a Christian context: 'to attribute actions that far exceed human power to God, to his angels, to demons, or to those granted power by God'.[19] Epic, for Tasso, must ultimately be informed by Christian values: 'The argument of the epic poem should be drawn, then, from true history and a religion that is not false.'[20]

In the Renaissance, the juxtapositions of romance with epic and that of Christian values with pagan ones stem from the common dilemma of how to write the epic in a Christian age. The charismatic chivalrous knights of medieval *chansons de geste* had been written, unlike their counterparts from the classical epic tradition, as consciously Christian heroes. Could they, therefore, provide a viable, Christianised alternative to their classical counterparts?

Beowulf

One heroic narrative that deals explicitly with the problem of Christian heroism in the pagan world is *Beowulf. Beowulf* recounts the story of the Geat prince Beowulf, who comes to the Danish kingdom of the Shieldings to save them from the monster Grendel. Beowuld successfully defeats both Grendel and Grendel's mother, thus preserving the great mead-hall Heorot, the 'hall of halls' (78), for their king, Hrothgar.[21] Though composed in ignorance of the legacy of classical Greek and Roman epic, *Beowulf* is a lengthy heroic narrative that posits a warrior code similar to the Homeric code of *kleos*. Its hero's mores are thus worth comparing not just with those of Homer's epic heroes, but with those of Virgil's Aeneas. However, Beowulf, for all his desire for earthly fame, crucially demonstrates an understanding of mercy and, by implication, a veneration for God-given life. His propensity for mercy sets him off, then, from the wrathful Achilles and wily Odysseus, Homeric heroes whose gods operate as dealers of destiny but not as judges of morality. Significantly, Beowulf's mercifulness is brought to the fore not in the exercise of it but in exceptions to it – at moments at which he kills rather than refuses to kill. This sets him off too, then, from the pious Aeneas, who at a crucial moment also refuses to show clemency, but only because it would be counteractive to the demands of nationhood and thus to the patriotism that underlies the specifically Roman *pietas*. Beowulf's rationale is not nationhood, or even, as we shall see, the primogeniture that so underlines it in Virgilian terms – it is simple moral good.

Moral good in *Beowulf* is aligned with a specifically Christian vision. Although Beowulf inhabits a pagan world that existed centuries before the Christian world of his poet, the spectre of Christianity stands over the poem as the only worthy solution to evil. The society of the Shieldings is clearly defined as pre-Christian, and their paganism renders them helpless against the embodiment of evil that is Grendel. Grendel is 'God-cursed' (711), for he is among the descendants of Cain, 'whom the Creator had outlawed / and

condemned as outcasts' (106–7). Such evil is more than a match for the
Shieldings' pagan beliefs:

> Sometimes at pagan shrines they vowed
> offerings to idols, swore oaths
> that the killer of souls might come to their aid
> and save the people. That was their way,
> their heathenish hope; deep in their hearts
> they remembered hell. The Almighty Judge
> of good deeds and bad, the Lord God,
> Head of the Heavens and High King of the World,
> was unknown to them. Oh, cursed is he
> who in time of trouble has to thrust his soul
> in the fire's embrace, forfeiting help;
> he has nowhere to turn.
>
> (175–6)

Against this backdrop of pagan impotence, the arrival of Beowulf is significant. Although, historically, he too belongs to a pagan society, he is depicted
as a Christian hero, enjoying the special favour of the Christian god:

> The King of Glory
> (as people learned) had posted a lookout
> who was a match for Grendel . . .
> And the Geat placed complete trust
> in his strength of limb and the Lord's favour.
>
> (665–7, 669–70)

Beowulf's victory becomes proof – as indicated in the parenthetical 'as people
learned' – that only Christian glory can defeat anti-Christian wickedness.
Though Beowulf is never depicted as converting the pagan Shieldings, it is
after his defeats of Grendel and Grendel's mother that, curiously, the
language of King Hrothgar first contains a monotheistic outlook. When his
first words to Beowulf after the triumph over Grendel are to 'let the
Almighty Father be thanked for this sight' (927–8), it is as if the pagan
mores of Hrothgar's people had never existed.

   In imposing Christian values on pagan heroism, the poet of *Beowulf*
carries out an important synthesis. His is not, as Roberta Frank has pointed
out, the simple rejection of pagan heroics as recommended in the writings
of early medieval theologians such as Bede, Alcuin and Aldhem, as much as

two centuries before the composition of *Beowulf*.[22] His narrative demon-strates a respect and, crucially, an enthusiasm for the wondrous deeds of Anglo-Saxon warriors, yet he must reconcile these with Christian concerns about mercy and restraint. In this, his objective is not dissimilar to that of later medieval and Renaissance epic poets, who would grapple with the pagan origins of men such as Aeneas. The heroism constructed by the *Beowulf* poet marries an element of astonishing strength and bravery with an obviously Christian morality. His hero's deeds are always the result of special favour from God. Significantly, too, this hero knows about mercy, a knowledge implied by his conscious decision to kill Grendel:

> But the earl-troop's leader was not inclined
> to allow his caller to depart alive:
> he did not consider that life of much account
> to anyone anywhere.

> (790–3)

Added to this is the poet's insistence on the monsters' inherent anti-Christian evil, so that their deaths are read as an affirmation, not a violation, of a Christian investment in good.

This is not to undermine Beowulf's thirst for glory, a desire for *kleos* that is Homeric in its magnitude. But Beowulf's glory is not just eternal; it is unearthly. It is not merely about fame in this world, everlasting as it may be; it is about heavenly recognition. Whereas Achilles had only the two earthly options of eternal posterity through heroic song or a happy life in unheroic peace, Beowulf can have the glory of god. Tellingly, Hrothgar, whose single advantage over Beowulf is age and therefore wisdom, instructs him to reject simple bloodlust and 'Choose, dear Beowulf, the better part / eternal rewards. Do not give way to pride' (1759). When Beowulf engages in his final fight – with the dragon that guards an ancient hoard of treasure – he does so prima-rily to protect his people and only secondarily to gain wealth. Though he signals this secondary desire with his dying wish to behold the hoard of gold, his people are ready to reject it, burying it with their king, and hence privileging the moral basis of Beowulf's heroism over the material one.

Beowulf, then, is a warrior for good over evil, almost a Christian soldier. By placing Beowulf's heroism within a Christian context, the *Beowulf* poet shows that thirst for glory is acceptable, for it is necessarily a force for good. His battles are not executed simply in the name of national preservation or expansion, even though the *realpolitik* of invasion and defence is inscribed in the setting of the poem by the threat posed by the neighbouring Swedes.

Thus, Beowulf fights not for simple personal posterity (as does Achilles) or for imperial interests (as does Aeneas). So little is he part of a monarchical line that he is never positioned as an heir apparent; after all, he inherits the kingdom from the Geat prince Hygealac not by birthright but by dint of valour and ability. Hygealac's gesture is foreshadowed by Hrothgar's construction of Beowulf as son (and possibly heir); it is subsequently echoed in the dying Beowulf's attitude to the brave young Wiglaf, who emerges at the end of the poem as an entirely plausible new leader for the Geats.

Beowulf, then, demonstrates the alternatives open to the poet in reconciling pagan heroism with Christian values. Importantly, it signals the usefulness of imposing a moral narrative of good over evil on to an existing story of heroic action, a Christianising tactic not unlike the allegorising treatment of Virgil that, we have seen, was also taking place in the Middle Ages. The two coincide in Dante's epic of the later Middle Ages – his *Divina Commedia*.

Dante's *Divina Commedia*

For Dante, the task of writing a heroic or, more specifically, an epic narrative had to be considered under the aegis of Virgil. Italy on the cusp of the Middle Ages and the Renaissance had designated Virgil a position at the head of the poetic canon. However, this position was morally problematic in a Christian age. For Dante, as for the *Beowulf* poet, the pre-Christian epic poet and his epic hero had to be accommodated and tolerated within a Christian vision. Notes Thomas Hill, 'Dante, like the *Beowulf*-poet, seems to have thought that some gentile "pagan" heroes could be saved but, unlike the *Beowulf*-poet, he is very cautious and hesitant about this possibility'.[23] Thus, for Dante, Virgil's poetic powers must be acknowledged, but so must their moral limitations. Dante is, like Virgil, self-consciously writing within and therefore alluding to the tradition of epic before him; he begins *in medias res* inasmuch as, at the start of the poem, we join the poet-narrator 'Halfway along the road we have to go' (I.i) and he descends down this road to the underworld. Most importantly, for Dante, the epic form was a vehicle for narrating great actions. However, there were actions greater than simple imperialistic endeavour to be narrated. Translating the epic from classical Latin into vernacular Italian, and transposing the form into the age in which he lived, Dante utilised epic to recount what, to the late medieval mind, could be the only heroic quest of any importance – the search of the Christian soul for divine knowledge and love.

Dante's narrative also demonstrates the medieval tendency to interpret heroic narrative allegorically, yoking its literal meaning to an abstract or moral one. This medieval allegorising of epic is specifically a subsumption of heroic conflict under the Christian aegis of the eternal battle between good and evil. That earthly narratives are allegorical of higher things is a standard of medieval poetics that is underpinned by religious belief; indeed, it may be traced to the allegorising nature of biblical exegesis from the early Church Fathers onwards. As Mindele Anne Treip has suggested, allegory is a logical outcome of Christian beliefs about the inherent, embedded and therefore discoverable power of the word.[24] The allegorical nature of medieval poetics, as Treip also points out, provided a basis for medieval and subsequently Renaissance epic: 'these increasingly elaborate allegorical expositions [of classical myth and epic] would seem to mark a new departure and lay the foundations for a designedly allegorical epic literature, the spiritual "progresses" of Dante, Tasso, Spenser, Milton'.[25]

Dante's concept of allegory is of a twofold structure – based on Augustinian ideas on exegesis – in which literal meaning is accompanied by an allegorical moral meaning.[26] According to Dante himself:

the subject of this work must be considered in the first place from the point of view of the literal meaning, and next of the allegorical interpretation. The subject, then, of the whole work, taken in the literal sense only, is the state of souls after death, pure and simple. . . . If, however, the work be regarded from the allegorical point of view, the subject is man according as by his merits and demerits in the exercise of his free will he is deserving of reward or punishment by justice.[27]

In other words, Dante's poem tells, on a literal level, of his journey through hell, purgatory and heaven, while demonstrating, on an allegorical level, the trials and tribulations of the soul (in this case, the soul not just of Dante but of Everyman) in its journey towards true divine understanding. Dante is guided on his quest first by Virgil and then by Beatrice, the girl Dante loved in his youth and idealised as the perfection of both womanly and human virtue. Virgil leads Dante through the regions of hell and purgatory, before this position is assumed by Beatrice, who takes the poet into heaven. Thus, Virgil represents, in Dante's poem, the human capacity for reasoning that may exist independently of and prior to the deeper, firmer knowing that comes with faith, which is represented by Beatrice. In his journey through hell and purgatory, Dante encounters various sinners; these become representative of the sins themselves, which the powers of reason, embodied by Virgil, overcome.

In narrating the soul's quest for divine knowledge and love, it is interesting – though, on reflection, unsurprising – that Dante saw Virgil as a logical emblem for reason. But the veneration with which Dante holds Virgil is made apparent on their first meeting:

> 'Are you indeed that Virgil, are you the spring
> Which spreads abroad that wide water of speech?'
> When I had spoken, I bowed my head for shame.
>
> 'You are the honour and light of other poets;
> My long study and great love give me strength
> Now, as they made me pore over your book.'
>
> (*Inferno* I.79–84)[28]

In Virgil, then, Dante makes explicit reference to past pagan epic, and signals his intentions to Christianise the form. His Virgil is prior to Beatrice in the same way that the classical epic precedes the Christian epic. Of course, Dante is also necessarily indebted to Virgil, for remnants of the Virgilian epic must form the basis of Dante's Christianised epic. The epic element of quest or journey is retained on the literal level, while it could be said that the implicit power attributed to Virgil's epic – its ability to provide commentary on so many aspects of human psychology – is made explicit by Dante's allegorical narrative. Thus, Dante intends to follow not just in Virgil's footsteps as supreme epic poet but in Aeneas' as epic hero. This becomes evident when Dante compares his quest with those of both Aeneas and St Paul. As he approaches the gates of hell, he says to Virgil:

> 'You tell me that the father of Sylvius,
> While still in nature, went to eternity
> And was there with all his senses.
> . . .
> It does not seem unsuitable to a man of intellect:
> Nor that he was chosen in empyreal heaven
> To be the father of bountiful Rome and her empire;
> . . .
> And afterwards the chosen vessel went there,
> To bring back reassurance for that faith
> Which is the beginning of the way of salvation.
>
> But I, why should I go there? By whose permission?
> I am not Aeneas; neither am I Paul;
> Neither I nor others think that I deserve it.
>
> (*Inferno* I.13–15, 19–21, 28–33)

Yet Dante does survive hell and, in doing so, demonstrates that the quest of the soul in search of its divine reward is as special a piece of heroic action as both the foundation of Rome and the foundation of the Church of Rome.

Significantly, Dante's comparison of himself with both Aeneas and Paul recalls too the poem's contemporary political context. For, in aligning himself with these two founders of empire, Dante is referring to his own hopes for a new form of Italian governance, which he set out around the same time in his *De Monarchia* ('On Monarchy'). Disillusioned with power struggles in the papacy, Dante hoped for a united Holy Roman Empire of the order of Augustan Rome. This is not to say, of course, that Dante positions himself in the role of founder, only that he is positing the ideal establishment of a new empire for the good of his people. In his own words, his intentions in writing the poem were to 'remove those living in this life from a state of misery, and to bring them to a state of happiness'.[29] Throughout his poem, references to the corrupt practices of contemporary Florentine public figures make clear his dissatisfaction with current political affairs.

These political references initially seem out of place in a text whose primary concern is spiritual, yet, as we shall see, they are wholly in step with Dante's conception of the soul and the nature of its progress. For Dante, the soul is characterised above all by its capacity for free will. After all, we have seen that the poem's allegory, as described by Dante, is about the spiritual outcome achieved by the man through the 'exercise of his free will'. If the soul is the hero of Dante's poem, the soul's capacity for heroism is an extension of its capacity for choice. This allegorical hero of the *Commedia* – the soul – is heroic in its achievement of heaven through its own exertions. Dante's depictions of various sinners are also innate criticisms of men, or souls, who have failed to exercise their free will heroically. Dante's location of epic heroism in the Christian soul's progress and its free will would resonate, to varying degrees, in the epics of Tasso, Spenser and Milton.

Ariosto's *Orlando Furioso*

Yet, between Dante on the one hand and Tasso on the other intervenes romance, most importantly, Ariosto's deployment of romance. The romance form develops from the *chansons de geste* of medieval France. Based on legends, these had been, to differing extents, redacted or composed into longer texts by anonymous poets and performed by travelling singers or *jongleurs*. These poems or songs were eventually grouped into three cycles, the first two dealing with Charlemagne and his knights and the third with William of Orange. The earliest extant example, belonging to the first cycle, is *Chanson de Roland*, dated to the end of the twelfth century. From this first poem onwards, the romance form is characterised by its feudal setting, by its concerns with knights and their adventures, particularly by the knights' chivalric efforts at defending the honour of king and country. These efforts provide the basis for the knight's own honour. Chivalric romance heroism, therefore, is shaped by patriotism.

Patriotism is, however, always underpinned by Christian morality. The *Roland* poet, for example, alters historical events – the ambush of Charlemagne's knights by Basques on return from war with Muslim Spain – to emphasise the conflict between Christianity and Islam (denominated, of course, as paganism). The ambush is blamed not on Basques but on Muslims, or Saracens, and it prompts religious conflict. The poem's larger context is therefore the holy war that is the First Crusade. The poem's nominal hero, Roland, Charlemagne's nephew, leads the rearguard into battle with the Saracens for the city of Saragossa and in doing so dies. That this crucial battle is fought on behalf of the Christian God is demonstrated by Roland in response to his compatriot's warning of imminent battle:

> Oliver said: 'Lord companion, I think
> We may have a battle with the Saracens.'
> Roland replies: 'And may God grant it to us.
> It is our duty to be here for our king:
> For his lord a vassal must suffer hardships
> And endure both great heat and great cold;
> And he must lose both hair and hide.
> Now let each man take care to strike great blows,
> So that no one can sing a shameful song about us.
> The pagans are wrong and the Christians are right.
> No dishonourable tale will ever be told about me.'
>
> (1006–16)[30]

For Roland, heroic glory in battle resembles the *kleos* desired by Achilles. His death, like that of Achilles, does not diminish this, for it is succeeded by the posterity of song. But Roland's heroism is tied, additionally, to feudal loyalty and, significantly, to Christian good. Little wonder, then, that the battle is actively decided by God, first in prolonging the day so that Charlemagne can defeat Marsile, the Muslim king of Saragossa, and then in sending Gabriel to Charlemagne's assistance in a grand second battle with the Muslim overlord Baligant. Although the Muslims are not the only villains of the piece – Roland is also betrayed by his stepfather, Ganelon – the poem makes clear that any enemy of the knights is an enemy of God. Thus, Ganelon is described as a 'living devil' (746) and his trial, following the death of Roland, is decided against him only through the direct intervention of God.

The knights of romance, as inherited by the Renaissance, are explicitly Christian soldiers. As compassionate Christians, they are also, of course, courtly lovers, defending not just the honour of their king, but that of damsels in distress. When Ariosto came to write his version of Roland's exploits, *Orlando Furioso* (after Boiardo's *Orlando Inamorato*), this added element of romance in the modern sense of the word provided a source of amusement and parody, as well as, importantly, a deviation from epic expectations. The titles of both Ariosto's and Boiardo's poems do not just signal their hero but, in line with conventional epic openings, align him with an overriding emotion or trait. However, here, these emotions are love and the fury that comes of love. Roland, or Orlando, is in both poems a lovesick knight in pursuit of the beautiful pagan princess Angelica. Ariosto's opening lines make clear his intentions to layer the chivalry of romance on the belligerence of epic: 'I sing of knights and ladies, of love and arms, of courtly chivalry, of courageous deeds' (I.1).[31]

Needless to say, Ariosto's positioning of love at the centre of epic heroism involves a significant revision of classical epic in terms of both character and plot. His heroes, Orlando and Ruggiero, are driven not by *pietas* in the Roman sense but by its romance derivatives – pity and love – in the same way, as we have seen, that Aeneas was being read by some in the Middle Ages and early Renaissance as displaying not stern piety but compassionate pity.[32] However, in a heroic narrative, pitying love lacks the teleological force of *pietas*, for it is about distraction, not action. The knights are not engaged in holy war; they are endlessly distracted from war by love, or, more accurately, by desire. Orlando forgets his duty to Charlemagne as a result of his blind love for Angelica; Ruggiero is similarly devoted to Bradamant, though his love does not preclude him from being tempted by such tantalising visions as the pagan Alcina in disguise, as desire comes to distract from desire. Each moment that an Ariostoan hero succumbs to love and desire marks a diversion from the conventionally epic plot of conquest or duty. The result is the continually digressive structure that has eventually come to be associated with romance. Romance, as Patricia Parker's influential analysis points out, is 'characterised primarily as a form which simultaneously quests for and postpones a particular end, objective, or object'.[33] The substitution of love for traditional epic concerns such as duty or glory is thus reflected on the narrative level in a constant deflection away from epic teleology, or unity of action, in the Aristotelian sense. As Colin Burrow puts it:

> The centralized devotion to an imperial cause which is manifested in Aeneas' *pietas* appears to be completely lacking from the poem. *Orlando furioso* seems indeed almost to be an explosively decentred revision of the epic plot, in which the multiplicity of episodes so violently prevented by Aeneas become the chief object of writing.[34]

Yet, it is possible to read such digression as a compulsory aspect of the Christianisation of the epic. This is not simply because the chivalric knight who displays Christian compassion is bound to be sidetracked by objects of pity, but because, as Andrew Fichter suggests, distraction and digression are part of the standard Christian narrative of temptation.[35] Thus, when Ruggiero is spirited away first to Alcina's island and then to her sister Logistilla's gardens, these episodes represent important stages in his moral development. The first represents a necessary temptation and the second a spiritual recuperation through the attainment of self-knowledge. Ruggiero, Fichter posits, is then ready to 'complete his epic journey in the terms laid down by Christian allegory, to advance from reason to grace' – much, we might note, like Dante.[36]

A Christianised narrative requires that digressions give way to resolution. As Burrow reminds us, Ariosto made substantial revisions to the poem, revisions that steer it towards an epic resolution of martial and Christian conquest. That this dénouement for both heroes is, in the final analysis, specifically epic in nature is made clear by allusions to both Homer and Virgil. Thus, Orlando's fury is channelled away from matters of love to matters of war when his friend Brandimarte is killed in battle, in an echo of the death of Patroclus and Pallas. He is finally more warrior than lover as he angrily avenges Brandimarte's death in explicitly Achillean fashion:

> When Achilles saw Patroclus staining the ground with his blood under his borrowed helmet, he was not satisfied with slaying his friend's slayer but had perforce to lacerate the corpse, dragging it about. /... To conclude, there is no anger to equal that which you feel on seeing your lord, your kinsman or boon-companion injured before your eyes. So Orlando was surely right to be cut to the quick, to flare up on so dear a friend's account, seeing Brandimart lying dead from the fearsome blow dealt him by King Gradasso. (XLII.2 and 6)

Just as *philia*, or friendship, in Achilles can be expressed only through a warrior's *menis*, or wrath, so Orlando's capacity for love is now inextricably yoked to belligerence, not to desire or pity. Similarly, Ruggiero's warrior credentials are highlighted when the poem ends not with his union to Brad-amante but with his subsequent defeat of the pagan Rodomont. His decision to kill Rodomont is one of pious self-defence, not patriotic revenge, but it is none the less compared to Aeneas' slaying of Turnus. Realising 'the trap into which he might fall if he delayed dispatching the impious Saracen' (XLVI.139), Ruggiero has no choice but to condemn his enemy to the fate that Aeneas doles out to Turnus: 'Released from its body, now ice-cold, the angry spirit which, among the living, had been so proud and insolent, fled cursing down to the dismal shores of Acheron' (XLVI.140). Both Orlando and Ruggiero are thus established as Christian epic heroes, their chivalric tendencies finally, if tentatively, pressed into the service of religious conquest. Ariosto's detailed revisions, then, demonstrate how the digres-sions of romance must be raised only to be defeated in order to satisfy the demands of Christianised epic.

Tasso's *Gerusalemme Liberata*

Tasso, writing in the wake of both Dante's use of Christianised allegory and Ariosto's deployment of romance, produces an epic in which romance provides a literal narrative, accompanied by an allegorical narrative that is informed by Christian morality. Crucially, the years that intervene between Ariosto's poem and Tasso's are marked not just by the Catholic backlash to the rise of Protestantism that was the Counter-Reformation but by the rela-tively late discovery of Aristotelian epic theory, referred to earlier. These renewed emphases on both religious orthodoxy and epic teleology are immediately evident in Tasso.

Tasso, as we have seen, insisted on a Christian foundation to epic poetry. He also later insisted on, and connected this Christian element to, the use of allegory in epic, stating, 'Allegory has rightly been said to resemble both night and darkness; it is therefore to be used in mysteries and in poems full of mystery like the heroic'.[37] For Tasso, it is only logical that the revelatory technique of allegory that lies at the heart of Christian scripture is utilised by the grand genre of epic. According to Tasso, epic must convey Christian morality using the modes of Christian didacticism, that is, by presenting 'images' with which the reader must interpret: 'to lead to the contemplation of divine things and thus awaken the mind with images, as the mystical theologian and the poet do, is a far nobler work than to instruct by demonstration.... The mystical theologian and the poet, then, are noble beyond all others'.[38]

Tasso's theories on allegory and its precise application in *Gerusalemme Liberata* are carefully worked out and explicated in an 'Allegoria del Poema' ('Allegory of the Poem'), which appeared with the Italian edition of the poem in 1581.[39] Echoing the Dantean concept of literal and allegorical levels, Tasso conceives of epic structure as consisting of an abstract moral idea clothed by heroic action. In the opening lines of his 'Allegoria', he states:

> Heroic poetry, like an animal in which two separate natures are joined, is composed of Imitation and Allegory. With the former it attracts the souls and ears of men and brings them wondrous delight, while with the latter it instructs men in virtue or knowledge or both. And as Epic Imitation is but a semblance and image of human action, so Epic Allegory must be the figuring forth of human life. Now Imitation regards men's actions as they present themselves to the outward senses. ... By contrast, Allegory regards the passions, the beliefs, and the moral habits, not only as they appear outwardly, but as they intrinsically and essentially are.[40]

Thus, for Tasso, the spiritual life, internal to humankind, is internal too to the epic form, which ostensibly concerns itself with the external show of heroic action. Unlike Dante, then, Tasso made use of the genre of romance and its trappings of chivalry. The epic's exterior is chivalric struggle, while its crucial interior is the Christian pursuit of moral good. Significantly, in other words, if Dante's allegorical key is the journey or quest, Tasso's is simply conquest, that of Christian knights over pagan enemies.

The poem tells the events of the First Crusade, in which Godfrey, identified throughout with the epithet 'pious', leads a Christian army to wrest Jerusalem from Muslims. According to Tasso, the army 'signifies the virile man, composed of body and soul', while Jerusalem 'signifies such Civil Happiness as would befit a Christian'.[41] Of his heroes, Tasso explains that Godfrey:

> stands in the place of intellect, in particular that intellect that judges not the necessary but the mutable – things that could fall out in any number of ways. By the will of God and of the princes he is chosen Captain over this enterprise, for the intellect is from God, constituted by nature Lord over the other powers of the soul and over the body, commanding the former with a civil and the latter with a kingly power.[42]

Godfrey therefore commands both the other princes and the mass of soldiers as the intellect does both 'the other powers of the soul' and 'the body'.[43] Of the other princes, Tancred and Rinaldo specifically represent concupiscence and ire: 'the love that caused Tancred and the other knights to behave like fools and abandon Godfrey, and the indignation that led Rinaldo to stray from the enterprise – these signify the strife between the rational faculty and the concupiscible and irascible faculties, and how these two rebel'.[44]

In Tasso's model of epic heroism, the intellect is a specifically Christian virtue in its powers of discernment and discrimination. The pious Godfrey, then, is crucially distinct from the pious Aeneas, for Godfrey's piety is of the pitying kind. This Christian intellect is wedded to anger and love; conversely, anger and love cannot function without the guidance of the intellect. In the ireful Rinaldo and the concupiscent Tancred, Tasso rewrites past epic and romance respectively into a Christianised mode. Rinaldo is a hero in Achillean mould, a boy-soldier whose 'thirst for honour is unquenchable' (I.10).[45] He abandons the Crusade after having slain a comrade who had been tempted by pagan magic to slander Rinaldo. Rinaldo's furious assault ('foolish fury in a petty cause / turning his sword against Christ's champions' [V.33]), his departure and his subsequent temptation by the pagan Armida are explicitly in defiance of Godfrey and of God. These are the actions of an ungodly epic hero, wrathful and misguided. So, crucially, Rinaldo's reconciliation with Godfrey heralds his destruction of the enchanted wood, which symbolises his triumph over earthly delusion and temptation. According to Tasso:

> In his duel with Gernando, trespassing beyond the bounds of civilly sanctioned vengeance, and in his servitude to Armida, Rinaldo may denote anger ungoverned by Reason. Thus Rinaldo's return and his reconciliation with Godfrey signify but the obedience that the irascible must render to the rational.[46]

More than this, in Rinaldo's return to the fold, an Achillean epic heroism of glory by wrath is symbolically subjected to Christian reason.

Tancred's follies, meanwhile, echo those of Ariosto's knights, when they eschew martial duty for love. Lovesick for the pagan Clorinda, Tancred wanders far from camp and falls into the clutches of Armida. Eventually, however, this concupiscence too is validated by being Christianised, when Clorinda, unwittingly fatally wounded by Tancred in battle, confesses her love for him and is baptised. For Tasso, love is a virtue only if it is harnessed to Christian reason, and is thereby rendered fit for epic action: 'if love is not merely a passion and a movement of the sensitive appetite, but a highly noble habit of the will, as St. Thomas held, love will be more praiseworthy in heroes and consequently in the heroic poem'.[47] Tancred's desire for Clorinda is acknowledged by her in virtually the same breath as her conversion to Christianity. It is therefore validated as the kind of constant love worthy of a Christian epic hero, the kind of love explicitly distinguished by Tasso from the passions displayed by classical heroes: 'This kind of love the ancients either did not know or did not wish to describe in their heroes. . . . But modern poets . . . can still in forming a knightly character describe love as a constant habit of the will.'[48]

When not ennobled into righteous anger or constant love, ire and concupiscence provide distractions from the drive of the narrative, just as the temptations of desire constitute digressions from plot in Ariosto's romance-epic. Yet, Tasso, more so than Ariosto, is committed to epic teleology, specifically to a dénouement whose allegorical function is to demonstrate the power of Christian reason to achieve divine and everlasting happiness. Ariosto's romance plot, in which the pursuits of love and honour are liable to take off in opposite directions, has therefore been revised, in order that the Christian knights might pursue martial glory and chaste love together, in an allegory – recalling Dante – of the pursuit of Christian good. However, not just the temptations of romance behaviour but the excesses of classical epic heroism – for example, wrath – are shown to be inimical to this linear trajectory towards both literal and allegorical fulfilment, towards an absolute goal in both narrative and abstract terms. In Tasso's poem, both epic and romance have been re-dressed and pressed into service to a Christian morality. His legacy to the epic tradition, then, is to insist on the epic's power to reveal gradually but insistently a message that is both divine and determinate in nature.

Spenser's *Faerie Queene*

Spenser's debt to Tasso is substantial, though the details of it are uncertain. Spenser was clearly aware of Tasso's epic, though possibly not so of Tasso's *Discourses on the Heroic Poem* and 'Allegory'.[49] Spenser was also indebted to Ariosto, whom he read, crucially, along with the full exegetical paraphernalia that built up quickly around Ariosto's work, in such writings as John Harington's English translation of *Orlando Furioso* and the Italian editions of Ariosto's epic by Simone Fornari and Giuseppe Bononome. Significantly, these attributed to it an allegorical impulse that it did not necessarily possess.[50] Thus, when Spenser came to write *The Faerie Queene* as an allegorical romance-epic, he perceived his work to be part of a tradition which, for him, had been signalled by Tasso and, before him, Ariosto, whose work he famously declared he intended to 'overgo' with his epic.[51]

Like Tasso, Spenser appears to harness the waywardness of romance to the teleology of epic using the tools of allegory, specifically Christian allegory. But the allegory of Spenser's rich and complex poem is not always easily pinned down, for correspondences seem to be lost in a bewildering array of episodes, characters and, significantly, quests and heroes. For there is more than one quest underway and more than one hero to deal with in the *Faerie Queene*. Each book of the epic tells of at least one quest; and most of the quests, though not all, are undertaken at the behest of the Faerie Queene. These quests run parallel with the overarching quest of the overall hero, Arthur, who rides in search of the Faerie Queene, in order that he might do her service. Through employing a number of sub-quests and sub-heroes, Spenser cleverly maintains the multifaceted quality of romance and preserves just the merest threat of digression. However, all this is eventually yoked to an ultimate goal, in both allegorical and literal terms.

The text's reluctance to delimit the excesses of romance within the bounds of allegory is suggested by Spenser's statement on the allegorical dimension of *The Faerie Queene*. Like Tasso in his 'Allegory', Spenser delineated the configurations of his allegory, in a letter to his patron Sir Walter Ralegh. Unlike Tasso, however, Spenser's text does not substantiate the ideas he sets out in his letter. Further, it is not enough to suggest that this incongruity is a result of Spenser's lack of opportunity either to finish his poem or to revise it, for the letter was written after the composition of Cantos I–III.

None the less, the letter usefully sets out Spenser's ideas on allegory and gives vital clues to some, if not all, of the poem's allegorical basis. Identifying his poem as 'a continued Allegory, or darke conceit', Spenser justifies his use of allegory by adverting to the now familiar Renaissance notion that allegory achieves both aesthetic and didactic effect through the use of gradual revelation:

> To some I know this Methode will seeme displeasaunt, which had rather haue good discipline deliuered plainly in way of precepts, or sermoned at large, as they vse, then thus clowdily enwrapped in Allegorical deuises. But...So much more profitable and gratious is doctrine by ensample, then by rule.[52]

The didactic intention of *The Faerie Queene*, according to Spenser, is 'to fashion a gentleman or noble person in vertuous and gentle discipline'; in other words, to undertake the political and moral education of the Elizabethan gentleman.[53] His central hero, Arthur, is, for Spenser, an obvious successor to past epic heroes because he is both 'a good gouernour and a vertuous man'. Homer, according to Spenser, had demonstrated both the public and personal virtues respectively with Agamemnon (not Achilles) and Odysseus, while Virgil and Ariosto combined them in their heroes, and Tasso 'disseuered them againe' in Godfredo and Rinaldo.[54] But Arthur is not to assume the position of moral exemplar alone. According to Spenser, Arthur represents the core virtue of 'magnificence', while each of the poem's six books (the poem was to have comprised twelve books) tells of an heroic quest undertaken by at least one knight, in representation of a distinct virtue: respectively, holiness, temperance, chastity, friendship, justice and courtesy.[55] Most of the knights are helped by Arthur, just as the virtues must ultimately be informed by magnificence, which 'is the perfection of all the rest, and conteineth in it them all'.[56] Most of the books follow a trajectory in which a knight sets off on a quest to destroy deceit or licentiousness. Thus, in Book I, the Redcrosse knight, signifying holiness, quests to free the kingdom of the Lady Una from a dragon. Crucially, Redcrosse must first overcome, with Arthur's help, the wizard Archimago, the 'master of false images', and Duessa, or duplicity, and must be restored to purity in the house of Caelia (whose name means, literally, 'heavenly'). Caelia is mother of Fidelia (faith), Speranza (hope) and Charissa (charity). Because Una is representative of truth, indeed of the One Truth of Protestant Christianity, the defeat of the dragon represents the liberation of truth and a triumph over deceit. Similarly, in Book II, Sir Guyon, as temperance, seeks to destroy the Bower of Bliss of Acrasia, whose name signifies that she is 'without control'. He is, in the course of his quest, tempted by Mammon; again, Arthur comes to the rescue. Once restored by Alma, whose name means 'nourishing' and thus signifies the soul, and whose house, in an extended metaphor, represents the human body, Guyon can go on to destroy the wanton excesses of the Bower of Bliss.

One knight not in need of Arthur's help is the female warrior Britomart. The association of Britomart's name with British martiality, and thus her identification with Elizabeth I, is unavoidable. So too is the allusion to Ariosto's Bradamante, who spends much of *Orlando Furioso* seeking her true love Ruggiero, with whom she goes on to found a royal line. Similarly, Britomart rides in search of Artegall, and the pair of lovers are destined to be dynastic founders of Britain. While Britomart may be betrothed from the outset of the book, she is in fact representative of the virtue of chastity. Chastity, therefore, is not a simple question of virginal abstinence; it connotes instead the fidelity that comes with wedded love. Not surprisingly, then, Britomart's heroic adventures include the rescue of Amoret, who represents love, and the reconciliation of Amoret with her lover, Sir Scudamour, the 'shield of love'. Through Britomart, Spenser clarifies the distinction, found in Tasso, between mere lust on the one hand and matrimonial love on the other. The one is digressive, suggestive of romance's distractions, the other is teleological, particularly in its performance of dynastic responsibility.

The ultimate goal in Spenser's moral allegory is Christian good, here specifically designated as glory. It is personified by the Faerie Queene, Gloriana, herself, for whom the knights fight and whom Arthur seeks. Thus, the allegorical message is that all the virtues must be harnessed under that of magnificence in order that glory may be achieved. Crucially, however, glory is polyvalent. Though it suggests primarily Christian glory, connoting the combination of beauty and goodness in the divine, it can also denote an earthly fame and honour outside a moral context. Thus, the Spenserian knight is allegorically an ordinary (Christian) man on a moral progress and literally an extraordinary hero on a wondrous quest. This doubling of Christian and heroic quest occurs in Tasso and Dante in terms of narrative, where it is split into the allegorical and the literal. Both poets, as we have seen, privileged the allegorised Christian quest, locating it, in Tasso's terms, at the core of the text or, in Dante's, at a higher level. Spenser, however, allows both Christian morality and simple heroism to share, in the word 'glory', the same semantic space, signalling that, even at the endpoint of his narrative, the two might coexist uneasily.

Ultimately, however, glory is associated by Spenser with patriotism. Of her several associations, Gloriana's most important, according to Spenser's letter to Ralegh, is with Elizabeth I, to whom the poem is dedicated: 'In that Faery Queene I meane glory in my generall intention, but in particular I conceive the most excellent and glorious person of our soueraine the Queene, and her kingdome in Faery land.'[57] The patriotic thrust of the poem can be discerned at several points in the narrative, for example, in the revelation that Redcrosse is actually St George, patron saint of England. England is thus aligned with Una's home, land of truth, which is saved by Redcrosse. Furthermore, the task allotted to Artegall, as justice, to save Irena from Gran Torto, the 'grand tyrant', is an allegory that heroicises the attempts by Protestant England to wrest control of Ireland from the perceived tyrannical influence of the Catholic Church. Thus, Faeryland exists on at least two allegorical levels: ruled by Gloriana as Elizabeth, it is a representation of Britain, but as the locus of glory and the end-goal of the progress of virtue, it is nothing less than heaven. The poem thus powerfully aligns Christian glory with Britishness.

Spenser's epic is not merely the first English epic; it is self-consciously an epic of England. It recalls the nationalistic rationale of Virgilian epic, but marries patriotism to Christianity. Significantly, all this it does within both an allegorical drive and a rich texture of multiple plotlines. The soul at the centre of Spenser's narrative is simultaneously the Christian soul in search of salvation, a model Englishman on his way to gentlemanly perfection and a magical quester in a never quite definable realm of faery.

Milton's *Paradise Lost*

By his own admission, Milton was long in preparing himself to write a conventional heroic epic before coming to compose *Paradise Lost*, considering as early as 1642:

> whether that epic form whereof the two poems of Homer, and those other two of Virgil and Tasso, are a diffuse, and the book of Job a brief model: or whether the rules of Aristotle herein are strictly to be kept, or nature to be followed, which in them that know art, and use judgement, is no transgression, but an enriching of art: and lastly, what king or knight, before the conquest, might be chosen in whom to lay the pattern of a Christian hero.[58]

Milton ranges over the intricacies of assuming a place in the epic tradition in line with Homer, Virgil and Tasso, of adhering to Aristotelian epic theory and, significantly, of Christianising the epic with the familiar tool of allegorical romance. Yet, eventually, he would reconsider and reformulate the problem of the Christian epic, redressing in particular the mode of allegorising the progress of the soul. Milton confronts the question by dealing with the classical epic on the one hand and the contemporary romance epic on the other. Though John Dryden would later label *Paradise Lost* a romance, in which 'the Gyant had...foil'd the Knight, and driven him out of his strong hold, to wander through the World with his Lady Errant', it can safely be suggested that Milton largely rejected romance epic and sought another approach to classical epic.[59] Acknowledging the power and stature of classical epic in both its own time and his, yet doubting the Christianising powers of romance allegory, Milton's solution is, in effect, to bypass romance and embrace more directly the trappings of classical epic. Romance, by then familiar to the epic as an allegorical mode and therefore a Christianising tool, is firmly set aside by Milton.

Milton eschews allegory in favour of Christianising epic in the most obvious way – by biblicising it.[60] Although he is not the first to turn to scripture for epic material, for he had before him the example of Marco Giralamo Vida's *Christiad* (1535) and Abraham Cowley's *Davideis* (*c.* 1650), Milton offers more than the versified scripture of Vida and Cowley.[61] He constantly juxtaposes classical concerns with Christian ones. Yet, although Milton placed the Bible above the classics in terms not just of moral power but of literary merit, he did not hesitate to exploit the veneration and stature afforded to the classical epic.[62] This appropriation of classical epic is evident in his ready use of the epic conventions that Virgil had consolidated through his borrowing of these from Homer. More than any other poet after Virgil, Milton brings back into focus a range of epic motifs. Beginning *in medias res* and descents to the underworld are features of many of the epics discussed here, but Milton reintroduces the epic catalogue, the war council and the heavenly scales. Thus, his list of fallen angels in hell echoes those of the Achaian ships in the *Iliad* and of the Italian chieftains in Book VII of the *Aeneid*; the devils' war council at Pandemonium recalls those of both Agamemnon and Aeneas before the main attack, and God, like Zeus and Jupiter, indicates his judgment with a divine set of scales. All these set Milton's poem in a direct line from the classical texts and challenge the reader to accept it as a Christian version of these legendary ancient epics.

In order to achieve the sense of decorum required of a biblicised epic, Milton had also to transpose the dignified style of Homer's and Virgil's dactylic hexameters into English. Rejecting Ariosto's and Tasso's rhymed ottava rima and Spenser's nine-line stanzas, Milton adopts blank verse, which he describes as 'English heroic verse without rhyme, as that of Homer in Greek and of Virgil in Latin; rhyme being no necessary adjunct or true ornament of poem or good verse', and further asserts that it is 'to be esteemed an example set, the first in English, of ancient liberty recovered to heroic poem from the troublesome and modern bondage of rhyming'.[63] Another attempt at injecting stylistic decorum can be seen in Milton's now infamous syntactic inversions, what Italian poets called *asprezza* and which Tasso recommended for heroic poetry.[64] Though not inherently Latinate in themselves, Miltonic inversions none the less recall the classical languages by their association with foreignness and difficulty. This is decorum by defamiliarisation; Milton achieves formality by calling attention to form.

Still, the juxtaposition in *Paradise Lost* between classical epic style and Christian content is necessarily an uneasy one. Charles Martindale suggests, however, that Milton 'was alive to these contradictions, and built the tensions between pagan and Christian, epic and Bible, into the fabric of his work'.[65] The precise problem of how to present Christian truth in classical mode, and the way in which Milton dealt with this, can be seen in Milton's

Christianisation of the classical epic convention of the invocation of the muse. Tasso's poem had suggested that the divinity of the muse was Christian, not classical, as though all muses had been mistakenly appropriated by the ancient Greeks and rightfully belonged in heaven:

> O Muse, who do not string a garland of
> the fading laurel fronds of Helicon,
> but far in heaven among the blessed choirs
> wreathe deathless stars into a golden crown,
> breathe into my heart the fire of heavenly love.
>
> (*Gerusalemme Liberata* I.2)

Spenser, meanwhile, had aligned his 'sacred Muse' (I.1) with Elizabeth, 'holy Virgin chiefe of nine' (I.2), thereby cleverly burying the question of the muse's pagan origins beneath his quasi-patriotic, quasi-mystical allegory. Milton, however, confronts the problem with an explication of the classical muses as mere bywords for deeper, Christian wisdom. Thus, although he invokes Urania, Greek muse of astronomy, he insists that 'The meaning, not the name I call: for thou / Nor of the muses nine, nor on the top / Of old Olympus dwell'st, but heav'nly born' (VII.5).[66] Urania is just a synonym for divine wisdom. Similarly, the muse, when invoked at the beginning of his poem, is no classical invention but an abstraction of God's omniscience:

> Sing Heav'nly Muse, that on the secret top
> Of Oreb, or of Sinai, didst inspire
> That shepherd, who first taught the chosen seed,
> In the beginning how the heav'ns and earth
> Rose out of chaos...
>
> (I.6–10)

The seriousness of the problem is clearly set out here. Milton cannot gloss over the pagan provenance of his muse because of the nature of his song, which is nothing short of divine truth. Thus, the inspiration for Milton in composing his poem is the same as that for Moses in the writing of the Bible. Both are relaying the word of God.

Milton's epic, then, must ultimately convey this truth. Thus, according to Martindale, although 'the classical and the Biblical are intertwined throughout the poem, there is some overall movement from classical to Biblical'.[67] The poem progresses from the flagrant epical heroism of Satan and the other fallen angels, through to a second, greater war in heaven, on to the scripturally true story of the fall. That Satan is evocative of an epic hero is evident at the outset, as he soars and strides magnificently across the poem's canvas. He is, according to Martindale, 'more closely associated with epic values and activities than any other of the poem's major characters'.[68] As Northrop Frye has noted:

> it is to Satan and his followers that Milton assigns the conventional and Classical type of heroism. Satan, like Achilles, retires sulkily in heaven when a decision appears to be favouring another Son of God, and emerges in a torrent of wrath to wreak vengeance. Like Odysseus, he steers his way with great cunning between the Scylla-like Sin and the Charybdis-like Death; like the knights errant of romance, he goes out alone on a perilous quest to an unknown world.[69]

And also like sulky Achilles, some of the battle-weary fallen angels retire to recite their heroism in a parody of Homeric *kleos*, to 'sing / With notes angelical to many a harp / Their own heroic deeds and hapless fall / By doom of battle' (II.547–50). Such narrow glory-seeking is merely a 'demonic' brand of heroism, set in context by the angels, who 'contented with their fame in heav'n / Seek not the praise of men' (VI.375–6).[70] The only song to attend the angels' heroism is the 'instrumental harmony' of God, 'that breathed / Heroic ardour to advent'rous deeds / Under their godlike leaders, in the cause / Of God and his Messiah' (VI.65–8).

However, the real watershed between the limitations of classical epic and the unbounded divine truth that is Milton's ultimate aim is to be found in Book IX, when, just before setting out the action of Adam and Eve's fall, the poem takes a dramatic pause:

> ... sad task,
> Not less but more heroic than the wrath
> Of stern Achilles on his foe pursued
> Thrice fugitive about Troy wall; or rage
> Of Turnus for Lavinia disespoused,
> Or Neptune's ire or Juno's, that so long
> Perplexed the Greek and Cytherea's son

(IX.13–19)

The sequence of events surrounding the fall – divine anger and retribution and ultimately expulsion – is, according to Milton, more heroic than the contents of either Homeric or Virgilian epic. Specifically, God's just wrath is more important than the furies of pagan epic's heroes and gods. Equally so, 'this subject for heroic song' is more worthy too than the chivalrous battles of romance. Milton describes himself as:

> Not sedulous by nature to indite
> Wars, hitherto the only argument
> Heroic deemed, chief maistry to dissect
> With long and tedious havoc fabled knights
> In battles feigned; the better fortitude
> Of patience and heroic martyrdom
> Unsung.
>
> (IX.27–33)

The knights of romance are 'fabled', their battles 'feigned', and theirs is not true 'heroic martyrdom'. This attack on romance is sustained through the lines that follow, with their disdain for:

> tilting furniture, emblazoned shields,
> Impresses quaint, caparisons and steeds;
> Bases and tinsel trappings, gorgeous knights
> At joust or tournament
>
> (IX.34–7)

Not only does the vocabulary imply show and superficiality, but the matter-of-factness with which romance's characteristics are listed also suggests unimaginative conventionality. In other words, romance posits 'The skill of artifice or office mean, / Not that which justly gives heroic name / To person or to poem' (IX.39–41). Milton's heroic song is concerned with neither pagan fury nor chivalric manners; it is a 'higher argument' (IX.42).

This crucial passage challenges the epic reader to find true heroism in the poem, heroism that surpasses the deeds of previous epic heroes. Furthermore, true heroism is thrown into relief by the antics of Satan and his crew, and situated in the actions of those who not only fight for good, but who choose to fight for good. Satan, up to Book IX, is defined by his decision to rebel. So is it that, beyond Book IX, Adam and Eve are defined by their decision to fall. And the decision is indeed theirs, for Adam is reminded that he is 'Left to his own free will, his will though free / Yet mutable' (V.236–7). Yet, there is a crucial difference between the two decisions: 'The first sort by their own suggestion fell, / Self-tempted, self-depraved: man falls deceived / By the other first: man therefore shall find grace' (III.129–31). As with Dante, Tasso and Spenser, then, Milton is concerned with the soul's heroic capacity, a capacity made possible by free will. But Milton is interested primarily in the circumstances that created the soul's heroic potential; he narrates not the struggle to achieve grace, but the way in which the need for that grace was established. He therefore does not relate a heroic allegory of the soul's progress towards divinity, but tells the heroic origins of that journey and anticipates the heroic triumphs with which it will end.

As a story of origins, *Paradise Lost* must purport to be truth itself, not truth shadowed – this would be simple allegory. Though the poem contains significant allegorical episodes, not least Satan's encounters with the figures of Sin and Death, its allegory is of a profoundly different nature from the romance epics of Tasso and Spenser. It is not that Milton disapproves of the moral efficacy of romance allegory (dismissive as his poem may be of its finery); indeed, in recounting his youthful reading habits in a pamphlet of 1642, he states, not without a touch of good humour:

> I betook me among those lofty fables and romances, which recount in solemn cantos the deeds of knighthood founded by our victorious kings, and from hence had in renown over all Christendom. There I read it in the oath of every knight, that he should defend to the expense of his best blood, or of his life, if it so befell him, the honor and chastity of virgin or matron.... Only this my mind gave me, that every free and gentle spirit, without that oath, ought to be born a knight, nor needed to expect the gilt spur, or the laying of a sword upon his shoulder to stir him up by both his counsel and his arms, to secure and protect the weakness of any attempted chastity.[71]

Yet, for Milton, there is a better way to instil virtue than by example, and that is by historical exposition; in other words, not by recreating through simple allegory, but by returning to first causes. When Milton states elsewhere that 'He that can apprehend and consider vice with all her baits and seeming pleasures, and yet abstain, and yet distinguish, and yet prefer that which is truly better, he is the true warfaring Christian', he is foreshadowing the possibility of two versions of Christian free will under trial, through an everyman or through the first man. Milton chooses the latter.[72]

This is not to say, however, that Milton's choice is anti-allegorical. For a committed Christian like Milton there must exist the acknowledgement that God cannot be known directly and is always to be shadowed somehow; that is, underlying the poem is the belief that all narrative, even biblical, can only point to a higher truth. As we have noted earlier, it is by dint of this strand of thought that allegory is read into Christian teaching, and exegesis is central to Christian understanding. If Milton's truth is to be of the same texture of the truth at the heart of scripture, then his allegorical mode too must be of the same woof as scriptural allegory. Milton's insistence on the ineffability of God's word emerges in Raphael's angelic discourse to Adam.[73] Raphael stands as 'Divine interpreter' (VII.72) between God and man, and, in Adam's words, 'hast voutsafed / Gently for our instruction to impart / Things above earthly thought' (VII.80–1). Milton, in presuming to 'justify the ways of God to men' (I.26), stands in precisely the same relationship to us as Raphael does to Adam. He must literalise the story of the fall in order that it may be understood. He must also narrativise it, even epicise it, endowing it with plot trajectory and character psychology. For this reason, it is possible to say that *Paradise Lost* is not an allegorical epic in the way that *The Faerie Queene* is.[74] Yet, for this reason, too, it is important to concede that *Paradise Lost* is allegorical in so far as all scriptural narrative is allegorical, and to note, after C. S. Lewis, that 'In the religious life man faces God and God faces man. But in the epic it is feigned, for the moment, that we, as readers, can step aside and see the faces both of God and man in profile'.[75] The face of God that we see in *Paradise Lost* is necessarily allegorical of an unknowable and unquestionable truth. Miltonic epic therefore reproduces the honest and objective assumptions of Homeric epic, that what is being narrated is an accepted and integral part of cosmic and human history.

These two questions – the extent to which Milton had successfully conveyed the imponderability of Christian thought, and the extent to which he had successfully rewritten the classical epic for a Christianised world – would dominate the eighteenth-century reception of *Paradise Lost*. The extent to which Milton, in grappling with these questions, personified heroism in himself would become a consideration for the nineteenth century. It is Milton, more than any other epic poet, who would enable the Romantic alignment of epic poet with epic hero, a situation which his own words seem to foreshadow:

> he who would not be frustrate of his hope to write well hereafter in laudable things, ought himself to be a true poem; that is, a composition and pattern of the best and honourablest things; not presuming to sing high praises of heroic men, or famous cities, unless he have in himself the experience and the practice of all that which is praiseworthy.[76]

It is Milton too, apparently, whose shadow is cast over epic attempts in the eighteenth century. Though there is little need here to rehearse the now too familiar and debated terms of Harold Bloom's concept of the 'anxiety of influence', it is worth noting that Milton decisively revised classical epic for a Christian age, a revision with consequences for epic in the eighteenth century and beyond.

Coda: Cervantes' *Don Quixote*

The significance of Milton's epic rewriting of romance and allegory is matched in terms of influence by one other seventeenth-century text, Miguel des Cervantes' *Don Quixote*. The novel was written in two parts in 1605 and 1615. In the intervening decade, Cervantes was outraged by the appearance of a spurious sequel, and wrote his own continuation in response. The novel as we have it now recounts the adventures of a middle-aged *hidalgo*, or Spanish gentleman, Alonso Quijano, who turns his back on his lifestyle of impoverished gentility to become Don Quixote, the kind of knight-errant of which he has read in his favourite romances. Convinced that such books are historically veracious, he decides to revive the golden age of chivalry and sets off to wander the countryside in the company of his squire, the simpleton Sancho Panza. Part I ends with Quixote's forced return to his village, which he again leaves in Part II. The final conclusion is brought about by Quixote's return to sanity and his death. The whole is supposedly based on texts discovered by the frame narrator, the first part originally written in Arabic by a Moor, Cide Hamete Benengeli, while the author of the second part is never identified. Indeed, the events of Part II are meant to take place after the publication not just of the first part but of the false second part, and Quixote and Sancho are by this time considered minor celebrities by those they meet.

The aim of the text, as stated in the frame narrator's prologue, is 'the demolition of the ill-founded fabric of these books of chivalry, despised by so many and praised by many more' (16).[77] Cervantes' objective is nothing short of the deflation of the epic form through burlesque. The way in which Quixote's adventures achieve this demolition is readily apparent from the knight's first adventures. The pattern of mockery is clearly set out: when Quixote is confronted with real events and phenomena, his interpretation of these events is translated by his romance-filled imagination, and his subsequent actions can only be described as insane and, what is worse, often result in grievous physical harm to himself. In other words, chivalric heroism, though regarded by Tasso and Spenser as exemplary Christian behaviour, is presented here as so out of step with the real and the everyday as to be insane and even pernicious. Thus, in tilting at windmills, Quixote predictably ends up bruised; in mistaking an inn for a castle and a prostitute for a princess, he eventually loses half an ear; in waging war against a flock of sheep he is battered beyond recognition. And such bodily harm is only half the problem. Quixote's delusions result in various moral and legal violations, from physical violence against innocent travellers to the freeing of sentenced prisoners. Through it all, Quixote appears ridiculous not just to the other characters, including the simple Sancho, but to the reader as well.

Such a pattern of mockery is burlesque inasmuch as an incongruity between the common and everyday with the heroic and elevated is exploited to achieve comic effect. Chivalric behaviour is, for Cervantes, no longer convincing as an allegory for Christian progress. One of the aims of Cervantes' burlesque moments is, as Anthony Close has shown, to:

> make fun of the pseudo-historicity of chivalric romances, with their sage chroniclers and their sources in miraculously preserved Oriental archives. More generally, they spoof the entire paraphernalia of epic grandiloquence, and thus create a festive and ironic atmosphere around all the hero's acts, predisposing the reader to consider them with amused detachment.[78]

However, though Close's careful analysis of Cervantes' use of high and low burlesque (the former when Quixote's elevated style is used absurdly to describe the trivial events that befall them, and the latter, less often, as when serious subjects such as Quixote's death are conveyed in an offhand manner) is admirable, he fails to make the important point that Cervantes' epic burlesque has the opposite effect of later mock-epic, such as Alexander Pope's. It is not the case, as Close suggests, that all burlesque works 'to ridicule another literary work or genre or style' (19), for, as with Pope's mock-epics, it is possible for burlesque to use the trappings of a given genre or style as a tool of ridicule, in other words, for its target to be strictly social and not literary. If Dido is made to talk like a fishwife, or indeed an epic warrior is invoked in a description of a belle of the *ton* such as Pope's Belinda, in order that fishwives or society dames may be ridiculed, then heroic seriousness has actually been preserved, because the point is precisely that it is so difficult to attain. On the other hand, if the gap between high and low, Dido and the fishwife, or knight-errants and sixteenth-century Spanish gentlemen is exploited in order to poke fun at the very concept of high seriousness, then the message is that the mighty are not as mighty as they seem, or that one simply cannot take heroic adventure too seriously.

In targeting chivalric romance Cervantes attacks the allegorical epic tradition as it had come down to him from Ariosto, Tasso and Spenser.[79] As Michael McGaha has suggested, Cervantes 'created a modern hero who, in his thoroughgoing humanity, was more "exemplary" to the suffering masses of mankind than the plaster saint which medieval and Renaissance commentators had made of Aeneas'.[80] More than this, Cervantes directly attacks the inadequacy of classical epic heroism to deal with the demands of everyday life. Don Quixote unquestioningly accepts the classical epic heroes as models of behaviour, explaining to Sancho that:

> what a man must do and what a man does if he wishes to achieve a reputation for prudence and long-suffering, is to imitate Ulysses, in whose person and labours Homer painted for us a living portrait of these two qualities, just as Virgil showed us in the person of Aeneas the courage of a dutiful son and the sagacity of a brave and able captain, not describing or revealing them as they were but as they should have been, to leave models of their virtues for future generations. (207)

Such epic heroism is shown to be spectacularly redundant in the prosaic business of life, as when, in an example of epic burlesque, Quixote engages in mortal combat with flocks of sheep. The epic resonance of this story is heightened by its origins in classical mythology (that is, the tale of Ajax being made by the gods to fight with sheep). Cervantes sets the scene of battle first by juxtaposing Quixote's illusory heroic world against 'reality':

> he was beside himself with joy, because he knew that these were two armies marching to clash in the middle of that broad plain. Every minute of every hour his imagination was filled with those battles, enchantments, adventures, extravagances, loves and challenges that books of chivalry recount, and everything he said, thought or did was channelled into such affairs. And the dust clouds were being raised by two great droves of sheep approaching from opposite directions along the same road, but the dust prevented the sheep from being seen until they came close. (139)

Here the burlesque attains its effect from parody, as Quixote strides into battle, ready to spear the sheep 'with as much fury and determination as if he really were attacking mortal enemies' (142) and is consequently counter-attacked by the shepherds, who 'drew their slings from their belts and started to salute him about the ears with stones the size of fists' (142). The outcome of this clash between literary fantasy and everyday reality is, predictably, injury to Quixote. Then, the burlesque is intensified by Quixote's reaction – he vomits. Such an animalistic response is, as L. A. Murrilo suggests, 'a counterforce to the learned materials of the epic'.[81] Indeed, we could think of the text's overall fascination with the body, particularly through Sancho, as a general critique, and additional burlesque, of the epic.[82]

Unsurprisingly, the opposition between high and low, between Quixote's epic fantasising and everyday reality, which undergirds Cervantes' burlesque is often expressed as the text's fundamental dichotomy between romance and reality.[83] It is tempting to think of this as a dichotomy between Quixote's world of chivalric romance, construed as insanity, on the one hand and the real world of sheep, inns and prostitutes on the other. So much is this so, one could argue, that even a fully conscious investment in the spectacle of romance, such as those of the Duke and the Duchess, is ultimately indistinguishable from madness: 'the Duke and Duchess, going to such lengths to make fun of two fools, were within a hairsbreadth of looking like fools themselves' (956). In such a formulation, reasonable characters, such as the barber and the curate, whom Maria DiBattista identifies as 'anti-questers', provide the rational element against which Quixote's, and to an extent Sancho's, madness is defined.[84]

This romance/reality dichotomy needs further explanation. For the 'real world' in which Quixote finds himself possesses only the most superficial trappings of reality. A closer inspection, particularly of the story of Luscinda, Dorotea, Cardenio and Don Fernando, reveals a place of pastoral and comedy.[85] As Felix Martinez-Bonati suggests, the 'reality' of the text is supplied not by this world in which Quixote finds himself but by the world inhabited by the reader:

> The fictitious world of the *Quixote*, then, is erected on a most solid *sense of reality*, common to the author and his readers, that is evoked in the work from the beginning. In the nonfictitious background of the book, the reality of life functions as a matter of firm and unquestioned consensus.[86]

The comic-pastoral 'real' world of *Quixote* functions to show up Quixotic epic and romance as one of the less reliable modes of literature. However, it could be suggested that the text queries all literature as a source of truth, as evidenced by its persistent ironic self-questioning, from the use of the untrustworthy narrator Cide Hamete to Sancho's absurd story of the goats, which subverts the idea of plot and dénouement. Nobody, Cervantes seems

to be saying, should invest wholeheartedly in any idealising form of literature, and most pernicious of all forms are the chivalric romances of the epic
tradition.

Don Quixote's most important contribution to the epic tradition, however,
is to allow for an alternative heroism to that of romance and epic, specifically an anti-idealistic heroism. In doing so, it opens up a space into which
the individual of early novel may step. It facilitates a comparison between
epic romance heroes and the 'real' people of the novel as it emerges in the
eighteenth century. Its legacy may therefore be seen in the consciously anti-
epic novels of the next century, particularly those of Henry Fielding and
Tobias Smollett.

3
The Eighteenth Century: Epic in the Modern World

The century or so after the appearance of *Paradise Lost* witnessed two significant developments in the epic tradition. The first is the tendency of poets such as John Dryden and Alexander Pope away from straightforward epic attempts towards related endeavours, namely, epic translation and mock-epic. Dryden's translation of the *Aeneid* appeared in 1697. Pope worked for ten years on his translation of the *Iliad*, which appeared in six volumes between 1715 and 1720, and for three years collaborated on the *Odyssey*, which appeared in five volumes (1725–6). Both poets also produced mock-heroic or shorter heroic poetry – Dryden's *Absalom and Achitophel* (1681) and *Mac Flecknoe* (1682), and Pope's *The Rape of the Lock* (1712–14) and *The Dunciad* (1728–42). The second, later development in the epic is the emergence of what Henry Fielding labelled the 'comic epic in prose', referring to his own *Joseph Andrews* (1742) and *Tom Jones* (1749). Alongside Fielding's 'comic epics' may be read Tobias Smollett's *The Adventures of Roderick Random* (1748) and *The Adventures of Peregrine Pickle* (1751).

The first trend represents the most notable contribution to the epic made by the major poets of the early eighteenth century. It is both a response to and an affirmation of an increasingly precise and comprehensive body of epic theory, based on the epic criticism of the Italian Renaissance, which emerged in France in the seventeenth century before later being exported to England. In particular, it is to be read in the context of the debate that flourished in both France and England over the value of classical thought and literature. Dryden and Pope seem to align themselves with those in support of the classics, inasmuch as their works gesture towards a veneration of the classical epic poets. As one scholar has described their epic efforts, Dryden 'chose rather than emulating Virgil to translate him', while Pope 'quietly refused the acknowledged responsibility of his office and fell to the altogether more comfortable task of polishing Homer'.[1] In a curious way, these epic gestures may also be read as a reaction against the robust challenge set by Milton's epic, in terms of their preference for epic in an ancient mode over a modern one. However, Dryden's and Pope's 'epics' do reluctantly express some doubt about the worth and relevance of classical literature and its norms. The effect of their epic attempts is not so much a lively continuance of the epic as a curatorial preservation of it.

The second trend is fruitfully read not so much as a response to Milton as the legacy of Cervantes' *Don Quixote*. As we have seen, *Don Quixote* brings into question the value of epic solemnity and classical heroism; those who write in the manner of Cervantes openly critique the epic form and emphasise the irrelevance of epic heroism. Yet, Fielding and Smollett, who consciously wrote under the aegis of *Don Quixote*, elaborate further on Cervantes' mode of comic epic. Where Cervantes so virulently mocks his own hero but refuses to provide an alternative to him, Fielding and Smollett posit a new set of heroics for the modern age. Their relationship to the epic is therefore a complex one, for while they criticise classical epic heroism, they retain an investment in the notion of heroism *per se*. These 'comic epics' imaginatively enlarge the critique of the epic form implicit in Cervantes, while displaying the marks of their indebtedness to the epic tradition. Though often positioned as milestones in the rise of the novel, they are worth considering here because they represent a significant innovation in the epic genre, to be set against the conservative gestures of Dryden and Pope.

This chapter will examine Dryden's and Pope's epic translations, as well as their mock-epics, paying particular attention to *The Rape of the Lock*. In turning to epics in prose, we will glance at the influential prose epic *Télémaque* (1699), by François de Fénelon, before discussing the 'comic epic' novels of Fielding and, to a lesser extent, Smollett. Finally, in a coda, we will look forward to Milton's influence in the Romantic age, by examining the scriptural epic *Der Messias* ('The Messiah') (1748–73) by Frederich Klopstock.

Eighteenth-century epic theory

In order to understand fully the context in which first Dryden and Pope, and then Fielding and Smollett, came to write their variations on the epic, it is important to look briefly at the state of epic theory in the late seventeenth century and into the eighteenth. English epic theory was extensively influenced by developments in France. Following the pattern set in the Italian Renaissance, French epic theory of the age had developed into a formidable collection of precepts about, for example, the necessity of unity of action or the permissibility of Christianised supernatural machinery. The most significant developments, however, were: the consolidation of the epic's status as the premier literary form, the emphasis on the epic's didactic nature and the continued narrowing of suitable epic exemplars to two poets – Homer and Virgil. Such notions were imported to England through several select texts, for example, René Rapin's *Réflexions sur la Poétique d'Aristotle* (1674) and René Le Bossu's *Traité du poëme épique* (1675), which was translated into English as *A Treatise on the Epick Poem* in 1695.

The popularity of Le Bossu's treatise in particular meant that the ground-rules of French epic theory became common critical knowledge in England.[2] These constituted, primarily, a restriction of epic practice to classical epic, particularly to Homer and Virgil, in an emphatic rejection of the epics of the Renaissance. But it is Le Bossu's central thesis that proved profoundly influential. Expanding on the idea that epic is necessarily allegorical, Le Bossu suggests that the underlying message or ideology of the poem – its 'fable' – is of greater importance than its surface narrative – its 'action'. So much is this so that, according to Le Bossu, the epic poet formulates this fable before anything else. The epic is therefore, for Le Bossu and those he influenced, fundamentally ideological. Such a proposition, as we shall see, lies at the heart of both Dryden's and Pope's epic efforts. Both were familiar with Le Bossu, Dryden having read him in French before the appearance of the popular English translation of 1695.[3]

However, the classical foundation on which such epic theory stood had to contend with the so-called *querelle des anciens et des modernes* ('the quarrel between the ancients and the moderns'). This debate about the value of the classics raged among poets, translators and critics in seventeenth-century France – for example, Boileau, the Daciers (the husband-and-wife team of respected classicists) and Le Bossu on the one hand and Charles Perrault, Antoine Houdar de La Motte (Madame Dacier's rival in Homeric translation) and Voltaire on the other. It was only slightly less hotly contested in England. The central question to the *querelle* was, as Joseph Levine puts it, 'Were the Greeks and Romans superior in all the ways of life and thought to everything that followed after? Or had the moderns in one field or another succeeded in equaling or surpassing them?'[4] The 'ancients' insisted that the classics provided models for emulation, and even for instruction, in contemporary life, while the 'moderns', investing in a belief in a general forward march of intellect, suggested that the classics were at best aesthetically interesting but at worst irrelevant and even barbaric. This was, of course, a modern take on Renaissance concerns about the gap between pagan values and Christian ones, being an extrapolation of the problem beyond religion to life in general (perhaps to be expected in an era in which the concept of a value system beyond the remit of religion was able to be countenanced). By the end of the seventeenth century and into the next, however, a compromise position began to emerge, that the classical age was a distant but valuable culture, particularly poetically and historically, but that humankind had obviously made advances in science and technology, which necessarily had an effect on art.[5] This veneration of the classics offset by a growing confidence in the abilities and values of modern society characterises in one way or another all the eighteenth-century epic efforts to be discussed here. However, this juxtaposition is, as we shall see, not always an easy one.

The sense of uneasiness concerning the ancients' place in a world of modern literature and thought may be seen in the reception of Milton's *Paradise Lost*. There was much discussion over the poem's position as epic, specifically as one of the major epics after Homer and Virgil, and approbation was not universal. Indeed, Joseph Addison, one of the poem's staunchest advocates, strikes a somewhat defensive tone in 1712 when he dismisses the question of the poem's epic status as immaterial to its greatness, stating, 'I shall wave [sic] any Discussion of that Point which was started some Years since, Whether *Milton's Paradise Lost* may be called an *Heroic Poem*? Those who will not give it that Title, may call it (if they please) a *Divine Poem*.'[6] In contending with the question of Milton's epic status in the context of the classical epic poets, poets such as Dryden and Pope were surprisingly ambivalent about Milton's relatively modern epic.

The way in which both Dryden and Pope positioned Milton vis-à-vis the classical poets is instructive. Dryden's famous 1688 epigram on Milton only *appears* to place him alongside Homer and Virgil in a triumvirate of epic poets:

> Three Poets, in three ages born,
> Greece, Italy, and England did adorn.
> The first, in loftiness of thought surpassed;
> The next in majesty; in both the last.
> The force of nature could no further go;
> To make a third, she joined the former two.[7]

These lines seem to present Milton as an amalgam of the two classical epic poets, and hence even to suggest his supremacy over them. Yet, the reference to Milton's ability as beyond the 'force of nature' suggests that his genius is neither natural nor original. It is as though nature, unable or unwilling to create another epic poet, has somewhat lazily produced a copy of the previous two. Though Dryden is often identified as a modern, his stance here is very much in line with that of the ancients.[8] As Levine notes of the question of imitation as handled in the *querelle*, 'The gap between the ancients and moderns on this point was not very wide'.[9] Dryden, like the ancients, seems to insist that the classics, as the true and great originals, can only ever be copied. Indeed, in the dedication to his translations of Juvenal's *Satires* in 1692, some three years before the appearance of his translation of the *Aeneid*, Dryden rejects outright the existence of a third great epic poet after Homer and Virgil, stating, 'if it may be permitted me to go back again to the Consideration of *Epique* Poetry, I have confess'd, that no Man hitherto has reach'd, or so much as approach'd the Excellencies of *Homer* or of *Virgil*'.[10] In the same essay, he questions the status of *Paradise Lost* as an epic poem:

> As for Mr. *Milton*, whom we all admire with so much Justice, his Subject is not that of an Heroick poem; properly so call'd: His Design is the Losing of our Happiness; his Event is not prosperous, like that of other *Epique* Works: His Heavenly Machines are many, and his Human Persons are but two.[11]

Crucially, he also renews the implication that Milton is unoriginal as an epic poet, stating that 'no Man has so happily copy'd the Manner of *Homer*; or so copiously translated his *Grecisms*, and the Latin Elegancies of *Virgil*'.[12] Yet it is worth pointing out that Dryden's denial of Milton's epic status is hardly a grudging one, for he is full of judicious praise of *Paradise Lost*. It is simply as though Dryden cannot construe of modern epic-writing as anything more than a translation or imitation of the classics.

Pope, perhaps more easily identifiable as an ancient, expresses a comparable view. Writing in 1717, in the midst of translating the *Iliad*, he makes his position on the classics very clear:

> All that is left to us is to recommend our productions by the imitation of the Ancients: and it will be found true, that in every Age, the highest character for sense and learning has been obtain'd by those who have been most indebted to them. For to say truth, whatever is good sense must have been common sense at all times; and what we call learning, is but the knowledge of our predecessors.[13]

In the Preface to his translation of the *Iliad*, he attributes Homer's greatness to his originality: 'Homer is universally allow'd to have had the greatest *Invention* of any writer whatever. The praise of judgment *Virgil* has justly contested with him, and others may have their pretensions as to particular excellencies; but his Invention remains yet unrival'd.'[14] As Kirsti Simonsuuri suggests, Pope opposes Homeric invention against Virgilian judgement, positing the former as the genius that inaugurates the epic form and the latter as the one that successfully refines it. Thus, invention becomes 'a mark of originality and directly opposed to imitation'.[15] Pope goes on to ally Homer's invention with the characteristic of poetic fire: 'It is to the strength of this amazing invention we are to attribute that unequal'd fire and rapture, which is so forcible in *Homer*.[16] No other poet, according to Pope, is able to produce this same quality of 'fire', presumably because he is doomed to imitate and not to originate. Pope's list of poets in comparison with Homer is telling:

> This *Fire* is discern'd in *Virgil*, but discern'd as through a glass, reflected from *Homer*, more shining than fierce, but every where equal and constant: In *Lucan* and *Statius*, it bursts out in sudden, short, and interrupted flashes: In *Milton*, it glows like a furnace kept up to an uncommon ardor by the force of art...[17]

After the Homeric originals, epics necessarily lack invention and, with it, fire. Hence, they are lifeless in comparison and, in Milton's case in particular, artificial. As with Dryden, there is no malice here, only the assumption that no modern epic poet can ever be as good as Homer (or, for Dryden, as good as Virgil).

So far it would seem that the deep respect Dryden and Pope demonstrate for the classical originals, and the fact of their absorption in the task of translating epic rather than composing it, attest to a preference for the classical epic over the modern. However, it is possible also to discern a contemporary ideology at the heart of the translations of both poets and therefore to discover a tension between this classical veneration on the one hand and a modern perspective on the other. Importantly, Dryden and Pope, after Le Bossu, are committed not just to the narrative of epic but to its ideology – that is, to fable as well as action. And, in attempting to translate a classical ideology, each poet in his own way ultimately admits its incompatibility with, and even irrelevance to, an Augustan worldview. The compromise position of the *querelle*, which offsets classical beauty against modern progress, is therefore discernible in both Dryden's and Pope's translations.

Dryden's *Aeneid*

Dryden wrote in a long line of English translations of the *Aeneid*, many of which he studied carefully in order to draw on them in his work.[18] He none the less developed his own theory of translation, first set out in 1680 in his preface to a collection of translations of *Ovid's Epistles*.[19] Here he enumerates the three strategies available to the translator, which Richard Thomas summarises as 'metaphrase', 'imitation' and 'paraphrase, or translation with latitude'.[20] For Dryden, the first method is a literal translation and the second a liberal one; his personal preference is for a third way, which he describes thus:

> since every language is so full of its own proprieties, that what is beautiful in one is often barbarous, nay sometimes nonsense in another, it would be unreasonable to limit a translator to the narrow compass of his author's words: 'tis enough if he choose out some expression which does not vitiate the sense. ... There is therefore a liberty to be allowed for the expression, neither is it necessary that words and lines should be confined to the measure of the original. The sense of an author, generally speaking, is to be sacred and inviolable. If the fancy of Ovid be luxuriant, 'tis his character to be so, and if I retrench it, he is no longer Ovid. It will be replied that he receives advantage by this lopping of his superfluous branches, but I rejoin that a translator has no such right...[21]

Dryden, then, sought to understand the spirit of the original poet and his poem rather than simply to reiterate its surface meaning. That is, true to Le Bossu, he aimed to get to the fable of the poem and convey this to the reader. The 'latitude' to which Dryden refers is evident not simply as expansion – which is, of course, immediately noticeable as he so often takes a greater number of lines to render the sense of the original – but also as his subjective construction of the poem's ideology. In other words, in the many elaborations of the original we find Dryden's interpretation of the spirit, or ideology or 'fable' of Virgil's *Aeneid*. As Dryden himself notes, 'Some things too I have omitted, and sometimes have added of my own...the Additions, I also hope, are easily deduc'd from Virgil's sense'.[22] More importantly, in Dryden's attempts at reconstructing the ideology of the classical original we find an unwitting acknowledgement of the differences between this apparently ancient ideology and a modern one. We find, in other words, a forced concession on Dryden's part of the irrelevance of a classical epic viewpoint to a neoclassical readership.

Dryden's version of Virgil's ideology is clearly indebted to Le Bossu. According to Le Bossu, Virgil sought to 'instruct *Augustus* as the Founder of a great Empire, and to inspire into him as well as his Successors, the same Spirit and Conduct which had rais'd this *Empire* to such a Grandeur'.[23] Similarly, Dryden believed that Virgil's main intention was 'To infuse an awful Respect into the People, towards such a Prince: By that respect to confirm their Obedience to him; and by that Obedience to make them Happy'.[24] Though Dryden does imagine Virgil as a reluctant propagandist for Augustus – for he is aware that 'this Conquerour, though of a bad kind, was the very best of it' – he nevertheless believes, following Le Bossu, that the underlying ideology of the poem is a description of good and pious government for the instruction of the emperor.[25]

However, this ideology of governmental prudence is conveyed in Dryden's translation not positively, by way of nationalistic celebration, but negatively, through sharp political critique. Dryden reflects in his translation on the government of his own day and implicitly comments on the efficacy of a new English *Aeneid* in influencing it. Crucially, Dryden, as we have seen, construes Virgil in his Preface as a fundamentally republican poet who tries to make the best of things by undertaking to advise his emperor. It is not surprising that Dryden set such store by this assumption, when he was a converted Catholic living in the reign of a Protestant king. Rather than translate the *Aeneid*, as some others had done, as a straightforwardly Royalist poem with Aeneas as a version of Charles II or even James II, Dryden aligns Aeneas with William III.[26] Significantly, in doing so, he underlines the points at which William diverges from the heroic ideal, and not where he approaches it. His translation is peppered with critiques, some subtle and others much more direct, of William and of the general political climate under his rule. This becomes apparent when we compare Dryden's *Aeneid* with both the original and with more literal translations. For example, in a number of passages, we find a marked preference for order and conservatism in Dryden's depictions of mobs and mob anger.[27] One instance is the famous epic simile in Book I of the *Aeneid*, which compares the storms to an angry crowd. Whereas Cecil Day Lewis's almost line-by-line translation of Virgil runs thus:

Just as so often happens, when a crowd collects, and violence
Brews up, and the mass mind boils nastily over, and next thing

Firebrands and brickbats are flying (hysteria soon finds a missile) –
That then, if they see some man whose goodness of heart and conduct
Have won their respect, they fall silent and stand still, ready to hear him;
And he can change their temper and calm their thoughts with a
    speech . . .

(I.148–53)[28]

Dryden's translation has:

As, when in tumults rise th' ignoble crowd,
Mad are their motions, and their tongues are loud;
And stones and brands in rattling volleys fly,
And all the rustic arms that fury can supply:
If then some grave and pious man appear,
They hush their noise, and lend a list'ning ear;
He soothes with sober words their angry mood,
And quenches their innate desire of blood.

(I.213–20)[29]

There is no denying that Virgil's mob is angry and threatening, yet Dryden portrays it as insanely and innately bloodthirsty; not just momentarily dangerous but inherently so. The people are, after all, 'ignoble' in the sense of being not just common but base. Similarly, the 'clowns', or peasants, who attack the Trojans in the misunderstanding over Silvia's pet deer in Book VII are, in the original, simply *indomiti agricolae* (VII.521), which Day Lewis translates as 'hardy countrymen' (VII.520), suggesting nicely both their occupation and their kinship with Silvia. However, they are turned by Dryden into 'a bois'trous, rude, ungovern'd crew' (VII.724), again hinting at an inherent tendency to violence. Dryden displays here what L. Proudfoot calls 'his hatred of disorder, and his equation of the mob with disorder', connected in part, it would seem, with his insistence on the preservation of hierarchy.[30]

A pointed critique of William III occurs in Book VI, in which Aeneas descends to the underworld and encounters those who are doomed to suffer for their various crimes. Those listed by Virgil are primarily those against kin: *hic quibus invisi fratres, dum vita manebat, / pulsatusve parens* (VI.608–9), which Day Lewis translates as 'Here are those who in life hated their own brothers, / Or struck their parents' (VI.608–9). In a striking move, Dryden translates this as 'Then they, who brothers' better claim disown, / Expel their parents, and usurp the throne' (VI.824–5). As Thomas notes, 'No reader would miss the conversion of the simply familial to the monarchical', and the resulting attack on William's ascension to the throne at the expense of his father-in-law, James II.[31] In addition, as both Thomas and Proudfoot show, a reference some lines later to the crime of treachery is elaborated by Dryden into a description of foreign invasion rather than domestic corruption.[32] The original states simply, *vendidit hic auro patriam dominumque potentum / imposuit* (VI.621–2), which appears in Day Lewis's version thus: 'One sold his country for gold, putting her under the yoke of / Dictatorship, and corruptly made and unmade her laws' (VI.621–2). In Dryden's translation, however, this becomes a strong statement against a very specific form of sedition: 'To tyrants other have their country sold, / Imposing foreign lords for foreign gold' (VI.845–6). It is not difficult, of course, to make a connection between this and the reign of a king who was also William of Orange.

Though Dryden refrains from making an all-out attack on the king, his critiques are well-placed reminders that William is hardly Aeneas. However, although Dryden believed that Virgil too had doubted whether his emperor was of the mould of his epic hero, he did not fully translate 'Virgil's sense', which, according to Dryden himself, was to instruct a potentially wayward ruler on the methods of good governance. For it would seem that Dryden knew how unlikely it was that *his* king would take his advice. His translation implies that, whereas Augustus could be expected to take on the qualities of Aeneas, William would do no such thing. Paramount here is the notion of *pietas*, which is instrumental to Aeneas's heroism. In his preface, Dryden states that:

> the Manners which our Poet gives his Heroe ... are the same which were eminently seen in his *Augustus*. Those Manners were Piety to the Gods, and a dutiful Affection to his Father; Love to his Relations; Care of his People; Courage and Conduct in the Wars; Gratitude to those who had oblig'd him; and Justice in general to Mankind.[33]

That William is lacking in *pietas* in particular is made apparent later in the preface, when Dryden writes:

> A Man may be very Valiant, and yet Impious and Vicious. But the same cannot be said of Piety; which excludes all ill Qualities, and comprehends even Valour it self, with all other Qualities which are good. Can we, for example, give the praise of Valour to a Man who shou'd see his Gods prophan'd, and shou'd want the Courage to defend them? To a Man who shou'd abandon his Father, or desert his King in his last Necessity?[34]

Just such a man – who 'shou'd abandon his Father' – is William, particularly in his joint reign with Mary, the Protestant daughter of the exiled James II. Dryden here is making painfully obvious how his king fails to match Aeneas or even Augustus. As Paul Hammond remarks judiciously, 'the possible addition of a third term to the comparison, making the parallel Aeneas/Augustus/William … is neither proposed nor denied'.[35] Significantly, then, Dryden 'cannot repeat Virgil's decision to accept the new order'.[36] Even more significantly, Dryden cannot fully assume Virgil's ideological position as royal adviser or court poet. The time for heroic kingship, and of the possibility of the epic poet encouraging heroic kingship, is long gone. Dryden's epic translation is informed not by imperialist optimism but by political pessimism.

If Virgil's epic represents for Dryden a standard of behaviour that cannot be recalled, it is of no surprise that the heroism of kingly piety that he views as the responsibility of the epic poet to celebrate works so well for Dryden elsewhere as an ideal but unattainable virtue, a foil against which to satirise or criticise contemporary events. Thus, in the mock-heroic mode of *Mac Flecknoe*, epic heroism clearly no longer exists in Dryden's time, and what makes Mac Flecknoe, the king of poetasters, so laughable is the gap between him and a truly heroic king of classical literature such as Aeneas. In *Absalom and Achitophel*, not so much a mock-heroic as a satirical heroic poem, the case is slightly different and more complex. Proudfoot notes that Dryden's *Aeneid* echoes *Absalom and Achitophel* in its political commentary.[37] As with the *Aeneid*, in which the allegorical correspondences that should tie Aeneas, Augustus and William never quite match up, here the links between Absalom and Monmouth, between Achitophel and Shaftesbury and, most importantly for the idea of heroic kingship, between David and Charles, are not tenable to their logical ends. None the less, with the precedent for this allegory having been established by pamphleteers and poets before Dryden, the likenesses are sufficiently recognisable. Indeed, to be fair to Dryden, in his portrayal of David/Charles, he comes closer than ever, certainly closer than he does in his *Aeneid*, to assuming the role of the Virgilian court poet, which is to aggrandise his monarch. In his glossing over Charles's various faults, he inhabits the ideological position he imagined for Virgil, that of propagandising on behalf of a potentially good king. What is significant, however, is that the poem, though written in heroic couplets and in a strikingly heroic manner, is never a heroic poem about David as Charles. In its title reference to the struggle between Absalom and Achitophel and its detailed descriptions of the various characters and their machinations, the poem is, in the final analysis, a political rather than heroic piece, and the possibility of an original modern epic of imperial heroism remains, for Dryden, elusive.

Pope's *Iliad* and *Odyssey*

Dryden's *Aeneid* was, for Pope, an inspirational model, which he called 'the most noble and spirited translation I know in any language'.[38] It is therefore of interest that Pope's Homeric translations display a similar mix of veneration for the classical mode and anxiety over its relevance to the modern age. Pope's decision to translate Homer was made out of the utmost respect, indeed a genuine childhood love, for the classical poet, and this is readily apparent in the preface to his translation of the *Iliad*. However, Pope was also pragmatic about Homer's relevance to the Augustans, and this is particularly evident in the way he handled the problem of Homer's morality. This question was at the centre of the Homeric war, an important tributary of the *querelle*. In France, the formidable Madame Dacier, whose prose translation of Homer appeared in 1711, conceived of early Greek culture as the site of what she called *goût*, an ideal of an 'original, uncorrupted state of civilization where moral and intellectual values were self-evident and where the individual could, without models, give expression to the imaginative activities of his age'.[39] For many others, such as Dacier's rival La Motte, the Homeric epics were morally suspect and had to be improved in order to be presented to a modern readership.[40] Pope's position on Homer's moral code was somewhere in between these. On the troublesome subject of the 'vicious and *imperfect Manners* of [Homer's] *Heroes*', Pope noted that:

> it is a Point generally carry'd into extremes, both by the censurers and defenders of *Homer*. It must be a strange partiality to antiquity to think with Madam *Dacier*, 'that those times and manners are so much the more excellent, as they are more contrary to ours'. Who can be so prejudiced in their favour as to magnify the felicity of those ages, when a spirit of revenge and cruelty, join'd with the practice of Rapine and Robbery, reign'd thro' the world; when no mercy was shown but for the sake of lucre, when the greatest Princes were put to the sword, and their wives and daughters made slaves and concubines? On the other side, I would not be so delicate as those modern criticks, who are shock'd at the *servile offices* and *mean employments* in which we sometimes see the Heroes of *Homer* engag'd. There is a pleasure in taking a view of that simplicity in opposition to the luxury of succeeding ages, in beholding Monarchs

without their guards, Princes tending their flocks, and Princesses drawing water from the springs. When we read *Homer*, we ought to reflect that we are reading the most ancient author in the heathen world; and those who consider him in this light, will double their pleasure in the perusal of him.[41]

Though Pope defends Homer's morals by placing them in their historical context, he concedes that they are unpalatable to those in the Augustan age. What is significant is that, although Pope believes in theory in an objective depiction of Homer in order that the reader may then accept Homer's morality for what it is, in practice he cannot help but update this for a modern readership.

As Dryden had done with Virgil, Pope saw his task of translating Homer as being one of interpreting the spirit of the original: 'That which in my opinion ought to be the endeavour of any one who translates *Homer* is above all things to keep alive that spirit and fire which makes his chief character.'[42] He would retain a basic belief in Homer's morality, but make necessary adjustments when it came to those individual incidents that proved potentially offensive. While Dryden tried but failed fully to translate what he saw as the celebration of kingly heroism at the heart of the *Aeneid*, Pope, it seems, quite knowingly conceded the impossibility of updating Homer's ideology and morality. Acknowledging that 'a meer modern wit can like nothing that is not *modern*, and a pedant nothing that is not *Greek*', he hoped to produce something that, neither thoroughly modern nor wholly Greek, would strike a compromise between the two.[43]

Pope believed in the fundamental didacticism of the *Iliad*, that 'the chief Aim of it is to instruct'.[44] In the face of doubts over the poem's moral standard, Levine suggests that 'The only way around was to insist on the morality of the whole: The *Iliad* is about the evil consequences that resulted from the (immoral) wrath of Achilles'.[45] This left Pope free to plaster over any cracks in decorum. The result, as so many have complained of Pope's Homeric epics, is a strikingly Augustan ideology of polite behaviour.

Thus, Homer's heroic code, based on the martial valour that is *kleos* and therefore on self-interest, is transformed by Pope into one of aristocratic disinterestedness.[46] This is what happens, for example, when Glaukos and Diomedes exchange armour in Book VI. The Greek Glaukos and Trojan Diomedes, recognising that the grandfather of one had once been the guest of the other, set aside hostilities to engage in gift-exchange, but Glaukos mistakenly trades his precious gold armour for Diomedes' bronze. This incident occurs in Richmond Lattimore's more literal translation of the *Iliad* thus:

> So they spoke, and both springing down from behind their horses
> gripped each other's hands and exchanged the promise of friendship;
> but Zeus the son of Kronos stole away the wits of Glaukos
> who exchanged with Diomedes the son of Tydeus armour
> of gold for bronze, for nine oxen's worth the worth of a hundred.
>
> (VI.232–6)[47]

Pope, however, apparently uncomfortable with the idea that Glaukos could only have been led into an unequal exchange by reason of temporary insanity, suggests a very different motivation:

> Thus having said, the gallant chiefs alight.
> Their hands they join, their mutual faith they plight,
> Brave *Glaucus* then each narrow thought resign'd,
> (*Jove* warm'd his bosom and enlarg'd his mind)
> For *Diomed's* brass arms, of mean device,
> For which nine oxen paid (a vulgar price)
> He gave his own, of gold divinely wrought,
> A hundred beeves the shining purchase bought.
>
> (VI.288–95)[48]

The 'gallant' and 'brave' Glaucus is also generous, and he thus has his heroism underlined by this noble-spirited act. Pope explains his decision in the following note:

> The words in the original...may equally be interpreted, *he took away his sense*, or *he elevated his mind*. The former being a reflection upon *Glaucus's* prudence, for making so unequal an exchange, the latter a praise of the magnanimity and generosity which induced him to it. *Porphyry* contends for its being understood in this last way. ...I have followed it, if not as the juster, as the most heroic sense, and as it has the nobler air in poetry. (VI.291n)

Pope's is an Augustan ideal of heroism as disinterested generosity rather than self-aggrandisement. This is particularly resonant, suggests Peter Connelly, in the face of the increasingly sophisticated commercialism and capitalism of the eighteenth century: 'The ideological matrix that organizes Pope's understanding of Homeric society [is based on the] real historical conflict between the emerging middle-class political order and the nostalgic dream of a virtuous aristocratic society.'[49]

This heroic ideal may also be seen in Pope's construction of Agamemnon's character, which is one of 'pride' intermixed with the recurring term of 'magnanimity' (I.105n). In Nestor's advice to Agamemnon, part of his speech to the Greek council of war in Book IX, we find Pope striving to clarify Agamemnon's responsibilities as leader and particularly to prioritise gentlemanly restraint over bellicose bravery. Nestor's words are meant to convey, very subtly, to Agamemnon his obligation to keep the peace among his troops rather than to initiate arguments such as that with Achilleus. Lattimore renders this very brief hint of Nestor's thus:

> But let me speak, since I can call myself older than you are,
> and go through the whole matter, since there is none who can dishonour
> the thing I say, not even powerful Agamemnon.
> Out of all brotherhood, outlawed, homeless shall be that man
> who longs for all the horror of fighting among his own people.

> (IX.60–4)

As Pope puts it himself, he translates this passage 'with liberty' (IX.87n):

> Age bids me speak; nor shall th' advice I bring
> Distast the people, or offend the King:
> Curs'd is the man, and void of law and right,
> Unworthy property, unworthy light,
> Unfit for publick rule, or private care;
> That wretch, that monster, who delights in war:
> Whose lust is murder, and whose horrid joy,
> To tear his country, and his kind destroy!

> (IX.85–92)

Kathryn Lynch points out that Pope insists on an 'Augustan social and historical context', by imagining a society whose order is manifested in laws, rights and private property.[50] More than this, however, the delayed reference in these lines to internal disorder in particular means that Nestor appears to expound against bloodlust and belligerence in general. The heroic ideal established here is a distinctly Augustan, class-based one of temperance as a foundation of wealth, status and authority.

The Augustan restraint of Pope's Homeric translations manifests itself too in his use of heroic couplets. The neat, epigrammatic style of Pope's couplets is achieved by their self-contained unity and enhanced by the tight internal balance of the regularly occurring caesurae. The illusion of control, as William Bowman Piper suggests in his study of *The Heroic Couplet*, conveys a sense of the politeness and civility of which the Augustans were so proud.[51] In addition, Pope's couplets are essential to his vision of Homeric life as antithesis, in which opposites are constantly juxtaposed with each other. Thus, Agamemnon's 'pride' is offset by 'magnanimity', Achilles' 'anger' by his 'courage', and so on.[52] In this way, Pope manages to downgrade the intemperate or offensive potential of Homer's heroes. This effect of a kind of genteel correctness is, as Piper points out, a trait of Pope's couplet technique in particular. In contrast, Dryden's couplets achieve urgency and drive by being 'yok[ed] into great movements of verse', and are thus instrumental to the political and satirical nature of a work such as his translation of the *Aeneid*.[53]

Pope's *Rape of the Lock*

In Pope's mock-epics, the question recurs of how to offset the immorality of classical epic behaviour with a sense of veneration for it. It is a critical commonplace that, as burlesques, *The Rape of the Lock* and *The Dunciad* derive their meaning from the gap between the high and the low, between the serious and heroic actions of epic on the one hand and the dull and trivial concerns of the modern day on the other. As high burlesques, these poems would seem to attach their loyalties to the epic form, and hence to ridicule contemporary life as resolutely non-epic. Mock-epics, the argument goes, do not mock the epic but employ the epic standards in order to mock others. Yet, the very redeployment of epic as satire suggests an over-familiarity that borders on disrespect. Moreover, the conventions of epic, thus removed from context, become reduced to the status of formulae, and thus run the risk of appearing mundane. Unsurprisingly, Pope, who so masterfully subsumes epic conventions under a satirical programme, was well aware of the potentially absurd nature of epic markers. In 'A Receipt to make an Epick Poem', which appeared in *The Guardian* in 1713, a year after the first version of *The Rape*, he runs mechanically through the gamut of epic conventions as listed by Le Bossu, from the 'Machines' to the 'Fable' to the 'Moral or Allegory. He jokes:

> For the Fable: Take out of any old Poem, History-books, Romance, or Legend (for instance Geffry of Monmouth of Don Belianis of Greece)

those Parts of Story which afford most Scope for long Descriptions: Put
those Pieces together, and throw all the Adventures you fancy into one
Tale. Then take a Hero, whom you may chuse for the Sound of his Name,
and put him into the midst of these Adventures: There let him work, for
twelve Books; at the end of which you may take him out, ready prepared
to conquer or to marry; it being necessary that the Conclusion of an
Epick Poem be fortunate. To make an Episode: Take any remaining
Adventure of your former Collection, in which you could no way involve
your Hero; or any unfortunate Accident that was too good to be thrown
away; and it will be of Use, applied to any other Person; who may be lost
and evaporate in the Course of the Work, without the least Damage to
the Composition.[54]

This less than venerable stance towards the epic is, indeed, crucial to the
mock-epic. The underlying belief in the dignity of the epic is always over-
laid in Pope's mock-epics by a playful attitude to its forms. In the first
instance, however, the aim in juxtaposing the two is merely to achieve
comic effect. On a more serious level, Pope's mock-epics make a sustained
critique of the shallowness of contemporary society, coupled with an
acknowledgement that epic heroism offers just as little social and moral
guidance. As with his epic translations, then, Pope's mock-epics ultimately
admit classical epic heroism to be anachronistic, and consequently imply
the existence of a code of behaviour that marries classical mores with
contemporary ones.

The Rape of the Lock tells of the not so shocking incident of the cutting of
the lock of hair of a vacuous young socialite by her rejected beau. The
comedy that lies between epic grandeur and everyday frippery is immediately apparent in this poem. When the protagonist Belinda prepares her
toilet, for example, she is likened first to a goddess administered to by her
priestess:

> And now, unveil'd, the *Toilet* stands display'd,
> Each Silver Vase in mystic Order laid.
> First, rob'd in White, the Nymph intent adores
> With Head uncover'd, the *Cosmetic* Pow'rs.
> A heav'nly Image in the Glass appears,
> To that she bends, to that her Eyes she rears;
> Th' inferior Priestess, at her Altar's side,
> Trembling, begins the sacred Rites of Pride.
> Unnumber'd Treasures ope at once, and here

> The various Off'rings of the World appear;
> From each she nicely culls with curious Toil,
> And decks the Goddess with the glitt'ring Spoil.
>
> (I, 121–32)[55]

as well as to a warrior preparing for battle:

> Here Files of Pins extend their shining Rows,
> Puffs, Powders, Patches, Bibles, Billet-doux.
> Now awful Beauty puts on all its Arms;
> The Fair each moment rises in her Charms...
>
> (I, 137–40)

The burlesques of Belinda as goddess and as warrior combine to echo, among other things, Athene donning her armour in Book V of the *Iliad*. The effect is to highlight the gap between the frivolity of Belinda's beauty regime and the seriousness of epic quest and conquest. The same may be said of the full range of epic conventions which Pope evokes, such as the appearance of supernatural machinery in the near-invisible sylphs and gnomes that attend Belinda (an addition made to the 1714 version of the poem); the battle in miniature that is the card game played between Belinda and her beaux; and the descent to the underworld that is the gnome Umbriel's visit to the Cave of Spleen – a jibe at the attacks of the vapours suffered by the denizens of the fashionable world.

Certainly, Pope's most obvious satirical target is polite society. The gap between epic form and trivial content that is evident in the burlesque is, after all, found in distilled form throughout the poem. Pope skilfully uses rhyming couplets to achieve this. Thus, for example, the sylphs are charged with defending young women in any dire event:

> Whether the Nymph shall break *Diana's* law
> Or some frail *China* Jar receive a Flaw,
> Or stain her Honour, or her new Brocade,
> Forget her Pray'rs, or miss a Masquerade,
> Or lose her Heart, or Necklace, at a Ball...
>
> (II. 105–9)

A similar effect is evident in these lines, in the immediate aftermath of the 'rape':

> But anxious Cares the pensive Nymph opprest,
> And secret Passions labour'd in her Breast.
> Not youthful Kings in Battel seiz'd alive,
> Not scornful Virgins who their Charms survive,
> Not ardent Lovers robb'd of all their Bliss,
> Not ancient Ladies when refus'd a Kiss,
> Not Tyrants fierce that unrepenting die,
> Not *Cynthia* when her *Manteau's* pinn'd awry,
> E'er felt such Rage, Resentment and Despair,
> As Thou, sad Virgin! For thy ravish'd Hair.

In the first example, the contrast between high and low, between moral lapses on the one hand and social or material accidents on the other, is readily apparent. In the second, the gap now exists between the broad – one might say, epic – sphere of action, inhabited by tyrants, kings and (true) lovers, and the narrow world of old maids and pretty young things. Needless to say, the masculinity of the epic form plays an important subtext. The trivial, feminised world of the *beau monde*, in which the cosmetic is valued above the heroic, is a ready target.

The climax of the poem is, of course, the cutting of that precious lock. With conflict already foreshadowed in both Belinda's toilet and the skirmishes in which she participates when playing cards, the decisive battle-scene is the assault on Belinda's lock and the fight that ensues. The gap between heroic and polite society is foregrounded with an epic simile that compares the situation with 'when bold *Homer* makes the Gods engage, /And heav'nly Breasts with human Passions rage' (V.45–6), and thus the epic is invoked in terms of both form and content. However, conventionally epic weapons are set aside in favour of glances and frowns:

> While thro' the Press enrag'd *Thalestris* flies,
> And scatters Death around from both her Eyes,
> A *Beau* and *Witling* perish'd in the Throng,
> One dy'd in *Metaphor*, and one in *Song*.
> . . .
> When bold Sir *Plume* had drawn *Clarissa* down,
> *Chloe* stept in, and kill'd him with a Frown;

> She smil'd to see the doughty Hero slain,
> But at her Smile, the Beau reviv'd again.

(V.57–60; 67–70)

The purpose of the poem, as conventional critical wisdom has it, is to demonstrate the absurdity of modern behaviour when it is set alongside the norms of classical epic.[56] Through it all, then, the dignity of epic would seem to be preserved, for such preservation is key to the poem's theme.

Yet, even in his mock-epics, Pope belies a mistrust of classical epic behaviour. As Howard Weinbrot's incisive analysis of *The Rape of the Lock* suggests, it is the uncivilised aspects of modern life – selfishness, anger, trivial quarrels – that Pope criticises. In other words, it is the interface between contemporary society and epic bellicosity that is depicted in his poems. Pope based his poem on real events, writing it at the request of his patron, John Caryll, in order to promote peace between two feuding families. In doing so, Pope is advocating an ideal of polite behaviour that stands above the aggression he sees in both the *belle monde* and the epic world.[57] Thus, although he venerates the classical epic tradition and trusts implicitly in its grandeur, Pope is distinctly uncomfortable with its morals and manners, and plumps in both his epic translations and his mock-epics for an Augustan ideal of politeness.

The same could be said for *The Dunciad*. The subject of the poem is the crowning of Tibbald (a figure based on the poetaster Lewis Theobald, who had dared to question Pope's edition of Shakespeare) as ruler of the empire of Chaos under the aegis of the goddess, Dulness. Like *Mac Flecknoe*, the poem satirises bad poets by setting them against epic heroes, for example, in the coronation games in which poets and critics participate, which reveal their sycophancy and pedantry. Even the paraphernalia of the poem – its copious notes, appendices and other commentary – reveal the gap between the majestic simplicity of epic and the plodding triviality of modern literary endeavour. None the less, the poem is a sustained critique of the self-importance and petty one-upmanship of literary life, precisely because such traits resemblance to the belligerence of war and hence to the behaviour of epic heroes.

In short, for both Dryden and Pope, the classical epics represent a high watermark of literary endeavour, but their morality and ideology are not always transferable to the modern age. Translating these ancient epics but conceding their ultimate irrelevance, they make doubly sure of the impossibility of epic-writing for the modern poet, for not only is ancient epic irrelevant in its worldview but modern epic is also always inferior. Indeed, their ambivalence towards Milton seems to embody just such concerns for the status of epic in the modern age. The net effect of their ambivalence is maintenance of the epic as an ideal, but in a way that stultifies it. Theirs, then, is a preservative, even fossilising, gesture, with little hope for any furtherance of the epic tradition.

Fénelon's *Télémaque*

Having addressed Dryden's and Pope's epic translations, it is worth discussing briefly one other ostensibly epic work of the late seventeenth century, François de Fénelon's *Télémaque, fils d'Ulysse* ('Telemachus: Son of Ulysses'). Its composition is roughly coterminous with Dryden's *Aeneid*, having been written around 1693–4 and published without Fénelon's consent in 1699. *Télémaque* is a prose work that narrates – and substantially augments – Telemachus' adventures as he searches for Odysseus in the first three books of Homer's *Odyssey*. Produced while Fénelon was tutor to the grandson of Louis XIV, the text is also a set of instructions for a future king. Fénelon described his epic as:

> a fabulous narration in the form of an heroic poem like those of Homer and Virgil, into which I have put the main instructions which are suit-able for a young prince whose birth destines him to rule ... In these adventures I have put all the truths necessary to government, and all the faults that one can find in sovereign power.[58]

To read Fénelon's work in the light of the epic translations and mock-epics of Dryden and Pope is to confront precisely the same issue that affected Dryden's and Pope's decisions to translate rather than compose epic – the question of how to emulate the classics. As we have seen, the increasingly sharp dichotomy between the ancients and the moderns produced, for potential epic poets, a dilemma. To write epic is to respect it, perhaps to revere it, and, according to a theorist such as Le Bossu, also to replicate the methods practised by the classical epic poets. However, the production of a new epic suggests competition with these poets and the possibility of the relative capability, perhaps the relative superiority, of modern poets. Dryden and Pope chose simply to resolve this by translating the great epics of the ancients; Fénelon selects a comparable route in writing a kind of sequel to one of these classical epics.

Fénelon's place in the *querelle* is easy enough to locate. For him, the ancient way of life was a model of simplicity and frugality, set against what he saw as the luxury and self-indulgence of modernity. According to Fénelon, 'it is our insane and cruel vanity, and not the noble simplicity of the ancients, which needs to be corrected'.[59] This is what he sought to do with *Télémaque*, which proposes a version of disinterested and frugal governance. The young Telemachus is advised throughout his travels by his wise companion Mentor on the importance of, among other things, simplicity over splendour, peace over war, agricultural labour over military glory. On their journey, the two come across – either through direct encounter or hearsay – various examples of good and bad government, for example, the industrious ways of the kingdom of Bétique and the wastefulness practised by Idomeneus, once king of Crete.

In doing so, then, Fénelon is writing a didactic epic in the manner described by Le Bossu. His intention is to educate his prince according to an ideology of simplicity, an ideology he attributes to the ancients. Fénelon's project contrasts with that of Pope, who imposes on his classical material a distinctly modern ideology, but it seems to resemble that of Dryden, whose position as princely adviser is built on an ostensibly classical ideology of virtuous and pious rule. Dryden, however, incorporates into his ideological stance a pointed political commentary on the government of his day, and he therefore belies a very modern sense of pessimism. Fénelon avoids making such contemporary criticisms and hence preserves his commitment to presenting his readership with what he sees as a distinctly classical mode of government. Compared to both Dryden and Pope, then, Fénelon seeks to produce an epic that is classical in both plot and ideology.

For the British epic writers who came after him, the importance of Fénelon's text to the epic tradition was considerable. *Télémaque* proved extremely popular in eighteenth-century England: the first English version ran to sixteen editions and was followed by at least ten more translations that century, including one by Smollett in 1776.[60] *Télémaque* was, according to Pope, important to any translator of Homer, for 'the Archbishop of Cambray's *Telemachus* may give him the truest idea of the spirit and turn of our author [Homer]'.[61] For Fielding, the text established an important precedent for prose epic:

the *Telemachus* of the Arch-Bishop of Cambray appears to me of the epic kind, as well as the *Odyssey* of Homer; indeed, it is much fairer and more reasonable to give it a name common with that species from which it differs only in a single instance, than to confound it with those which it resembles in no other.[62]

Both Pope and Fielding place *Télémaque* firmly with its forebear, the *Odyssey*. It is perhaps appropriate that Fénelon's nostalgically 'ancient' epic text seems to occupy a place alongside classical epic as far as his near-contemporaries are concerned, for it offers little direction for modern epic. In a sense, *Télémaque* is an even more conservative epic gesture than either Dryden's or Pope's. Though it spawned its own countless versions, 'as plentiful as blackberries to satisfy the palates of readers young and old', it did not profoundly inspire the epic attempts of Fielding.[63] Fielding's texts resemble Fénelon's staunchly classical epic only in their use of prose, for they mark out a new direction for epic in the eighteenth century.

Fielding's *Joseph Andrews* and *Tom Jones*

The second major development for the epic in the eighteenth century is an innovative one, though its innovation is achieved through compromise rather than outright revolution. The path assumed by Fielding is one which takes as its point of departure Cervantes' *Don Quixote*, a work that, as we saw in Chapter 2, embodies a critique of epic heroism. Fielding's interest in Cervantes is obvious: he wrote a farce entitled *Don Quixote in England* (1733), identified *Joseph Andrews* on its title-page as 'Written in Imitation of the *Manner* of Cervantes, Author of *Don Quixote*' and even came himself to be labelled the '*English* Cervantes'.[64] The Cervantine elements of Fielding's *Joseph Andrews* and *Tom Jones* are readily apparent. These works present, for one thing, a pair of travellers whose wanderings constitute a series of ridiculous episodes. Fielding also recalls Cervantes' parodies of romance and epic with mock-heroic battle scenes and pseudo-classical imagery, such as his extravagant descriptions of the morning sun. However, as we shall see, the experiments with epic carried out by Fielding differ in one substantial way from those of Cervantes'. Indeed, in doing so, they could even be said to gesture towards a Miltonic conception of epic and to conform, in crucial respects, to traditional epic.

Whereas Cervantes makes explicit an anxiety about the pernicious effects of romance and epic heroism, Fielding sets out to renovate, not repudiate, the epic. His Preface to *Joseph Andrews*, which is where he famously labels his work a 'comic epic in prose', is a manifesto for this new generic innovation.[65] Though Fielding is sometimes inconsistent in his terminology, it is possible to discern here a working definition for this new type of epic.

Allowing first for the possibility of the epic in prose in the style of Fénelon's *Télémaque*, he then proceeds to define the comic epic as epic by virtue of its 'action being more extended and comprehensive; containing a much larger circle of incidents, and containing a greater variety of characters'. In other words, comic epic is to epic what comedy is to tragedy. Fielding posits that the key characteristics of this comic variety of epic lie (in a borrowing from Le Bossu) in its 'fable and action', its 'characters' and its 'sentiments and diction'. Though he goes on somewhat confusingly to apply the label 'serious' or 'grave romance' to the epic form, Fielding makes a clear enough distinction between the comic and serious epic:

> [Comic epic] differs from the serious romance in its fable and action, in this: that as in the one these are grave and solemn, so in the other they are light and ridiculous: it differs in its characters, by introducing persons of inferiour rank, and consequently of inferiour manners, whereas the grave romance, sets the highest before us; lastly in its sentiments and diction, by preserving the ludicrous instead of the sublime. In the diction I think, burlesque itself may sometimes be admitted...[66]

For Fielding, the comic epic is more than a simple burlesque of the epic, though it may contain parodic moments. The comic epic is marked by, among other things, its relative levity. Fielding goes on to elaborate on the concepts of levity and ridiculousness, explaining that:

> the only source of the true ridiculous (as it appears to me) is affectation. ...Now affectation proceeds from one of these two causes, vanity, or hypocrisy: for as vanity puts us on affecting false characters, in order to purchase applause, so hypocrisy sets us on an endeavour to avoid censure by concealing our vices under an appearance of their opposite virtues.[67]

What Fielding does not say, and probably does not need to say, is that such ridiculous behaviour is largely an antagonistic force in his epic narratives, displayed mainly by unpleasant or bad characters, and sometimes by basically good 'sidekicks'. It falls to the comic epic hero to triumph over affectation. Though Fielding never outlines the characteristics of his heroes, he does hint at how affectation is to be neutralised. In his remarks on his portrayal of Parson Adams, Fielding states: 'It is designed a character of perfect simplicity; and...the goodness of his heart will recommend him to the good-natur'd'.[68] Such truth of character, 'goodness' and 'perfect simplicity' are what also define Fielding's 'epic' heroes, Joseph Andrews and Tom Jones. Thus, in Fielding's texts, the ridiculousness of affectation is to be offset by the equally light – but certainly never ridiculous – simplicity of the hero.

Fielding's other important specification for the comic epic is its emphasis on 'persons of inferiour rank'. Fielding's epic protagonists are of the working classes, though significantly the antagonists of his narratives usually belong to the aristocracy or else to what Michael McKeon has termed the 'progressive' classes of upwardly mobile tradesmen and the like.[69] Crucially, the problem of affectation, though not the sole preserve of these social orders, is prevalent in them – as demonstrated by the behaviour of Lady Booby in *Joseph Andrews* and Aunt Western, the Blifils (both senior and junior) and Lady Bellaston in *Tom Jones*. It is worth noting that affectation also manifests itself in the class pretensions of those who, on the periphery of the aristocracy, imagine themselves to be part of it. The alignment between aristocracy and affectation is made most apparent in the incident in which the only person on the stagecoach to offer Joseph any clothing after his attack by highwaymen is the lowly postillion. Thus, these epics would seem to embody the triumph of a strikingly working-class hero over the hypocrisies and vanities displayed in the main by those stationed above him. To emphasise this further, Fielding's heroes find themselves initially on the utmost margins of society. If class is about one's place in a social network, then Joseph Andrews and Tom Jones are extravagantly displaced, the one being an orphan, the other identified on the title-page as a 'foundling', that is, of course, a bastard.

Yet, Fielding's narratives ultimately fulfil a fantasy of familial reunion, as his heroes discover their rightful place not just within a family but within the aristocracy. With this, the potency of possible class conflict is nullified. The potentially explosive alignment of affectation with the upper classes becomes unfeasible when the truly good hero is shown to be a rightful member of them. Indeed, the ridiculing of aristocratic aspirations displayed by those without a legitimate claim to do so may then be seen to undergird such class conservativism, implying that the worst kinds of vanities and hypocrisies are committed by those who do not know their place. Fielding's heroes are rescued from the margins by these resolutions of family reunion, not least because the discovery of blood connections also does away with the spectre of incest, that most stigmatised of deeds. With the hero's social credentials in place, the narratives are not so much about a challenge of the working-class man to the establishment as they are stories of simplicity triumphing over affectation. We see this in the unions of the strikingly good – and aristocratic – lovers, Sophia and Jones, and Fanny and Joseph. The resolution is, as McKeon puts it, one whereby the initial promise of a triumphant progressive ideology – in which the upwardly mobile supplant the aristocracy – gives way to the establishment of a conservative ideology, which signals something like a return to aristocratic values under an ostensibly progressive cover.[70] It is therefore not possible to say, with Lennard Davis, that the 'comic epic' as defined by Fielding 'describe[s] a longish piece of prose fiction that depicts the life of the common or middling man or woman', for it resolves into a narrative of fairly conservative aristocratic heroism.[71]

Fielding's epics, then, establish an epic heroism that is not all that unconventional. Fielding, like Cervantes, sets his work against traditional epic but, unlike Cervantes, he offers a version of traditional epic and, with it, a version of traditional epic heroism. Crucially, his heroes set a positive, not a negative, example. Correspondingly, the world they inhabit is pernicious and problematic rather than a reality that must be accepted. Where Quixote sallies forth in a delusive state that requires correction, Tom Jones and Joseph Andrews, as well as Parson Adams, exhibit behaviour that, if not always exemplary in itself, arises from exemplary character. Where Quixote's actions often bring about adverse consequences for the ordinary and largely innocuous folk he encounters, Fielding's heroes are the targets of the rampant hypocrisy of their times. Cervantes' 'epic hero' is a fool, while Fielding's truly good, aristocratic heroes are little different from their forebears in the epic tradition. The epic is, for Fielding, a fundamentally positive term, one to be improved on rather than subverted.

This shift in emphasis from Cervantes to Fielding is partly explained by the general shift in attitude to Cervantes' text that commenced in the eighteenth century, the very beginnings of what Anthony Close has called the 'romantic approach' to *Don Quixote*.[72] This approach, simply put, consists of a profound sympathy with Quixote. The immense popularity of Cervantes' text in Augustan England rests in no small part on the tendency of eighteenth-century English readers to rehabilitate Quixote in order to identify with him. Ronald Paulson has shown how, under the influence of Locke's empiricist philosophies and their insistence on the primacy of individual perception in understanding the world, quixotism could be revisioned as a sign of the rationalising and aestheticising mind.[73] The resulting idea is that a little bit of quixotism resides in all of us. In Addison's *Spectator* essays, for example, Quixote is reimagined as the comparatively harmless Sir Roger de Coverley, someone to be laughed with rather than at. It is not difficult to see how Fielding's *Don Quixote in England* could conclude sympathetically that, after all, 'All Mankind are mad, 'tis plain' and further to exhort his audience thus:

> *Since your Madness is so plain,*
>   *Each Spectator*
>   *Of Good-Nature,*
> *With Applause will entertain*
> *His Brother of* La Mancha;
> *With Applause will entertain*
> Don Quixote *and* Squire Sancho.[74]

Quixote as an emblem of harmless eccentricity becomes a possible model for heroic individuality and therefore enables Fielding's characterisations of not just the thoroughly good Adams, but also the uniquely innocent and chaste Joseph, and the goodhearted outcast Jones. Admittedly, Parson Adams is guilty of a single instance of affectation, in his excessive pride in his capacities as a teacher: 'if this good Man had an Enthusiasm, or what the Vulgar call a Blind-side, it was this: He thought a Schoolmaster the greatest Character in the World, and himself the greatest of all Schoomasters' (215).[75] Yet, Adams's pride is innocuous since it arises not from hypocrisy but from vanity (or more accurately, 'Ostentation'), which Fielding identifies in his preface as the less pernicious form of affectation.[76] Adams therefore bears up under scrutiny as an example of sympathetic quixotism grounded in truth and not duplicity. As Paulson argues, 'It is Fielding's Quixotic adaptation [of Adams] that makes him comic *and* sympathetic, a completely new combination'.[77]

Fielding's 'light and ridiculous' 'comic epics', then, with their 'light' heroism set against the 'ridiculous' villainy that is affectation, fill the heroic vacuum threatened by the Cervantine reaction against epic, but do so by gesturing back to the aristocratic heroism of traditional epic. Fielding's insistence on a resolution of familial and social recovery preserves some link between the old epic and new. Epic, as we saw in Fielding's own formulation, sets the 'highest' of ranks and manners before us. In the final analysis, Fielding's comic epics do just that, and indulge in a combination of what is construed as a classical emphasis on nobility with a progressive ideal of inherent virtue to form the basis of its heroism.

As Paulson has pointed out elsewhere, Fielding's narratives play out, in the terms set up by Milton in *Paradise Lost*, the myth of fall and redemption.[78] The wanderings of Fielding's heroes and their sidekicks may resemble those of Quixote and Sancho Panza, but they are also stories of paradises lost and regained. After they are cast out from a less than desirable home run by less than desirable parents (in *Joseph Andrews* emblematised by the Boobys and their estate, and in *Tom Jones* represented by the rather obviously named 'Paradise Hall' and the Allworthys), the heroes set off on a journey of self-discovery which is crowned by restoration to an aristocratic familial seat, which becomes the setting for future connubial bliss. Fielding makes the suggestion of *felix culpa* especially obvious in *Tom Jones*, when Jones's journey begins with the narrator's observation that '*The world*, as Milton phrases it, *lay all before him*, and Jones, no more than Adam, had any man to whom he might resort for comfort or assistance' (288).[79] Furthermore, the requisite return to aristocracy ensures that these heroes are restored not by dint of their own unique strengths and virtues but, in a roundabout way, by superior character born of superior class, and indeed by the machinations of Fielding the author and narrator. Thus, the paradise that is regained is indeed God-given rather than entirely self-made, inasmuch as it is authorially induced and socially determined.

For the heroism of the truly self-made man, standing apart from social class and even apart from overt authorial intrusion, it is necessary to look to Smollett rather than Fielding. Smollett, like Fielding, was influenced by the popularity of Cervantes' work; indeed, he contributed to it, translating many of Cervantes' texts, including *The History and Adventures of Don Quixote* (1755). The typical trajectory of narratives such as *Roderick Random* and *Peregrine Pickle* seems to resemble that of Fielding's novels, from the picaresque plotting to the resolution of family reunion (which, in *Roderick Random*, even involves a discovery of the long-lost father). Yet when Smollett's heroes return to the familial home from which they had been banished, there is no simple aristocratic elevation. Any sense of resolution is to be gleaned from their acquisitions of money and love, enabled by their journeys of self-discovery. Smollett's refusal of the kind of godlike narrative authority assumed by Fielding shows up, according to John Richetti, his disaffection with the conservative ideology preferred by Fielding.[80] It indicates too that Smollett was willing to take Fielding's 'comic epic' heroism further, towards an inner strength of character and away from the insistence on social status.

To turn from the 'comic epics' of Fielding to the works of Smollett is to venture into the territory of the novel. The so-called 'rise of the novel' has been well theorised, most notably by Ian Watt and subsequently by McKeon as part of a changing social climate, in which individualism, capitalistic venture and middle-class ambitiousness supplanted hierarchy, aristocracy and conventionality as desirable virtues.[81] In theorising the novel as the

primary expression of modern life, however, it is easy then to assume that
the epic becomes correspondingly irrelevant and obsolescent. This critical
thinking may be traced at least as far back as G. W. F. Hegel, for whom the
epic was superseded by the novel, since epic-writing was incompatible with
a modern worldview.[82] For Hegel and those influenced by him, the novel is
the modern incarnation of the epic, for it expresses the modern preoccupation with subjectivity, immediacy, egalitarianism, the everyday, and so on,
as opposed to objectivity, hierarchy and the extraordinary. Echoes of
Hegel's thesis may be found in critics as apparently disparate as Georg
Lukács and Mikhail Bakhtin, who see the novel as the true expression of
modernity.[83]

None the less, in acknowledging the place of Fielding and Smollett in the
epic tradition, it is possible to view this preoccupation with the individual
and the so-called 'rise of the novel' as part of the development, not the
extinction, of the epic. Fielding's and Smollett's individualistic epic heroes
herald a new direction for *both* epic and novel, for, though they are the
precursors of the novelistic heroines and heroes of the next century, particularly in the development of the *Bildungsroman*, they are also factors in the
rising concern with selfhood that we see in the Romantic epics.

Coda: Klopstock's *Messias*

What marks the Romantic epics as epic, though, is that they combine this
interest with the self with a renewed fascination with Milton. Milton's influence on nineteenth-century epic poets was aided by the publication in
Germany of Frederich Klopstock's *Der Messias* ('The Messiah'). Klopstock's
poem saw a number of English translations, the most popular being the
prose version begun by Mary Collyer and completed by her husband Joseph
after her death.[84] *Der Messias* is an elaboration of the life story of Christ as
told in the New Testament, and contains a significant number of non-biblical
scenes, for example, the reaction of the souls of Adam and Eve to the
redemption brought about by the crucifixion and a climatic dénouement in
heaven upon Christ's ascension.

It is not surprising that Klopstock's method of scriptural enhancement
recalled, for many readers, Milton's epic. Indeed, Klopstock's poem was
perceived as surpassing *Paradise Regained* as the logical continuation of *Paradise
Lost*. In the words of Joseph Collyer:

> Mr. KLOPSTOCK has receiv'd from his MESSIAH the honour of being
> esteem'd the MILTON of Germany, and is consider'd as having completed

what that favourite son of the British muse had left unfinish'd. I shall not here examine, whether the beauties of the MESSIAH equal those of PARADISE LOST. It is sufficient for me here to observe, that Milton's PARADISE REGAIN'D, or in other words, his MESSIAH, though far from being destitute of merit, is universally allow'd to fall much below the work which has done such honour to his name and his country; and is acknowledg'd to be deficient in that unbounded invention, that beautiful machinery, and variety of characters, which distinguish the first and more vigorous effort of his genius; and has justly plac'd the name of MILTON in the same rank with that of the Father of the Epic muse.[85]

But Klopstock's position as the obvious epic successor to Milton was not accidental. In writing his *Messias*, Klopstock had been deeply influenced by a certain conception of Milton's poetic method, put forward by the Swiss philosopher-critics Johann Bodmer and Johann Breitinger. Bodmer and Breitinger theorised that good poetry influences the reader by moving him emotionally, and further posited Milton's work as the best example of this.[86] This poetics, inspired by Milton, was developed by the profoundly religious Klopstock into a model of the poet as secular prophet, and of poetry as an expression of deeply held beliefs. Klopstock saw his *Messias* as a work that, like *Paradise Lost*, would allow him to be not just an epic, but a vatic, poet.

Though little considered as a pre-Romantic today, Klopstock was influential to nineteenth-century British poets. He contributed to a newly energised veneration for Milton among the Romantics, particularly to a conception of Milton's poetry as an expression of his personal beliefs and emotions. As the next chapter shows, this Miltonic impulse motivates a dialogue between self and society that Romantics such as Blake, Wordsworth, Keats and Byron thought crucial to the idea of heroism and therefore to epic.

4

The Nineteenth Century: Epic and the Self

By the time we arrive at the nineteenth century, there exists an epic tradition constituted generally by the classical and Renaissance epics, but more particularly emblematised by Milton's *Paradise Lost*. The epics of the nineteenth century, beginning with the Romantic age, acknowledge this epic influence in one way or another. But these epics are also implicitly indebted to another tradition, represented more explicitly by Fielding and the Cervantine comic epic tradition, with its interest in matters of selfhood and self-development.

What we see in the Romantic age is a construction of the epic as an expression and celebration of individualism, a construction that the Romantics traced in the first instance to Milton. Milton was, as Joseph Wittreich puts it, 'the literary hero of the Romantic period'.[1] More importantly, as Wittreich suggests, the Romantics overturned an earlier conception of Milton, as expressed, for example, by Samuel Johnson, according to whom Milton was 'an acrimonious and surly republican'.[2] Wittreich states:

> Romantic criticism is, in large measure, a response to Johnson's censures and a reorientation of literary values. That Johnson's remarks were inordinately colored by personal preference and public prejudice was readily discernible, but that an element of truth lay in what he said was equally apparent. Johnson had told the truth but not the whole truth: more important, he had attacked assumptions that the Romantics held as incontrovertible truths, namely, that the heroic poet leads a heroic life, that there is a direct relationship between the character of the poet and the magnitude of his achievement. As these critics surveyed the life of

Milton, they uncovered the 'truth' in what Johnson had told them: Milton's uncongeniality, his cantankerousness, his domestic shortcomings; his liberal politics and unswerving conviction in the face of impending disaster; and his conventionality in the early poems. But they uncovered and were impressed by more: his dignity, his majesty, his solemnity, his seriousness, his sublimity, his learning, his acumen, his virtue, and his art.[3]

The assumption that 'the heroic poet leads a heroic life' was, it would seem, at the bottom of Milton's achievement, as far as the leading Romantics were concerned. The Romantic epic is therefore an elaboration of what many Romantic-age poets saw as the aim of the Miltonic epic – to demonstrate the heroism of the poet within the context of the poem as well as to reveal that heroism in the completion of a majestically impressive poem.

Thus, on the one hand, the texts discussed in this chapter advertise themselves as epics not just through scope or length, but with an obvious nod at the epic tradition of narrating extraordinary events or deeds. On the other hand, though, these texts express the growing preoccupation with self-development, both individual and psychological, that begins to be seen in Western literature in the novels of the eighteenth century and is consolidated in the *Bildungsromane* and domestic fictions of the early nineteenth century. The result is a type of epic that insists that the individual is heroic, specifically where that individual is the poet himself. This poet, as we shall see, must undergo a kind of self-interrogation prior to writing his epic, and it is this that establishes him as heroic. He is capable of writing an epic as he begins it, and the metatextual proof of this is the poem in which is embedded the story of that act of writing.

Of course, it is Blake who explicitly invokes the poet-hero and names him as *Milton* (1804). This chapter will deal briefly with this poem as a way forward to discussing poet-heroism in the Romantic epic. The most obvious example of this is *The Prelude* (1805, 1850) by William Wordsworth. The same phenomenon may be observed in John Keats's *Hyperion* (1818) which, when revised as *The Fall of Hyperion* (1819), inserts into the epic mode the epic poet – or, more precisely, inserts into the epic mode the poet attempting to write an epic. It is present also in Lord Byron's *Don Juan* (1819–24), which foregrounds the poet's self at the expense of his nominal hero and of the society that surrounds that hero. This supplanting of external heroism with internal psychology has notable effects on epic attempts later in the nineteenth century. Indeed, Elizabeth Barrett Browning, in *Aurora Leigh* (1857), demonstrates that self-awareness is the programme for epic-writing in the nineteenth century when she marries the very private and internal heroism of the Romantic epic to the story of negotiating one's place in the world that is typical of the nineteenth-century female *Bildungsroman*. This chapter also deals with a work from outside the British epic tradition – Leo Tolstoy's *War and Peace* (1869) – not simply because this work is so often labelled epic by virtue of its scope and its concern with historical events, but because it deals with the same questions of the relationship between society and the self that are at the heart of these Romantic and post-Romantic epics discussed here. Finally, in a coda, we look at two Victorian epics – Alfred, Lord Tennyson's *Idylls of the King* (1869) and Robert Browning's *The Ring and the Book* (1868–9) – that demonstrate an awareness of the slipperiness of subjectivity. Such an awareness points ahead to the fragmented viewpoints and shifting subjectivities of the modernist epics of the twentieth century.

Nineteenth-century epic theory

First, however, a brief overview of Romantic-age attitudes to the epic is necessary. Most of the major Romantic poets not only expressed veneration for Milton, but also respected and consciously attempted the epic form. Keats, indeed, declared that 'a long Poem is a test of Invention which I take to be the Polar Star of Poetry, as Fancy is the Sails, and Imagination the Rudder'.[4] Yet, an apparent paradox of the epic in the nineteenth century is that the age witnessed a decline in theories of the epic. Indeed, late eighteenth-century critics shook their heads over the strictures that had been placed on epic-writing by earlier theorists, particularly by René Le Bossu, who was singled out for special condemnation. An extract from William Hayley's influential *Essay on Epic Poetry* (1782) is representative of the attitude towards neoclassical epic theory:

> where the settled Rules of Writing spread,
> Where Learning's code of Critic Law is read,
> Tho' other treasures deck th' enlighten'd shore,
> The germs of Fancy ripen there no more.[5]

Furthermore, Hayley demonises Le Bossu as a 'subtle Pedant' at the head of this rigid 'System' which stifles poetic innovation.[6] Lord Kames, referring to Bossu's insistence on the importance of fable over action, sneered of his definition of epic that it 'excludes every epic poem founded upon real facts, and perhaps includes some of Aesop's fables'.[7] The Romantic age, in other words, saw a shift in attitude to genre, expressed in the late eighteenth century as a relaxation of generic boundaries and a dislike for generic conventions and rules. There was little of the kind of fussing over what did or did not constitute an epic that marks neoclassical epic theory. Epic was seen primarily as synonymous with narrative, and many concluded that epic and romance, for example, were closely related, if not identical. The epic-related novels of the eighteenth century were also readily included under the rubric of epic. Thus, James Beattie, writing in 1783, defines epic as narrative and therefore determines that romance and, with it, novel could be epic in nature; indeed, he concludes of Fielding's *Tom Jones* that 'Since the days of Homer, the world has not seen a more artful Epick fable'.[8] This new sense of informality towards epic is expressed, most famously, by Clara Reeve, who defends romance in *The Progress of Romance* (1785) by railing against the Renaissance-inspired rules that distinguish epic from romance, insisting that 'they spring from the same root, – they describe the same actions and circumstances, – they produce the same effects, and they are continually mistaken for each other'.[9]

In the wake of this new leniency in epic criticism of the period, innovation in the epic was acceptable, if not to be encouraged. Those epics thought to be the result of spontaneous, even primitive, genius were therefore venerated. In addition to Milton, then, Homer and Dante – but not Virgil – offered themselves as exemplary epic poets.[10] The age saw a marked increase in epic production. This feverish activity Robert Southey proudly labelled 'epomania', a phenomenon to which he contributed.[11] 'Epomania' affected too the major Romantic poets, as they sought to introduce an epic heroism on the premise constructed by Milton.

Blake's *Milton*

Hayley's vitriolic attack on epic theory was, as Stuart Curran suggests, the hornbook for epic poets of the age.[12] Hayley was also Blake's patron. Northrop Frye asserts that 'The immediate effect of Hayley on Blake was to sharpen his sense and increase his knowledge of the epic tradition'.[13] Both, it would seem, shared a disdain for the more rigorous aspects of epic-writing. Moreover, both felt that it was Milton who demonstrated precisely how to write epic outside the strictures of epic theory, preserving the essence of epic but experimenting with generic expectations. Wittreich states that 'Hayley not only contributed to Blake's knowledge of epic poetry but also honed his comprehension of Milton'.[14] In his *Essay*, Hayley suggests that Milton did not merely 'rehearse / The sacred, old traditionary verse' (I.167–8) of epic, he renovated it. What enabled him to do so was poetic genius of the first order. As Hayley asserted in his *Life of Milton*, Milton 'was a poet of the most powerful and, perhaps, most independent mind that was ever given to a mere mortal'.[15] Wittreich also reminds us that their shared interest in Milton is most clearly manifest in Hayley's commission to Blake to produce a portrait of Milton for Hayley's library. This *Head of Milton* reproduces traditional attributes of Milton iconography – a bay and oak wreath encircles the head, and a serpent with an apple in its mouth lies beneath it – in close adherence to Hayley's instructions.[16]

Yet, Blake revised and transformed Hayley's veneration for Milton into a heroicisation in *Milton*. As Lucy Newlyn demonstrates, the poem takes issue with those who would blindly deify Milton and his *Paradise Lost*.[17] Thus, the poem imagines Milton on a spiritual pilgrimage in which the poet learns of and overcomes the error of his ways in order that he might become a true poet and prophet. Milton's errors are manifest, for one thing, in his failings as a husband and father, failings which Hayley glosses over in his *Life*. Most significantly, however, Milton must develop from the poet who wrote *Paradise Lost* to the one who wrote *Paradise Regained*, which, for Blake, 'contains the highest, fullest, the most intense, the most valuable mental experience imaginable'.[18] *Paradise Lost*, in contrast, expresses both error and the potential for prophecy; Milton learns, in Blake's poem, to divest himself and his poetry of such error. The two proofs of Milton's error – his flaws as both husband and poet – are linked, for Milton must discover within himself a capacity for feminised compassion and polyvalence. For at the heart of Milton's error, according to Blake, is a belief in dualism and hence hierarchy and authority; Milton must therefore become aware of the capacity in his poetry to convey eternal wisdom. *Paradise Lost*, in its insistence on the absolute authority both of God and the poet, embodies the first stance. Yet, the poem, in offering glimpses of a multi-vocal, all-embracing divinity, does show the way towards the second. As David Riede puts it, Blake portrays Milton's poetic development from the 'divinely authoritative voice of *Paradise Lost*' to an acknowledgement of 'the myriad voices of the living Judaeo-Christian tradition'.[19] Thus, the poem, from advocating a rejection of the 'False Tongue' (pl. 13, 10) of religious orthodoxy in favour of the 'Eternal Great Humanity Divine' (pl. 3, 8), expresses Blake's own theological vision of God as an all-embracing and eternal truth present in everyone, but turned by the church into a symbol of authority and hence enslavement.[20]

Blake's Milton then is an heroic figure whose realisation of this allows him to complete himself as man and as poet and thence as prophet. The sternness and lifelessness of the *Head of Milton* is barely recognisable in Blake's vibrant, muscular illustrations for *Milton*.[21] This hero must endure a pilgrimage marked by a series of encounters with various emanations of himself and his beliefs – for example, Los, who represents poetic creativity defeated by religious hierarchy; Urizen, who appears in so much of Blake's poetry as the emblem of a fettered God; the virgin Ololon, who represents Milton's feminised poetic side which is capable of expressing eternal truth; and Satan himself, who embodies the evils of institutionalised religion that Milton had perpetuated in *Paradise Lost*. The Milton who begins the pilgrimage is one who writes blindly in the tradition of the classical epics, reproducing their bellicose and divisive tendencies and running counter to the true revelatory aims of poetry. In his preface, Blake makes this point emphatically:

> The Stolen and Perverted Writings of Homer & Ovid, of Plato & Cicero, which all Men ought to contemn, are set up by artifice against the Sublime of the Bible...Shakespeare & Milton were both curb'd by the general malady & infection from the silly Greek & Latin slaves of the Sword.... We do not want either Greek or Roman Models if we are but just & true to our own Imaginations, those Worlds of Eternity in which we shall live forever in Jesus our Lord.[22]

At the start of the poem, Milton is in heaven, having 'walk'd about in Eternity / One hundred years, pondering the intricate mazes of Providence' (pl. 3, 16–17). Upon hearing the prophetic song of a Bard, he resolves to descend to earth, and confront Satan, who represents his selfishness both as man and poet: 'I will go down to self annihilation and eternal death, / Lest the last judgement find me unannihilate.../ I in my Selfhood am that Satan; I am that Evil One!' (pl. 12, 22–3, 30). The Milton who achieves the pilgrimage has done battle with the dualistic, differentiating forces of false religion which had marked his poetic and personal lives. In confronting Satan he defeats selfhood, and hence acknowledges his power as a prophet of eternity and truth:

> In the Eastern porch of Satan's Universe Milton stood & said:
> 'Satan! my Spectre! I know thy power thee to annihilate
>   ...know thou, I come to Self Annihilation.
> Such are the Laws of Eternity that each shall mutually
> Annihilate himself for others' good, as I for thee.
> Thy purpose & the purpose of thy Priests & of thy Churches

> Is to impress on Men to despise death, to teach
> Trembling & fear, terror, constriction, abject selfishness.
> Mine is to teach Men to despise death & to go on
> In fearless majesty annihilating Self, laughing to scorn
> Thy Laws and terrors, shaking down thy Synagogues as webs.
>
> (pl. 39, 29–30, 34–42)

In defeating Satan, Milton opens himself to union with Ololon; to her he is able to 'come in Self-annihilation & the grandeur of Inspiration' (pl. 43, 2). In a spectacular conclusion, Ololon reveals herself as the 'Feminine Portion' of Milton, a 'Six-fold Miltonic Female' (pl. 43, 30). Dividing herself thus, the virgin unites with Milton, while the essential Ololon heralds the coming of Christ to Blake himself, thus evoking Milton's prophetic powers and implying the transfer too of these powers to Blake.

In envisaging Milton as a prophetic poet, Blake captures an attitude that is repeated in the epic attempts of his Romantic contemporaries, Wordsworth, Keats and Byron. However, in rejecting the epic form, and indeed *Paradise Lost* as an expression of that form, for perpetuating difference, selfhood and therefore tyranny, and in insisting on true poethood as 'Self-annihilation', Blake differs substantially from these poets. As we shall see, the model epic poet, for Wordsworth, Keats and Byron, was a man who had gained self-knowledge. It was the process of close self-interrogation that rendered him heroic and able to write of the heroic.

Wordsworth's *Prelude*

The Prelude is a blank verse poem in fourteen books, detailing the poet's development from childhood through young adulthood to his attainment of real poetic ability in his thirties. At the core of any reading of the poem as epic is the question of epic heroism. That the poem aspires to epic, particularly to epic in the Miltonic tradition, is made clear within the poem itself. In Book I of the poem, the poet recalls the subjects he had considered for his epic, and echoes the decisions made by Milton himself in writing *Paradise Lost*:

> Sometimes the ambitious Power of choice, mistaking
> Proud spring-tide swellings for a regular sea,
> Will settle on some British theme, some old
> Romantic tale by Milton left unsung;

> More often turning to some gentle place
> Within the groves of Chivalry, I pipe
> To shepherd swains, or seated harp in hand,
> Amid reposing knights by a river side
> Or fountain, listen to the grave reports
> Of dire enchantments faced and overcome
> By the strong mind, and tales of warlike feats,
> Where spear encountered spear, and sword with sword
> Fought, as if conscious of the blazonry
> That the shield bore, so glorious was the strife...

$$(I.166-79)^{23}$$

Yet, it is also made clear here that this is epic with a twist. The poet lists such traditionally epic matters in order to emphasise his rejection of them, settling instead on:

> ... some philosophic song
> Of Truth that cherishes our daily life;
> With meditations passionate from deep
> Recesses in man's heart, immortal verse
> Thoughtfully fitted to the Orphean lyre

$$(I.229-33)$$

At the heart of this preference for a 'song / Of Truth' over apparently superficially epic subjects is Wordsworth's complex relationship with Milton and with the epic tradition. In other writings, Wordsworth records his belief that sublimity, a term that for Wordsworth connoted great power and truth, was necessary for epic.[24] Like Milton, then, Wordsworth invests heavily in the solemnity of the epic form and, also like Milton, he rejects the allegorical heroism of earthly wars and chivalrous deeds for a true heroism of universal resonance. Unlike Milton, however, Wordsworth establishes this truth not by pushing outwards to the cosmological or theological, but inwards to the psychological. Wordsworth makes explicit what was viewed as being implicit in Milton – that the epic deed is a product of the poet's imagination, no matter how much it seems to appeal to the exterior standards of religion and nationhood, and that to tell of the poet, specifically the poet in the act of creating an epic, is to sing the truest song there is.

It is worth bearing in mind, however, that *The Prelude* was originally intended to be precisely that – a prelude to the much larger but never completed *Recluse*. The 'song / of truth' that Wordsworth intends as his epic is not automatically *The Prelude*, but just as likely *The Recluse*. Particularly in the earliest stages of the project, real epic ambition lay with the imagined superstructure of *The Recluse*, a poem that was to be, as we know, 'On Man, on Nature, and on Human Life'.[25] Thus, the autobiography of *The Prelude*, rather than simply Wordsworth's intended response to the epic tradition, represents, in the first instance, the psychic probing that he saw as a precursor to that response. Yet, as Jonathan Wordsworth's careful editorial work has demonstrated, the revisions that Wordsworth made over a lifetime clearly enhanced the epic tendencies of *The Prelude*.[26] Embedded in the final product, published posthumously by Wordsworth's wife in 1850, is a growing awareness of the heroic potential of the epic poet. As Jonathan Wordsworth's analysis suggests, as Wordsworth came to realise that *The Recluse* would never be completed, emphasis shifted from making a display of the achievement of poetic heroism to telling the narrative of its development, and allowing that narrative to become the proof of that achievement.[27]

The hero of *The Prelude* is not simply the poet but, more specifically, his mind and his soul (the two terms are used by Wordsworth with little real distinction between them). The heroic action is the poet's mental and psychological maturation, the trajectory a fairly conventional one of early development and promise, moving to a time of crisis and a falling-off, and on to resolution and success. In other words, Wordsworth tells of the development of his mind from his infancy through to the tribulations of young adulthood and thence to the poetic maturity of his thirties. When the poem is read this way, other epic conventions, in addition to the fore-grounding of heroic action, reveal themselves. The poem begins *in medias res*, with the poet recalling his decision to write the poem, before initiating the trajectory of mental development. The poem also possesses a muse of sorts, as the poet dedicates and addresses his verse to his fellow poet Coleridge.

But there is another player in this epic's heroic action. Wordsworth's mind is assisted throughout by Nature. In the developmental phase of the trajectory – the childhood of Books I and II – Nature is essential to the growth of the young mind's creative powers. 'Fair seed-time had my soul', Wordsworth famously declares, 'and I grew up / Fostered alike by beauty and by fear' (I.301). For the boy Wordsworth, Nature's teachings range from the transports inflict by the terror of a mountain, which almost comes alive when seen at night, to the beauties of a frozen lake and sky observed while skating on a winter's afternoon. All this results in a 'sanctifying, by such discipline, / Both pain and fear, until we recognise / A grandeur in the beatings of the heart' (I.413–15). The precise conditions of Nature's tutelage become clear as we progress through the poem. The poem's many natural metaphors for the poet's mind – the river, the breeze and finally the moon of the final book – alert us to the fact that Nature's creative powers mirror the poet's. Nature, by demonstrating the full range of her workings, is demonstrating the full range too of the human mind, particularly the poet's mind.

Yet, we must not imagine that Nature as the mind's teacher is therefore a superior agent in this heroic action. She – for Wordsworth's Nature is always a 'she' – merely 'fosters', inasmuch as she cultivates what already exists. Wordsworth is careful to make clear that his mind works as a creative force independently of Nature and that, eventually, Nature must yield responsibility for the poet's imaginative development to the poet himself.[28] According to the poem, the human mind, even in infancy, is able to 'Create, creator and receiver both, / Working but in alliance with the works / Which it beholds' (II.258–60). And Wordsworth's mind is no exception:

> But let this
> Be not forgotten, that I still retained
> My first creative sensibility;
> That by the regular action of the world
> My soul was unsubdued. A plastic power
> Abode with me; a forming hand, at times
> Rebellious, acting in a devious mood;
> A local spirit of his own, at war
> With general tendency, but, for the most,
> Subservient strictly to external things
> With which it communed.
>
> (II.358–68)

It is no coincidence that Wordsworth's earliest memories are recalled by the image of the River Derwent (I.269). Though this suggests the primacy of the natural, when read retrospectively against the poem's recurring motif of the river for the mind, it also invokes the autonomy of the mind. And again the temptation to read subordination when there is really self-assertion occurs in Book IV, when the poet's creative faculties begin to affirm themselves later in life: 'Gently did my soul / Put off her veil, and, self-transmuted, stood / Naked, as in the presence of her God . . .' (IV.150–2). The 'as' signals to us that things seem to be what they are not. The poet's soul may *seem* to resemble an acolyte before its deity, but it is assuredly not.

Possessed, we learn some lines later, of a 'God-like power' (IV.166), the poet's soul is itself a creative force, in open encounter with the creative force of Nature.

The question of who emerges victorious from this encounter is never really in doubt. Already, early on in its development, we find hints that the poet's mind will emerge as a solely capable creative force. It is significant, for example, that the poet's pilgrimage to the Alps, an emblem of Nature at its most sublime and powerful, actually results in an affirmation of the poet's creative powers over Nature's. When the poet comes within sight of Mont Blanc, this geographical pinnacle of the journey is not transformed into a neat metaphor for the achievement of mental perfection on the poet's part. The symbolism behind the attainment of the summit is surprisingly anticlimactic, for the mountain represents a challenge to the poet's creativity, rather than an objective correlative for it:

> That very day,
> From a bare ridge we also first beheld
> Unveiled the summit of Mont Blanc, and grieved
> To have a soulless image on the eye
> That had usurped a living thought
> That never more could be
>
> (VI.523)

Implicit in these lines is the superiority of the poet's creativity, since the image of the mountain that had been developed by his imagination is equivalent, indeed preferable, to the vision that offers itself to his naked eye. Mary Jacobus suggests that, 'At once overwhelmed by the spectacle of the Alps and yet adequate to it, the imagination sees in alpine grandeur the simultaneous sign and guarantee of its own sublimity – a consoling mirror of its limitlessness'.[29] It is possible to argue, however, that the actual Alpine view is construed, somewhat perversely, as inadequate to the imagined view, for the purely visual is limited in a way that the imaginative can never be. For example, the poet's crossing of the Alps is described as a disappointment, but, significantly, it is his imaginative expectation of that crossing that yields true creative glory, for it contains 'hope that can never die, / Effort, and expectation, and desire, /And something evermore about to be' (VI.607–9). Poetic maturity is marked by the triumph of the theoretical over the empirical, of mind over Nature. The sheer power of the poet's mind indicates its capacity for epic heroism.[30]

But poetic creativity, whether ultimately arising solely from the mind or initially assisted by Nature, is to be appreciated in solitude, away from the intervening, distracting world. And this is where it is important to recognise Wordsworth's investment in a Cartesian distinction between mind and man. The mind reigns supreme, whereas the dust of man is, for Wordsworth, utterly expendable. The poet wonders of the mind: 'Why, gifted with such powers to send abroad / Her spirit, must it lodge in shrines so frail?' (V.48–9). Significantly, such musings on the imperfectability of man are prompted in this passage by the epic burlesque of *Don Quixote*. But whereas Cervantes, and the tradition of comic epic and novel initiated by him, had implied that modern man is not made for epic action, Wordsworth finds and detaches the one element of man that *is* made for such action – the mind. If, for Cervantes, epic heroism cannot exist in the modern age, for Wordsworth, modern epic heroism can only exist, and does exist, in the mind of the poet.[31]

So much does Wordsworth insist on detaching the mind from men that the world of men becomes the antagonist of his epic action. The poet's entry into the world of men precipitates the crisis phase of the poem's heroic action, in which the poet loses faith in the powers of the mind and his mind consequently stumbles in its development. 'The central problem in *The Prelude*', as Richard Bourke sees it, 'is not that of the self but the difficulty of adequate socialisation'.[32] This central problem comes to the fore in the books that deal with Wordsworth's residence first in London and then in France during the Revolution. The sights of London quickly reveal themselves to be all external and superficial show and the promise of the Revolution ultimately ends in terror. Though Wordsworth portrays himself as believing still that 'A sovereign voice subsists within the soul, /Arbiter undisturbed of right and wrong' (X.183), the ways of the world are eventually depicted as antithetical to the ways of Nature. Wordsworth recalls how his was:

> . . . a heart that had been turned aside
> From Nature's way by outward accidents,
> And which was thus confounded more and more,
> Misguided and misguiding.

> (XI.291)

To turn from Nature is to turn from the most obvious source of the mind's inspiration. The outcome of his time in France is Wordsworth's loss of faith in men and, by extension, in himself and his own creative powers. In this state of despondency, Wordsworth loses his sense of creativity and becomes enamoured of the superficial rather than the truly poetic, of objects that appeal to the eye rather than to the mind. This is the nadir of his poetic pilgrimage, for he becomes seduced by the cult of picturesque poetry.[33]

This crisis is soon resolved, however, by a return to self. Wordsworth's sister Dorothy comes to the rescue, 'Maintain[ing] for me a saving intercourse / With my true self' (XI.341–2). Dorothy's intervention is followed by that of Nature, who, 'By all varieties of human love / Assisted, led me back through opening day / To those sweet counsels between head and heart' (XI.350–2). The result is the triumphant restoration of the poet's creative powers, the successful rehabilitation from mere picturesque to profoundly poetic:

> I shook the habit off
> Entirely and for ever, and again
> In Nature's presence stood, as now I stand,
> A sensitive being, a *creative* soul.

> (XII.204–7)

This triumph is finalised in the last book, Book XIV, and emblematised by the ascent of Snowdon. As the poet attains a summit for the second time in the poem, the moon appears out of cloud and over the distant ocean:

> When into air had partially dissolved
> That vision, given to spirits of the night
> And three chance human wanderers, in calm thought
> Reflected, it appeared to me the type
> Of a majestic intellect, its acts
> And its possessions, what it has and craves,
> What in itself it is, and would become.
> There I beheld the emblem of a mind
> That feeds upon infinity, that broods
> Over the dark abyss...

> (XIV.63–72)

The natural wonder that was Mont Blanc had figured to the young poet as a usurpation of the imagined beauty of the mountain. For the fully tested and triumphant mature poet, it is possible to go one step further. The wonder of Nature as seen in the moon is a 'type', a representation of the human mind. The natural world is no longer a challenge to the mind, but a metaphor for it. Thus subordinated to mental process, it is incapable of usurping it. Whereas the young poet had seen the mountain and lamented the loss of his own imagined vision, the mature poet sees only an image of the mind. The mind encounters only itself and is the stronger for this sense of duplication. The heroic action is complete.

For Wordsworth, therefore, creative power is established when it has risen, fallen and been triumphantly restored. More importantly, this rise and fall must be examined and understood by the poet himself. It is the knowledge gained from this experience that would enable an epic. It is this Wordsworthian construction of the epic poet as fully self-interrogated in order to write his epic that is worth keeping in mind when considering the epics of Keats and Byron. Neither Keats nor Byron, of course, could have read *The Prelude*, which was published in 1850, after the deaths of all three; it is worth considering, none the less, that the subjectivity that is so often associated with the Romantic age emerges in the epics of Wordsworth, Keats, and Byron in interesting, and comparable, ways.

Keats's *Hyperion* and *The Fall of Hyperion*

Like Wordsworth, Keats had Milton in his sights as he considered the epic form, and, also like Wordsworth, his innovations with the form are centred on the question of identity, particularly the identity of the poet. Keats's *Hyperion* hints at a challenge to the kind of grand majestic heroism that is suggested by Milton's lofty style (as opposed to the implicit heroism of Milton's poetic self), but it falters in its search for a suitable heroic substitute. The revisions that constitute *The Fall of Hyperion* serve to clarify this challenge while postulating an answer, one that rests on the establishment of a poet-hero whose identity is forged in a crisis of selfhood and, further, whose experiences are aligned with the protagonists of his own epic.

However, it is one thing to say that Keats intended to revolutionise the epic form, but quite another to demonstrate precisely how he did this. Stuart Sperry, in his influential analysis, suggests that Keats sounds his challenge to the old order of poets within the action of his poem; this challenge is to be found, straightforwardly enough, in his representation of the Olympian overthrow of the Titans. The fall of the Titans dramatises, according to Sperry, 'a sense of failure of the generation of poets before [Keats's] own'.[34] Sperry, indeed, correlates Keats's depiction of the overthrow of the Titans to his rejection of the old epic sense of history and objectivity. The passing of power from Titans to Olympians is 'a fall of timelessness into time that Keats had for some while come to sense as fundamental to the modern consciousness'.[35] For Sperry, moreover, the revisions of *The Fall of Hyperion* are a deliberate rejection of the Miltonic tone of *Hyperion*, as Keats struggled for a less consciously epic style in imitation of Dante.[36] However, the problem with this, as has more recently been pointed out, is that even a cursory reading of *Hyperion* will reveal that Keats's attentions, and thus his loyalties, appear to lie more with the old Titans than with the new Olympians.[37] It would seem that Keats's political investment in progress and revolution ultimately proves incompatible with his poetic interest in the tragic and elegiac Titans.

It is possible, though, to reconcile Keats's sympathetic portrayal of the fallen, broken Titans with his apparent desire to reject the constraints of the old epic tradition and embrace a new subjectivity. For a division of loyalties between the Titans and the Olympians, between the Miltonic epic and a new innovation in form, is inherent in the first *Hyperion*. The need to iron out this division is what brings about Keats's failure to complete the poem and it is this that Keats endeavours to resolve by writing *The Fall of Hyperion*. His radical revisions in this second poem constitute an attempt to clarify the Titans' position as well as his own position within the Miltonic epic tradition. And, contrary to recent analyses that insist that *The Fall of Hyperion* fore-shadows a postmodern model of poetic identity in flux, it is possible to see how Keats's version of the creative self puts forward a coherent subjectivity not unlike that proposed by Wordsworth.

Hyperion initially presents the Titans within the paradigm of traditional epic heroism. Keats experiments with what he called Miltonic 'stationing or statuary', that is, Milton's habit of posing his figures, fixing them in majestic stillness. Milton, according to Keats, "is not content with simple description, he must station . . . . So we see Adam 'Fair indeed and tall – under a plantane' – and so we see Satan 'disfigured – on the Assyrian Mount'".[38] Keats's epic inhabitants, like those of Milton, appear in all their statuesque glory. The physical presence of the fallen Saturn, like that of Satan lying in the fiery lakes of Hell, is all the more appreciable for being absolutely prone and still:

> Deep in the shady sadness of a vale
> Far sunken from the healthy breath of morn,
> Far from the fiery noon, and eve's one star,
> Sat grey-haired Saturn, quiet as a stone,

> Still as the silence round about his lair;
> Forest on forest hung above his head
> Like cloud on cloud.
>
> (I.1–7)[39]

The breathtaking proportions of a Titan such as Thea, next to whom 'the tall Amazon / Had stood a pigmy's height' (I.27–8), indicate that Keats is presenting a deliberately Miltonic – and beyond this classical – epic heroism, for the stature of these immortals recalls the proportions of Homer's gods. Even time is scaled up: Thea and Saturn remain motionless in their grief for four months.

But the lifelessness of these statuesque Titans means that they have been set up in order to be brought down. As Michael O'Neill puts it, the poem expresses 'Keats's studied determination to breathe new life into epic tradition by conceding its potential deathliness'.[40] It is tempting to read the Olympians' usurpation of these monstrous Titans as an attempt to shift this unattainable and therefore irrelevant heroism on to a more sympathetic and human scale, particularly when we consider that the Olympians promise a greater motility and emotionality than the Titans. Apollo, when he appears in Book III, is, in striking opposition to the stony Titans, all aquiver, marked by the 'trickling' of his 'bright tears' (III.42–3), the throbbing of his 'white melodious throat' (III.81) and his strumming on the 'lyre golden by his side' (III.63). Keats links this quivering, crucially, to Apollo's status as god of the poets, 'the Father of all verse' (III.13). It would seem that, as is explicit in Wordsworth and only implicit in Milton, the real hero here is the poet, particularly a very human, very feeling poet. Gone is the overtly Miltonic stationing; in its place are sensuousness and movement as Apollo attains godhead:

> His very hair, his golden tresses famed
> Kept undulation round his eager neck.
> During the pain Mnemosyne upheld
> Her arms as one who prophesied. – At length
> Apollo shrieked – and lo! from all his limbs
> Celestial . . .
>
> (III.131–6)

But if Apollo is indeed Keats's version of the poet-hero, this point would mark the beginning of the poem's celebration of this heroism. Yet, this is precisely where the fragment breaks off. Apollo's tremblings and hesitations on the verge of apotheosis make him temporarily a poet-hero, but this apotheosis will lead simply to godhead and, presumably, to a statuary presence and an untouchable epic heroism. For this humanity that Apollo momentarily possesses we should be looking, rather, to the fallen Titans. In order for the Olympians' promise of a new kind of epic heroism of humanity and emotionality to be convincing, the remote and gloomy Titans would have to be consistently rendered unsympathetically. However, the insistently epic stature of these gigantic Titans is juxtaposed with their vulnerability. Their position within the poem as fallen is precisely what renders them potentially human – as Jonathan Bate persuasively argues, they become tragic rather than epic.[41] Their loss of immortality confers on them the shadow of mortality, and just the kind of human heroism that places in relief their prior godlike heroism. Keats breaks off the poem at this point because Apollo cannot retain the fallen state Keats desires and admires and, in order fully to explore the human condition, he must return to the Titans.

The Fall of Hyperion is, as its title suggests, precisely about a fall, and it therefore puts into focus the Titans' experience. The Titans are now heroicised for their suffering. In *Hyperion*, Mnemosyne, the personification of memory and thus the mother of the muses, had overseen Apollo's transformation into the god of poets. In *The Fall of Hyperion*, she is replaced by her alter-ego Moneta, goddess of wisdom. Because Moneta as guardian of memory is no longer a maternal guide to Apollo but a priestess to the posterity of the fallen Titans, it is the Titans' fall, and not Apollo's apotheosis, that is the centrepiece here. Though Apollo is her 'dear foster child' (I.286), she is identifiable not so much as the mother of the Olympians but as the last of the Titans, the 'pale Omega of a withered race' (I.288).[42] What 'in [her] brain so ferments to and fro' (I.290) is not Apollo's birth but Saturn's death. What she reveals to the poet, and what emerges therefore as the theme of this second *Hyperion*, is the heroic struggle and fall of the Titans.

The most radical revision of *The Fall of Hyperion* is the insertion of the poet into the action of the poem. With this, the Titanic fall is witnessed directly by the poet, and, more significantly, it is mirrored in his own suffering as he strives to prove himself worthy of the task of recording their tribulation. But what is the nature of the poetic subjectivity that Keats imagines for himself? The answer to this question lies in two difficult moments within the poem: the first is the opening passage, with its discussion of the distinction between the poet and the dreamer, and the second is the poet's encounter with Moneta, who posits a notoriously slippery logic on the same theme.

The poem states, in the very first line, that 'Fanatics have their dreams, wherewith they weave / A paradise for a sect' (I.1–2), although, it insists, 'Poesy alone can tell her dreams' (I.8). Fanatics' dreams, unspoken, are merely dreams, whereas poets' dreams, when told, become poetry. The subtitle of the poem – 'A Dream' – tantalises us with the question of whether the text in hand is dream or poetry, and whether the poet is a mere dreamer or a real poet. Indeed, Keats makes explicit this question in the poem: 'Whether the dream now purposed to rehearse / Be Poet's or Fanatic's will be known / When this warm scribe my hand is in the grave' (I, 16–18). This question is placed firmly in focus when the poem becomes the retelling of a dream. In it the poet finds himself standing in a garden and then taking of the scattered remnants of a feast, which, resembling 'refuse of a meal / By angel tasted, or our Mother Eve' (I, 30–1), is emblematic of the decay of the old epic tradition of Miltonic grandeur.

What follows is a dream within a dream, which contains the confrontation with Moneta. In this second dream, any hope that the poet will prove himself a poet rather than a dreamer is problematised, though finally affirmed. When he passes the agonising test set by Moneta of ascending to her altar, he learns that 'None can usurp this height . . . / But those to whom the miseries of the world / Are misery, and will not let them rest' (I, 147–9). It would seem, then, that he is set apart from the apathetic masses that remain unmoved by fellow suffering. But any smug superiority on the poet's part is premature, for Moneta insists that because he has made the effort to reach her altar he is actually inferior; he is 'less than they' (I, 166). He is merely 'a dreaming thing, / A fever of thyself' (I, 168–9), one who 'venoms all his days, / Bearing more woe than all his sins deserve' (I, 175–6). According to Moneta, the troubled and troublesome dreamer willingly ventures into the kind of tribulation found in her temple, while the true poet is content with enjoying and spreading happiness. Our poet's success in suffering at the hands of Moneta only underlines his status as a dreamer. Moneta's distinction between the true poet and the mere dreamer runs thus: 'The one pours out a balm upon the world, / The other vexes it' (I, 201–2) and, presumably, vexes himself in the process.

None the less, the poet refuses this distinction, and the forcefulness of his response, as much as its argument, is crucial to the poetic identity he will forge for himself in the course of the poem:

> Then shouted I,
> Spite of myself, and with a Pythia's spleen,
> 'Apollo! faded, far-flown Apollo!

> Where is thy misty pestilence to creep
> Into the dwellings, through the door crannies,
> Of all mock lyrists, large self-worshippers
> And careless hectorers in proud bad verse.
> Though I breathe death with them it will be life
> To see them sprawl before me into graves...'
>
> (I.202–10)

Implicit in this outburst is the poet's successful defence of himself as a poet, for what he condemns in poetasters are insincerity, selfishness and carelessness. They practise Moneta's brand of poetry, which seeks merely to please. For Keats, the poet must cause suffering, in both himself and others, as he sets about recording but finally healing suffering. That he invokes Apollo here is significant, for at least two reasons. First, the reference to Apollo's mythical association with disease underlines the necessity of the poet's association with suffering. In addition, as Moneta relents in the face of this argument and enables the poet to become the witness and recorder of the Titans' desolation, the poet takes a crucial step towards poethood under her aegis, and thus embraces the part played by Apollo in the earlier *Hyperion*.

But there is a crucial difference in this transformation. Apollo's deification had been captured in his memorable assertion that 'Knowledge enormous makes a god of me' (*Hyperion* III.113). However, the poet of *The Fall of Hyperion*, though he does acquire 'A power...of enormous ken/To see as a God sees' (I.302–4), is called on to identify gods who are suffering and broken. The poet acquires not the invincibility of divinity, but the power to see and understand the Titanic pain that is the focus of this second version. Indeed, the agonies he undergoes as he watches Moneta, Thea and Saturn echo those that he experienced at the foot of Moneta's steps. The 'load of this eternal quietude,/ The unchanging gloom, and the three fixéd shapes/Ponderous upon my senses' (I.390–2) recall the 'stifling, suffocating' (I.130) cold and numbness of that earlier trial. He is able to sing of the Titans' fallen state because it is a state that he has himself attained in becoming a poet. Crucially, too, the yet to be written story of Hyperion, the title-hero, will presumably afford the opportunity to witness the unfolding of another lapsarian trajectory and reaffirm the parallels between the poet's fall into knowledge and the Titans'.

The question remains, however, of the stability of the self-knowledge achieved by the poet. Recent analyses of *The Fall of Hyperion* agree that it may be read as narrating the path towards poetic identity, but, drawing on Keats's concept of 'negative capability', they insist that the selfhood acquired by the poet is necessarily fluid and open-ended.[43] The poem presents, in Christopher Bode's recent analysis, 'a fallen world, forever falling'.[44] Similarly, O'Neill suggests that 'in *The Fall* the poet's burden is not to know so as to be in a position to prophesy or control, but rather to know so as to suffer'.[45] Yet such an argument does not attend to the way in which the poem gestures towards a coherent subjectivity and creative power forged out of this suffering and falling. While the poem's self-reflexivity seems to compromise the authority of the poet (for the suffering, becoming poet who inhabits the text appears to be a wonderfully postmodern critique on authorial stability), it could be read as confirming this authority because it necessitates the existence of a recovered poet who has undergone suffering in order to write the text. Bode describes the poem as 'a radically post-metaphysical epic, an epic without a metaphysical frame of reference, [which] is solely founded on the subjectivity of the poet and is enacted exclusively in his mind'.[46] Yet, it could be argued that, in foregrounding the poet's mind as the site of the poem's action, Keats makes a claim for its sovereignty and, consequently, for a stability of subjectivity. Carol Bernstein offers, in her discussion of *Hyperion*, this useful description of the way subjectivity can inhere in an apparently postmodern instance of self-questioning:

> ironically, the postmodern questioning of the subject, especially insofar as it is understood to be unitary and conscious, assumes a certain self-consciousness in the act of questioning itself....Thus a postmodern stance would want to have it both ways, placing thoughtful man 'under erasure' at the same time that its critique incorporates fragments of subjectivity: those fragments are now part of the mind's machinery and the relics upon which that machinery focuses.[47]

In *The Fall of Hyperion*, Keats questions the nature of poetic identity, in, for example, the seeming illogic of the poet's dialogue with Moneta, yet such questioning requires a state of rest, a coherence on the part of he who questions. For all its emphasis on unknowability, 'negative capability', after all, is also about the negatively *capable* poet who knows of unknowability. As with Wordsworth, so for Keats, the poet's experience under self-interrogation is what enables him to go on to construct an epic.

Byron's *Don Juan*

Byron's response to the epic tradition is the seemingly endless, frequently digressive *Don Juan*. That Byron did, in half-seriousness, intend to write an epic is suggested by remarks attributed to him by Thomas Medwin: 'If you must have an epic, there's "Don Juan" for you. I call that an epic: it is an epic as much in the spirit of our day as the Iliad was in Homer's.'[48] A comparable sentiment is to be found in the text of the poem:

> My poem's epic, and is meant to be
> Divided in twelve books, each book containing,
> With love and war, a heavy gale at sea,
> A list of ships and captains and kings reigning,
> New characters; the episodes are three.
> A panoramic view of hell's in training,
> After the style of Virgil and of Homer,
> So that my name of epic's no misnomer.
>
> (I.200)[49]

In other words, *Don Juan* is more comic epic than mock-epic. Where a preservative epic burlesque such as *The Rape of the Lock* gains its meaning by largely respecting epic conventions, *Don Juan* violates as many of these as possible, from refusing to begin *in medias res* ('That is the usual method, but not mine;/My way is to begin at the beginning' ([I.7]) to eschewing both blank verse and heroic couplets for stanzas in *ottava rima*. In the face of such rampant mockery, the poem's epic status has been granted by virtue of the sheer force of Byron's personality. Jerome McGann has stated simply that 'The work is epic because Byron wanted it to be thought of as such'.[50] Others have tentatively suggested that the poem's apparent nihilism (a mainstay of criticism of the poem since Harold Bloom dubbed it a 'spectre of meaninglessness') actually represents a radical innovation of the epic form.[51] Thus, Donald Reiman, in direct response to McGann, argues that *Don Juan* is an epic because its digressiveness and open-endedness reflects the growing uncertainty of its times.[52] Others have termed the poem an 'epic of negation' and an 'epic of indeterminacy'.[53]

It is a mistake, however, to construe Byron's epic response as simply free-for-all irony. This epic is intended as 'epic satire' (XIV.99), particularly as satire with a single, albeit broad, target. Just like *Don Quixote*, which Byron describes as a 'real epic' (XIII.9) for its ability to expose the false heroism of chivalry and therefore 'redress/Men's wrongs' (XIII.8), *Don Juan* seeks to reveal truth. It is not merely the life-story of the infamous lover Don Juan; it is a satire on hypocrisy, from the combination of political self-interest and literary pretentiousness Byron perceives in Southey and Wordsworth to the cant that abounds in fashionable society.

This writing of satire necessarily supposes the existence of a coherent self, for, as with all satire, it requires a dualism of satirist and satirised. Even where there exists the possibility for self-criticism on the part of the satirist and reform on the part of his target, the opposition between satirising subject and satirised object must exist as a foundation to the satirical act. So it is with *Don Juan*. It satirises the hypocrisies of society and preserves the possibility of truth as an antidote to this. This truth must emanate from a knowing, meaningful self, for the authority that the satirist has over both himself and his target must be especially consistent when what he is attacking is duplicity. The satirist of *Don Juan* must know the truth about himself that he may consequently expose the lack of truth in others. Frederick Garber points out of *Don Juan* that cant, as the expression of hypocrisy, says one thing and means (as well as conceals) another. Satire, 'standing in symmetrical opposition' to cant, replays this disparity between saying and meaning, but *reveals* this disparity as it does so.[54]

The poet of *Don Juan* constantly exposes this gap between saying and meaning, first by demonstrating it in his target and then acknowledging it in himself. In this way, his self-knowing and honesty emphasise the other's unknowing and hypocrisy. Thus, Juan's first lover, Donna Julia, is ridiculed for failing to resist Juan's charms only because her vows to her husband have been made with so little integrity and resolution:

> Julia had honours, virtue, truth, and love
> For Don Alfonso, and she inly swore
> By all the vows below to powers above,
> She never would disgrace the ring she wore
> Nor leave a wish which wisdom might reprove.
> And while she pondered this, besides much more,
> One hand on Juan's carelessly was thrown,
> Quite by mistake – she thought it was her own.

> (I.109)

Julia's resolution is only feigned; the structure and rhythm of the stanza suggest that the final line is merely bathos and, if it is bathos, then the pathetically insistent voice the poet assumes for Julia must culminate in the undermining of this protested resistance. Julia is being dishonest to herself and to Juan, not to mention to her husband Alfonso. And the consummation of the deed several stanzas later confirms this: 'A little still she strove and much repented, / And whispering 'I will ne'er consent' – consented' (I.117). Julia literally says one thing and means another. Her duplicity is captured in the gap between word and deed.

It seems, however, that the poet is not as hard on Julia as he could be, for he gallantly admits that he too finds vows of celibacy difficult:

> I make a resolution every spring
> Of reformation, ere the year run out.
> But somehow this my vestal vow takes wing;
> Yet still I trust it may be kept throughout.
> I'm very sorry, very much ashamed,
> And mean next winter to be quite reclaimed.
>
> (I.119)

The poet is as irresolute as Julia, and his insistence – that he will do the right thing – sounds as hollow as hers. But there is a crucial difference, one that overrides this irony. The poet, unlike Julia, recognises his hypocrisy in failing to keep his word, as well as his further hypocrisy in not really caring whether he keeps it or not. He is knowing enough not only to inform us of his inconsistency, but also to ironise his shame at this inconsistency. Such recognition is crucial, for it reveals the difference between knowing and unknowing, as well as the existence of a greatly superior brand of ironic self-knowing, that constitute *Don Juan*.

One is tempted to say that this knowing self (who bears a curious resemblance to Byron) is the real hero of *Don Juan*. Yet the poem already has a nominal hero – Don Juan – and the poet insists that the identity of his hero should not be conflated with his. Significantly, Juan displays an incapacity for hypocrisy that chimes with the poet's own capacity for truth. He is 'without malice; if he warred / Or loved, it was with what we call "the best / Intentions"' (VIII.25). He is truthful, if not always aware that he is being so. Importantly, though, it is the poet who supplies us with the commentary that makes explicit Juan's truthfulness. His knowledge, both of himself and of Juan, underpins the poem's drive against unknowing and, thus, hypocrisy. Juan and his adventures furnish the narrator with material to demonstrate Juan's truthfulness and the poet's knowledge of what truthfulness is. The poem itself informs us fairly late in its progress that 'This narrative is not meant for narration, / But a mere airy and fantastic basis / To build up common things with commonplaces' (XIV.7). In other words, the story provides a pretext for the theme of truth. The poem is, therefore, simultaneously about both Juan's adventurous heroism and the poet's superior self-awareness.

Thus, the poet and his hero are combined in such a way as to critique hypocrisy. The omnipresence of the poet is in keeping with this, since it averts, and subverts, the pretence that is realism. When the poet opens his epic by declaring, 'I want a hero' (I.1), he is drawing attention away from, not to, his hero, for he is making transparent the epic poet's task. Similarly, his many mockeries of epic conventions, such as Canto III's infamous invocation of 'Hail Muse! et cetera' (III.1), function not merely as gibes at the epic tradition, but more specifically as exposés of the workings of that tradition. Byron makes his critique of traditional epic heroism a meta-textual one. He reminds us that epic heroes, and epic events, are the product of the poet's imagination. It is he who whisks Juan from adventure to adventure, who leaves him dangling at each canto's cliff hanger. It is not so much that the poet usurps his hero; it is simply that he forces us to acknowledge his rightful place as the creator of that hero.

The poet at the heart of *Don Juan* has earned that place by virtue of his self-knowledge, knowledge gained through experiences that are only ever implied. Yet, the poem's persistent ironies problematise, for some, this sense of a consistent self. For McGann, it renders the critique of hypocrisy in *Don Juan* a purely negative gesture, for it means that Byron demolishes the spectre of hypocrisy but leaves nothing in its stead. McGann warns that, 'In laying "Byron" open to criticism, the writing takes away a fundamental Romantic truth-function. Sincerity, the integrity of the "veracious self", will not survive the poem's own processes'.[55] Aligning truth with the self and emphasising the many self-contradictions that abound in the text, McGann argues that 'what is "true" in the poem...always depends on context and circumstances. The concept of truth itself is revealed as open to change.'[56] But this begs the question – who, or what, is responsible for revealing the true nature of truth? Even if such motivation and volition is assigned to the text rather than the author, the text's insistence on the existence and the superiority of a Byronic persona must be accounted for. The text advertises his existence and then positions him as one who opens himself to criticism and, moreover, does the criticising. This forcefully established poetic presence *within* the text paradoxically points to a poet who inhabits an Archimedean point *above* the text, from which he reveals life's many ironies, even when those ironies seem to inhere in him.

The self-knowing satirist of *Don Juan*, the poet who must suffer in order to write of the sufferings of *The Fall of Hyperion*, and the self-interrogated poet envisaged by Wordsworth in *The Prelude* are versions of a poetic identity imagined as special self-understanding gained from experience or crisis. For all three poets, this making of the poetic self is depicted as central to the task of writing epic, and emerges from their interpretations of Miltonic epic. The poet-hero is one of the defining characteristics of Romantic epic.

It could be said, using the terms set by Mikhail Bakhtin to describe the shift from epic to novel in the modern age, that the traditional epic is monologic, that is, it presents a single, authoritative point of view. First, the epic poet always speaks in his own voice and, second, he assumes a coherence of values and morals between himself and his audience. For Bakhtin has suggested that the novel, with its multiple discourses and shifting viewpoints, seeks to represent 'heteroglossia', or linguistic diversity, which is the true state of language that the novel. The heteroglossic nature of the novel is distinctly tied to its depiction of a diversity of identities, specifically to its polyphonic representation of different characters.[57] According to Bakhtin, since 'the human being in the novel is first, foremost and always a speaking human being; the novel requires speaking persons bringing with them their own ideological discourse, their own language'.[58] For our purposes, then, we could identify the Romantic epic as acknowledging the existence of heteroglossia, inasmuch as it acknowledges the subjectivity of the poet's voice – the existence of a speaker, after all, posits the existence of an inter-locutor.[59] Yet, ultimately, the Romantic epics insist on the superiority of the poet's voice, for they insist on the significance of their self-experience and self-knowledge. More importantly, they insist on the primacy of the poet's creative power. For this reason, they do not wholeheartedly invest in heter-oglossic representation, and they specifically do not employ polyphonic depictions of different characters. Certainly, we could count *Don Juan* as an exception, what Bakhtin calls, indeed, a 'novelised' epic.[60] We could argue that its representations of a range of characters and their dialogue, as well as its use of irony, undermine the reliability and the uniqueness of the poet's voice. Yet, as we have seen, Byron too ultimately points up the supremacy of his voice, not only because of the authority he assumes as satirist but also because of the text's transparency as his creation.[61] It would seem that the inauguration of the truly novelised, that is, heteroglossic and polyphonic, epic occurs only with Elizabeth Barrett Browning's *Aurora Leigh*, with its attempt to place the poet-hero within the world and to make that placement part of the achievement of heroism.

Barrett Browning's *Aurora Leigh*

Aurora Leigh traces the life-story of the poet from childhood to young adult-hood and poethood. The young orphaned Aurora moves from her mother's native Italy to live in England with her aunt. At nineteen, she rejects her cousin Romney's hand in marriage, disapproving of his soulless brand of socialist philanthropy as much as he disapproves of her poetic ambitions. She subsequently moves to London, eventually becoming a poet of some popularity. But the poem also traces her personal development, as the love she has for Romney haunts her throughout. She becomes involved in the intrigues that surround him, when he decides to wed the poor but thoroughly good Marian Erle in order to realise his socialist theories, but is instead lured into (almost) marrying the evil Lady Waldemar. Eventually, Aurora takes Marian with her and returns to Tuscany. Finally, Romney, his socialist experiments shattered but his faith in humanity restored by Aurora's poetry, comes to Italy and is reunited with Aurora.

What this synopsis demonstrates is that *Aurora Leigh* possesses a novelistic plot of love frustrated but eventually triumphant. Yet, the poem also shows the effect of the Romantic epic form. It is, after all, a narrative of the self, specifically the poet's self. Strikingly, it narrates, like *The Prelude*, the development of the poet. That Barrett Browning was interested in the major Romantic poets and their poetics has been well documented.[62] As Kathleen Blake suggests, though Barrett Browning makes no direct reference to *The Prelude*, there is little doubt that *Aurora Leigh* was influenced by it, since it had appeared six years earlier in 1850.[63] Barrett Browning's remarks on Wordsworth's earlier poetry are worth noting, since they describe accurately his heroicisation of the poetic self. In an essay of 1842, she labels Wordsworth 'the poet-hero of a movement essential to the better being of poetry', and praises him for being 'eminently and humanly expansive; and, spreading his infinite egotism over all the objects of his contemplation, reiterat[ing] the love, life, and poetry of his peculiar being in transcribing and chanting the material universe'.[64] But it would seem that Wordsworth's example was inadequate to Barrett Browning's intentions. In the same essay, she notes, in terms that anticipate Bakhtin's, that he is 'rather intensely than actively human; capacious to embrace within himself the whole nature of things and beings, but not going out of himself to embrace anything; a poet of one large sufficient soul, but not polypsychical like a dramatist'.[65] The ability to celebrate not just the self but the self's place in society is something Barrett Browning felt she had discovered in another Romantic epic – *Don Juan*. In 1844, she wrote of her desire:

> to go on, & touch this real everyday life of our age, & hold it with my two hands. I want to write a poem of a new class, in a measure – a Don Juan, without the mockery & impurity, ... under one aspect, – & having unity,

as a work of art, – & admitting of as much philosophical dreaming & digression (which is in fact a characteristic of the age) as I like to use.[66]

Yet, this statement implies a rejection of Byron's poetics too. Crucially, in writing a 'Don Juan, without the mockery', Barrett Browning writes, in effect, a poem that is about the self *in* society rather than, as with Byron's poem, the self in opposition to society. We imagine that it is to Byron's incessant satire that Barrett Browning refers when she describes his poetry as having 'discovered not a heart, but the wound of a heart; not humanity, but disease; not life, but a crisis'.[67] In contrast, she writes a poem capable, in her own words, of 'running into the midst of our conventions, & rushing into drawing-rooms & the like "where angels fear to tread"; & so, meeting face to face & without mask the Humanity of the age, & speaking the truth as I conceive of it, out plainly'.[68]

Barrett Browning's fictionalisation of that self – the most obvious difference between her text and the Romantic epics before it – is a function of that insistence on placing the self in the world rather than above it or against it. Though it is certainly difficult not to compare Aurora Leigh with her creator, the point remains that Aurora is an intentionally fictitious creation with a name, history and personality of her own. By fictionalising her poet, Barrett Browning ensures that this poet is as much a poetic creation as the world she inhabits, and may therefore be firmly located within it.

Barrett Browning also makes clear that writing within the world is precisely the province of epic. This she does in Book V of *Aurora Leigh*, which Holly Laird astutely labels Barrett Browning's 'epical *ars poetica*'.[69] Here, Aurora considers her poetic progress so far. We already know that she has produced prose to support herself, writing for 'cyclopaedias, magazines, / And weekly papers, / holding up [her] name / To keep it from the mud' (III.310–12), and she adds to this list her attempts at ballads and pastorals.[70] What Aurora really wants (as, we assume, does Barrett Browning) is to produce an epic. She insists that epics have not 'died out / With Agamemnon and the goat-nursed gods' (V.139–40) and posits a description of heroism that sounds, for a moment, like that implied by the Romantic epics: 'All actual heroes are essential men, / And all men possible heroes' (V.151–5). But we have seen that Romantic epic heroism carried the taint of singularity and inaccessibility. The true epic poet, according to Barrett Browning, will embrace the age rather than stand aloof from it:

> if there's room for poets in this world
> A little overgrown (I think there is),
> Their sole work is to represent the age,

> Their age, not Charlemagne's – this live, throbbing age,
> That brawls, cheats, maddens, calculates, aspires,
> And spends more passion, more heroic heat,
> Betwixt the mirrors of its drawing-rooms,
> Than Roland with his knights at Roncesvalles.
>   . . .
>   Never flinch,
> But still, unscrupulously epic, catch
> Upon the burning lava of a song
> The full-veined, heaving, double-breasted Age
>
>   (V.200–8; 213–16)

Barrett Browning, in presenting these criteria for epic poetry, establishes her own poem as epic. Furthermore, she posits a poet's heroism based on an integration of self and society, not on the isolation of self that she discerned and criticised in both Wordsworth's solipsism and Byron's mockery. Poetry, she insists, is about the 'Inward evermore / To outward – so in life, and so in art / Which still is life' (V.227–8). As Laird sees it, Aurora Leigh is 'double-faced', in as much as she is able to look both inward to herself and outward to the world around her.[71]

Yet, Barrett Browning's poet-hero must first develop the self just as the poet-heroes of the Romantic personal epics do, in order that, unlike the Romantic poet-heroes, she will eventually be able to position that self in the world. That is, Aurora learns first to be a poet. Significantly, her quest for poethood is made possible only by her rejection of society's expectations for womanhood. She moves to London to begin her writing career immediately after rejecting Romney and, more specifically, rejecting his interdictions against women poets. But, having turned her back on femininity, Aurora has turned her back on femaleness, for she is rendered curiously asexual by her vocation. As a poet, she 'stand[s] outside / ...of the common sex' (III.406–7) and is, by her own admission, 'a printing woman who has lost her place / (The sweet safe corner of the household fire / Behind the heads of children)' (V.806–7). Most tellingly of all, she fails to recognise her love for Romney, correcting herself rather feebly and unconvincingly when she inadvertently recognises him as 'the man I love – I mean / The friend I love...as friends love' (VII.173–4). In her desperation, she even questions the value of poetry over that of love:

> 'Now, if I had been a woman, such
> As God made women, to save men by love –

> By just my love I might have saved this man,
> And made a nobler poem for the world
> Than all I have failed in'.

(VII.184–8)

Eventually, she must come to the conclusion that 'The end of woman (or of man, I think) / Is not a book' (VII.883–4).

Aurora, then, learns to embrace the womanhood she had initially rejected in her quest to become a poet. Yet, this is not a matter of regression, for Aurora must not simply exchange the hard-won independence of poethood for the submissiveness of wifehood. She must, as Beverly Taylor puts it, 'conceive of herself as a woman-poet rather than one of the alternatives she earlier imagined – a man-poet or a woman-wife'.[72] In other words, Aurora must develop as *both* a woman and a poet, and the one role ultimately and ideally augments the other. It would seem that the profoundest expression of this integration of roles is Aurora's marriage to Romney, since he comes to her as living proof of the power of her poetry to change lives, and therefore of her capacity as a poet to integrate with and influence humanity. Aurora had earlier wondered how she would be able to write an epic 'in mysterious tune / With man and nature' (V.2–3) when she had failed even to connect with the one man who had loved her:

> ... can I speak my verse
> So plainly in tune to these things and the rest,
> That men shall feel it catch them to the quick,
> As having the same warrant over them
> To hold and move them if they will or no,
> Alike imperious as the primal rhythm
> Of that theurgic nature? – I must fail,
> Who fail at the beginning to hold and move
> One man – and he my cousin, and he my friend

(V.24–32)

Thus, the acknowledgement of Aurora's poetic influence by that one man – Romney – expresses the extent of her influence over all men. Yet, what is significant is that Aurora is truly a woman poet before this reunion with Romney, for the poem that so affects him is written before she even leaves for Italy. Romney returns to Aurora not because she is a woman but because she is a woman-poet, pronouncing her 'My teacher, who has taught me with a book,/My Miriam, whose sweet mouth, when nearly drowned/I still heard singing on the shore!' (VIII.333–5). The success of Romney's second proposal of marriage is not the symbol of Aurora embracing womanhood; it is its logical outcome.

What this means is that it is not her love for Romney alone that allows Aurora to develop as a woman. Presumably, she attains this development through her experiences in London, crucially her encounters with two women who represent the extremes of womanhood – the archetypally good Marian, a virginal mother whose Madonna-like qualities are underscored by the virtually fatherless conception of her baby, and the archetypally bad Lady Waldemar, who is figured as a Lamia, a sexually corrupt and corrupting serpent woman. Her reactions to each are equally polarised. She absolutely rejects Lady Waldemar, writing a letter that breaks off any communication between them. This absolute estrangement Lady Waldemar's response confirms rather than denies, by declaring simply, 'I hate, hate, hate you' (IX.166). In contrast, Aurora embraces Marian as 'my sister Marian Erle,/My woodland sister, sweet maid Marian' (V.1095–6), and sets up home with her. So insistent is the text on the sisterhood of Marian and Aurora that Angela Leighton has read the poem's central quest as one of seeking a sister rather than a husband.[73] Yet, the text actually strives to show how Aurora's links with both women are made through their connection with Romney. Aurora wonders if:

> ...Lady Waldemar
> Succeeds my Marian?
> After all, why not?
> He loved not Marian, more than once he loved
> Aurora. If he loves at last that Third,
> Albeit she prove as slippery as spilt oil
> On marble floors, I will not augur him
> Ill-luck for that.

> (V.1106)

We could extend Laird's analysis of Aurora's position as 'double-faced' and say that Aurora looks out from between these two extremes; she is, after all, loved first and last by Romney. But it is more accurate to read Aurora not as the median between Marian and Waldemar, but as the sum of them and possibly of all womanhood. The poem's recurrent motif of female breasts is significant here. It is Aurora who learns to trace the 'impress' of the 'full-veined, heaving, double-breasted age' and it is she who becomes poet, woman, wife, potentially mother. Marian and Lady Waldemar, in contrast, each offers only one dimension of womanhood, the one defined by the child at her bosom and the other sexualised by her 'bare breasts, / On which the pearls, drowned out of sight in milk / Were lost' (V.164).

But it is not only that Aurora must become a woman in order to be a good poet, she must be a poet in order to be happy as a woman. For it is only once she is a poet that, as Dorothy Mermin puts it, 'the demands of love... will cost her nothing'.[74] As Blake suggests, '*Aurora Leigh* must end with a promise of marriage, a reconciliation of love and art, which is never even a matter of question in *The Prelude*'.[75] Yet, it is worth contesting Blake's conclusion that Barrett Browning's heroine struggles with a dilemma which Wordsworth does not even bother considering and that, therefore, she 'must attempt to achieve at the end of her story the stage at which he starts'.[76] Aurora Leigh integrates herself into society as poet and woman, or, more accurately, as a woman-poet. Wordsworth, in contrast, fails fully to consider the demands of social bonds and so severs himself from society and imagines his achievement solely in terms of becoming a poet. In other words, Barrett Browning achieves the end of a journey on which Wordsworth *never* begins. 'By the end of the poem, Aurora recognises no split between her identity as poet and as a woman', no division, that is, between self and society.[77]

It is, of course, the poem's dual trajectory towards poethood and wifehood that underlies much critical discussion about *Aurora Leigh*'s generic hybridity. Barrett Browning herself called the work a 'novel-poem'[78] and a 'poetic art-novel',[79] while her contemporaries freely used both the labels 'epic' and 'novel'.[80] Aurora's double quest combines the concerns of both the Romantic epic and another genre of self, the *Bildungsroman*. The *Bildungsroman* emphasises the need for the self to adapt to the society in which it finds itself.[81] The heroine of the female *Bildungsroman* in particular must compromise her integrity of self in some way in order to achieve marital bliss and social approbation; in contrast, as we have seen, the hero of the Romantic epic must turn his back on society in order to preserve his self-knowledge. Yet, Aurora Leigh manages to find love *and* to preserve her creative core. The poem's triumphant ending, in which Aurora and Romney's love is aligned with the building of a New Jerusalem, is a fusion of novelistic 'happily ever after' with an epic cosmic significance.[82]

We could adopt Bakhtinian terms and say that the poem's novelistic tendencies arise from its polyphonic representation of fictitious voices. Though it adopts the then experimental form of the first-person narrative, it does not subordinate other voices to that of its narrator and it maintains that all voices are apparently equally fictitious. The poet, like the novelistic narrator, never presents herself as a monologic epic poet reporting the deeds and words of others, but insists on depicting a range of speakers in dialogue and ostensibly speaking for themselves. Thus, in terms of character representation too Barrett Browning marries the concerns of self with those of society, and builds further on the innovations of the Romantic epic.

Tolstoy's *War and Peace*

There remains another possibility for epic in the age of the realist novel if we consider the one major text of late nineteenth-century world literature that is most often described as epic – Tolstoy's *War and Peace*. Discussed by many critics, particularly Russian critics, as an epic novel, and apparently compared by Tolstoy himself to *The Iliad*, the text occupies an almost legendary place in Western literature and popular imagination for its sheer size.[83]

As we have seen, the classical epics insisted on relating extraordinary deeds, particularly the deeds of an extraordinary individual, because those deeds became somehow central to his community, perhaps as an act of nation-building or as a model of exemplary behaviour. The Romantic epics, however, suggest that the individual's deeds, specifically the deeds of the poet, may appear to be ordinary but are more important than the immediate concerns of his community, because by being psychological and internal they are universal and timeless and therefore infinitely more relevant. Tolstoy's epic stands in contrast to both these epic modes. Though it suggests that the extraordinary public deeds of the classical epic are not very special at all, it does not do so in order to elevate the individual's private deeds, that is, his psychological or creative development, in their stead. Indeed, Tolstoy suggests that the individual cannot be separated from the community, for the community consists of individuals. Therefore, there can be no external heroic deeds, only internal everyday ones. In order to make his point, Tolstoy narrates the events surrounding Russia's victory over Napoleon in 1812. He demonstrates how this ostensibly epic triumph is due not to a single heroic achievement but to a myriad of actions carried out by an ensemble of ordinary men and women.

Unsurprisingly, then, *War and Peace* is concerned not with a single hero but with the fates of several families and, more specifically, the lives of several key characters: Prince Andrew Bolkonsky; his friend Pierre Bezukhov; the woman they both eventually love, Natasha Rostova; her brother Nicholas Rostov, and Andrew's sister, Princess Mary. As Napoleon makes his way through Russia, taking Moscow in 1812, each of these individuals is affected. Throughout the text, the public exploits of warriors and the private concerns of families are juxtaposed and eventually the two are shown to be indistinguishable. In other words, war is compared with peace, history combined with fiction, and the typically epic domain of war is set alongside the domestic interiors and familial relations of the novel.

We are called on to align these two realms from the outset. The text begins in the salon of the St Petersburg society hostess Anna Pavlovna Scherer, whose first words, and the opening lines of the novel, concern Napoleon and the prospect of war:

> 'Well, Prince, so Genoa and Lucca are now just family estates of the Buonapartes. But I warn you, if you don't tell me that this means war, if you still try to defend the infamies and horrors perpetrated by that Antichrist – I really believe he is Antichrist – I will have nothing more to do with you and you are no longer my friend ...' (3)[84]

Already, the problems of war intrude into drawing-rooms and private conversations. As the text progresses, this intrusion only exacerbates: Andrew and Nicholas go to war, the Rostovs flee Moscow on the eve of invasion, the Bolkonskys' country home is taken, Pierre becomes a prisoner of war and fantasises about killing Napoleon. What is more, historical figures mingle with fictional characters, as scenes of battle jostle with love stories and private tragedies.

Yet, this text is more than a narrative about the effects of war on private lives. It delineates the way in which war consists primarily *of* these private lives. Thus, by the time battle-scenes occur, these involve not just faceless soldiers but individuals who are tied to other individuals, lives that are part of a complex of many other lives. The text's descriptions of battles, significantly, are concerned less with military tactics or instances of bravery and more with the responses of ordinary soldiers, with Andrew's delirium on seeing the blue sky as he lies on the ground wounded, with Nicholas's enthusiasm at his first battle, with the humorous exchanges between Pierre and the men manning Raevsky's Redoubt at Borodino. This is Tolstoy's main point about war, that it is really a collection of individual actions by individual men, and not, crucially, the outcome of any amount of military planning. As Prince Andrew comes to realise:

> What theory and science is possible about a matter the conditions and circumstances of which are unknown and cannot be defined, especially

when the strength of the acting forces cannot be ascertained?...Sometimes – when there is not a coward at the front to shout, 'We are cut off' and start running, but a brave and jolly lad who shouts 'Hurrah!' – a detachment of five thousand is worth thirty thousand, as at Schön Graben, while at times fifty thousand run from eight thousand as at Austerlitz. ...The success of a military action depends not on [the commanders], but on the man in the ranks who shouts 'We are lost!' or who shouts 'Hurrah!' (687–8)

For this reason, the traditional 'heroes' such as Napoleon and Alexander I present as ultimately ineffectual, and only Kutuzov, of all the historically 'real' military commanders, comes closest to heroism because he rejects military strategy and accepts that the outcome of the Battle of Borodino is out of his hands.[85] This is the point that Tolstoy labours in his notoriously diffuse second epilogue, in which he propounds his theory of history as a playing out not of individual will or even of 'the transference of the collective will of a people to certain historical personages' (1282), but of an impossibly intricate network of actions determined – if determined at all – by God. For Tolstoy, heroism in the traditional sense does not exist because free will does not exist. As Rimvydas Silbajoris says of *War and Peace*, 'there really are no heroes; rather, there are men whose deeds emerge from the common fabric of life and who unconsciously enact the life-force that in Tolstoy is destiny'.[86]

Unsurprisingly, then, war, for Tolstoy, is a strange and curiously unmanageable, because unknowable and unpredictable, affair. Indeed, Tolstoy regularly employs the technique of what the Formalist critic Viktor Shlovksy called *ostranenie*, or 'making-strange', in his battle-scenes. War as witnessed by Pierre, for example, is nothing but a collection of absurd and apparently random sounds and sights.

Pierre glanced round at the first cloud, which he had seen as a round compact ball, and in its place already were balloons of smoke floating to one side, and – *'puff'* (with a pause) – *'puff, puff!'* – three and then four more appeared and then from each, with the same interval – *'boom – boom, boom!'* came the fine, firm, precise sounds in reply. It seemed as if those smoke-clouds sometimes ran, and sometimes stood still while woods, fields, and glittering bayonets ran past them. From the left, over fields and bushes, those large balls of smoke were continually appearing followed by their solemn reports, while nearer still, in the hollow and woods, there burst from the muskets small cloudlets that had no time to become balls, but had their little echoes in just the same way. '*Trakh-ta-ta-takh!*' came the frequent crackle of musketry, but it was irregular and feeble in comparison with the reports of the cannon. (845–6)

War is neither glorious nor strategic, but simply alien and alienating. The traditional epic model of heroism, a heroism of martial leadership and victory, is a futile attempt to impose order where, for Tolstoy, there is none to be found. 'The ancients', says Tolstoy, 'have left us model heroic poems in which the heroes furnish the whole interest of the story, and we are still unable to accustom ourselves to the fact that for our epoch histories of that kind are meaningless' (808).

If war is meaningless particularly because individual martial heroism is impossible, the real quest for the men and women of *War and Peace* is in preserving the community and collectivity that is threatened by war. Andrew and Pierre, often identified as the two main heroes, find death and life respectively; the failure of the one and the success of the other are determined by how much each invests in love and union. Andrew mistakenly pursues military glory at the expense of marital love, a pursuit first signalled when he leaves his wife Lise, the 'Little Princess', to join the army, but more emphatically demonstrated by his apparent embrace of death as he lies on the fields of Austerlitz, an acceptance that later makes him such an incompatible suitor to the life-affirming Natasha. As John Bayley has suggested, 'Andrew is created for death. He looks towards death as something true and real at last; and after all the false starts, alternations and reprieves, he achieves his right end'.[87] One could add that Andrew's death is 'right' for him in the light of his relentless pursuit of heroism in war, a heroism that, in this text, cannot exist. He is a '"generic refugee' from epic placed in a novelistic world, where all epic heroism is an illusion'.[88] Because Andrew rejects the familiar and familial, he necessarily rejects life on Tolstoy's terms.

Pierre's quest, in contrast, is for life, again on Tolstoy's terms. He seeks 'nothing less than the entire meaning of life', so much so that when he sets out to bring death to Napoleon he ends by saving the life of a child.[89] Specifically, Pierre seeks a life of honesty, good humour and, significantly, love. None of these exists in his first marriage, to Hélène, but they define his life with Natasha. Their immediate and almost unnatural fondness for one another when they first meet prefigures their future union, and suggests as well the weight that this union bears in the text as a signifier for connectivity and community.

This sense of community is what Bayley has labelled 'understanding' and has also associated with 'family'.[90] The victory sought in *War and Peace*, the object of its quest, is that element of immediate – in the sense of being both instant and unmediated – understanding that exists between members of a family. It is such understanding that defines the Russian nation in its opposition to Napoleon, in, for example, the Muscovites' seemingly spontaneous desertion of their city which gives the French a hollow victory. It is such an understanding, too, that marks Tolstoy's technique of characterisation, which Ernest Simmons describes thus:

> Their total personalities are revealed as they would be in real life. That is, we meet them first in customary settings and our initial impression of their external appearance is usually limited to what Tolstoy conveys in a few descriptive touches. Though we learn little more at this point, as times goes on, often a matter of years and many pages, our knowledge of them grows through innumerable small actions and intimacies, conversations, self-examinations, and especially by the remarks of others about them, until finally we obtain a complete image of each.[91]

As Simmons suggests, we come to feel that we instinctively understand the characters of *War and Peace*. And we feel also that they understand each other.

The fundamental 'war and peace' opposition of the text, then, is not just one of public and epic heroism against private and familial lives, but, put another way, one of selfishness against community.[92] That is, it is war that is somehow connected to the personal and private, and peace that is public and communal. This is not the contradiction in terms that it appears to be. For Tolstoy, the celebration of public heroism is selfish, greedy, ambitious, since it places the responsibility for community on one man, when, in actuality, 'The life of the nations is not contained in the lives of a few men' (1282). The 'life of a nation' is to be found in the lives of all its men and women. For Bayley, this opposition may be expressed as the difference between 'family' and 'system', the one associated with Russia and the other with France, or, more accurately, Francophilia.[93] There are 'bad' characters, who display shallowness, avarice or lust, and there are the 'good' ones, who display 'understanding' for one another.[94] And the triumph of understanding and community – of Russia, of love, of life – is encapsulated in Natasha. This is first captured, when, as a girl, she shows an instinctive feel for Russian folkdance and it is affirmed when, later barely recognisable as the plump materfamilias of the text's first epilogue, she presides over the text's dénouement of peaceful domesticity. Silbajoris explains this thus:

> Natasha's dowdy ordinariness, prolific motherhood, clarity of purpose, simplicity, and devotion *is* the country, and it, this country, can rise to grand epic heights when the occasion calls for it. It would have rung false note for Tolstoy to have closed the book with anything more grandiose.[95]

Natasha, in other words, plays a part in Tolstoy's larger critique of the individuality and free will that underlies heroism.

It would seem, at a glance, that Tolstoy rejects the epic tradition by rejecting its model of heroism, a model based on the glory-driven heroic code of the classical age and modified by the emphasis on Christian free will in the Renaissance. Yet, it is possible to read Tolstoy's historical novel as a qualified return to traditional epic. For many, its sheer scope, its presentation of what N. N. Strakhov called 'a complete picture of human life', qualifies it as epic.[96] This comprehensiveness, indeed, is the reason behind Tolstoy's own insistence that the text was 'not a novel', 'because I cannot and I do not know how to set fixed limits to the characters I have invented'.[97] Yet, *War and Peace* gestures towards the traditional epic not simply because of this, but because it circumvents the insistent subjectivity that marks both epic and novel in the early nineteenth century. It replays the classical epic attribution of communal glory to individual actions; where it differs is in its insistence that these actions are performed by all rather by one. In other words, Tolstoy rejects the implication of representativeness in epic heroism, but reiterates its epic intentions in celebrating nationhood and community.

Tolstoy's epic celebration of community extends to his own readership. Recalling Lukács' Hegelian formulation of epic tone as a hermeneutically sealed worldview between poet and audience, Tolstoy's founds his relationship with his readers on a shared perspective. This shared perspective is achieved by Tolstoy's historical thesis, or, more specifically, by Tolstoy's frequent reiteration of this thesis. This thesis is established not just by what Andrew Wachtel has astutely analysed as the text's 'metahistorical' narrator, who inhabits an Archimedean point above the text from which he philosophises on the gap between the 'fictional' and the 'historical', the individual and the collective, or free will and determinism.[98] It is also conveyed through a shared understanding between the reader, Tolstoy, and his key characters, particularly their organic, intrinsic development. For as we come to a gradual understanding of Tolstoy's men and women, so they (with the exception of Andrew) come to a gradual understanding of Tolstoy's view of history.[99] And this notion of understanding, common to author or narrator, character or reader, replays that *understanding* that is so significant to Russia and its victory within the text and that signifies community. Thus, the text's celebration of community is replayed in our own reading of it and the conjunction of our view with Tolstoy's.

In returning to the epic's assumption of shared perspective between poet and audience, Tolstoy returns also, in Bakhtin's terms, to the monologic quality of epic. Though he attempts a comprehensive depiction of the range of individual lives that constitute communal life, Tolstoy's characters, in the final analysis, serve to play out his hypothesis in their actions and even their words. This paradox between plurality and singularity explains why *War and Peace* may be described simultaneously, and by the same critic, as displaying both a 'polyphony of incident' and an 'absolute voice'.[100] It is as though, as Wachtel suggests, the text captures a tension between the modes of fictitious incident, historical fact and metahistorical hypothesis, a dialogue between 'distinct monologic narrative voices'.[101] In other words, the text posits an epic assumption about the mutuality signified by community while taking on a novelistic interest in the many lives that make up that community. It suggests a return of the epic to its position before the nineteenth century while looking forward to the attempt to capture a comprehensiveness of experience that marks the epic in the twentieth century.[102]

Coda: Tennyson's *Idylls of the King* and Browning's *The Ring and the Book*

The creative, knowing self at the heart of epic, which Wordsworth celebrated and which Keats and Byron, in their separate ways, struggled to achieve, was reconciled by Barrett Browning with society at large. That self was demonstrably diffused into that society by Tolstoy. For Tennyson and Browning, the single, coherent self is an impossibility, for oneself consists of the perceptions of that self by others. If there are as many selves as there are others, subjectivity is necessarily conceivable only as shifting and multifaceted. The role of the epic, then, is to capture that polyphony.

Thus, Tennyson's *Idylls of the King*, rather than a single narrative, is a collection of narratives centring on the figure of King Arthur.[103] The *Idylls* were written over a period of some forty years – the very first inspiration for the *Idylls* was the 'Morte d'Arthur', which was composed in 1833–4 and published in 1836 and the final idylls were not completed till 1874. Yet, Tennyson, it would seem, intended for this work to appear as a coherent whole, and it was published as such in 1891. Tennyson particularly intended this text as an epic and, according to his son Hallam, he recalled when the *Idylls* were almost completed that, 'At twenty-four I meant to write an epic or a drama of King Arthur; and I thought that I should take twenty years about the work. They will now say that I have been forty years about it'.[104] In the early idyll 'Morte d'Arthur', which evolved in time into the final idyll, 'The Passing of Arthur', Tennyson tentatively flagged up his epic intentions in a frame narrative entitled 'The Epic'. In this frame, the fictionalised poet of the 'Morte' reveals that he has burned most of his twelve-book epic, because it consisted of mere 'Homeric echoes'. The *Idylls*, then, are no simple imitation of classical epic.

It would seem that the *Idylls* make a claim to epic not simply by virtue of its length – Tennyson took great pains to ensure that the final number of idylls equalled the twelve books of traditional epic – but by their unquestioned celebration of chivalric codes as all that is good and pure, and their depiction of Arthur as the source of these values. However, this sense of epic is countered by the lack of narrative structure and the overall theme of disappointment and decay.[105] Thus, Tennyson does allow for a unified and tightly focused heroic action. Instead, he develops Arthur's rise and fall through the perspectives and experiences of those around him, and challenges the notion of stable self at the heart of epic. As Robert Pattison has put it:

> *Paradise Lost* is not so much about the Fall as about the psychology leading to it. Wordsworth's *Prelude* takes this psychological dimension of epic to its logical conclusion in an examination not of some exterior mentality but of self. Tennyson's epic steps away from Wordsworth's subjectivity . . . [106]

It might be possible to read the poem as an exploration of selfhood by over-reading the narrative as allegory, and constructing Arthur as emblematic of the soul.[107] Read carefully, however, the poem yields an exploration of differing subjectivities. The extent to which the heroic leader represents his community is not taken for granted, but carefully established through the people who make up that community. Arthur's chivalric code and, more importantly, the failure of that code, are determined and indeed brought about by the varying success and failure of his people – and, more specifically, his wife and his knights – to preserve and practise his principles.

Moreover, it is the failure of the chivalric code with which the poem ends. 'The narrative', notes Alastair Thomson, 'is about the decline of a man's kingdom'.[108] Arthur's passing is not just the death of one man but the extinction of the values he tried to instil in his knights. Heroism, it seems, cannot exist when coherent subjectivity itself does not. In writing of the death of Arthur (and in mourning the death of that other Arthur, Tennyson's friend Hallam), Tennyson is grieving for the loss of that shared objective worldview that constituted epic, a loss precipitated by Romantic solipsism and sealed by the rejection even of subjectivity in Tennyson's age. As Herbert Tucker reminds us, in recreating and reflecting on Arthur's chivalric heroism, Tennyson is also self-consciously reflecting on the role of epic. He acknowledges that, by the time he comes to write his epic, it can only be as an artificial resuscitation of a redundant heroism: 'The poet's need of a myth to write, and the public's need of a myth to live by, conspired to produce Victorian epics whose values center in the making, breaking, and dissemination of myth'.[109]

More so than Tennyson, Browning presents, in *The Ring and the Book*, a pastiche of multiple viewpoints. The genesis of the poem, according to Browning himself, lay in his discovery, at a flea market in Florence, of a book containing documents pertaining to a seventeenth-century murder trial. The murder in question was that of a girl and her lover at the hands of her husband. The girl had been married at the age of thirteen in order that her parents might obtain a substantial dowry and had, three years later, fled her husband's house with a priest, charging her husband with cruelty. Out of this, Browning produced a poem of nine books, each one relating the events from a different viewpoint, including the girl, her husband, and the pope.[110]

The result is 'an interplay of points of view through a series of individual monologues'.[111] The effect is a dizzying range of ways to tell the truth, the differentials arising not just between the various speakers but between what they say and what they might really mean. As Richard Altick and James Loucks remark:

> It is not easy to conceive of a method of narration more capable of leading one away from the truth. In this series of dramatic monologues, which contain stories within stories and reveal (or imply) motives within motives, truth is wrapped in layer upon layer of possible misrepresentation, the exact amount and purpose of which it is constantly the reader's task to determine.[112]

No wonder, then, that the critical search for an underlying message in Browning's poem has been fraught with debate. Some have decided that the final word belongs to the pope, whose rational overview of the events and sympathising conduct seem to evoke the only strategy available in a world of multiple knowledges. Altick and Loucks suggest, for example, that the poem's 'ultimate meaning' is that 'The search for truth in the midst of deceit and illusion, for stability in the midst of flux, turns out to be the search for the principles of right conduct'.[113] Yet, it is possible too that Browning's sympathies lie not with the pope but with the heroine, Pompilia, in which case the poem's abiding investment is in her simple and unquestioning faith.[114] The seeming critical dissension, then, does fall into agreement. The only solution in a world of varying degrees of truth was, for Browning, to be found in sincerity.

Tennyson and Browning were dealing with a particularly late nineteenth-century problem – how to heroicise in an age that increasingly questions heroism. Their rising awareness of shifting subjectivities problematises either a Romantic conception of the self-reliant poet-hero or a classical construction of the hero as representative of his people. It could be argued that the very idea of epic heroism, with its connotations of stability of identity, would eventually become untenable under the burden of such speculation. It is this uncertainty that marks what we call Modernism, and emerges in the epics of the twentieth century.

5
The Twentieth and Twenty-first Centuries: Modernist Epic

The twentieth century saw the dawn of a realisation that the world comprises not one reality but a variety of shifting subjectivities, that the old assurances of linear history and theology can no longer hold true in the face of mass production (the technologisation of popular culture) and mass destruction (two world wars). The realisation that this new world required a new way of telling it underlies Modernism as a literary and cultural movement. From the art of Picasso to the music of Stravinsky, to the work of literary modernists such as James Joyce and T. S. Eliot, there emerges a common thread: a 'high aesthetic self-consciousness and non-representation towards style, technique, and spatial form in pursuit of a deeper penetration of life'.[1]

This, far from heralding the end of the epic, inaugurated a new stage in epic. The modernist epic looks back to the mythical beginnings of ancient epic in order to make sense of the world while attempting to capture something of the uncertainty of the twentieth century. It is defined by its allusion to early epic narrative – usually, because of its peculiar connotations of both restlessness and return, to the *Odyssey* in particular – as well as by a fragmentation of this narrative – using a range of stylistic and technical innovations. Such an attitude to traditional epic arises out of a concern, even anxiety, that its old, stable teleology is simultaneously irrelevant to the modern world and a necessary antidote to it. The foundational text in this regard is Joyce's *Ulysses* (1922). Two comparable responses to Joyce – Eliot's *The Waste Land* (1922) and Ezra Pound's *Cantos* (1917–70) – consolidate this new development in the genre. Meanwhile, H. D.'s *Helen in Egypt* (1961) and Derek Walcott's *Omeros* (1990) posit feminist and postcolonial versions of modernist epic respectively, simultaneously venerating and interrogating the epic canon as the province of the white male. Finally, this chapter glances

155

at a very recent epic venture – Tom Paulin's *Invasion Handbook* (2002) – to ascertain whether the form might persist into the twenty-first century. Before proceeding to our discussion of modernist epic, however, this chapter will consider briefly an early twentieth-century contribution to epic literature – Thomas Hardy's *Dynasts* (1904–8) – which, in the light of the definition of modernist epic offered here, may be read as a 'pre-modernist' epic. First, however, we shall deal with the state of epic criticism.

Twentieth-century epic theory

The idea of epic theory in the twentieth century is oxymoronic, because much epic criticism of the twentieth century is devoted to proclaiming the death of the epic, particularly at the hands of the now ubiquitous literary form of the novel. The Romantic disdain for generic fixity in epic theory was paralleled, as we have seen, by an increasing innovation in epic practice. However, the suspiciousness towards traditional epic that it engendered grew into a tendency to equate epic itself with stultification. Such, for example, was the spirit of the influential analysis of epic put forward by G. W. F. Hegel in his *Aesthetik* of 1835. In the twentieth century, such an attitude would continue, particularly in the work of the Russian critics Georg Lukács and Mikhail Bakhtin. Both Lukács and Bakhtin formulate, variously, generic theories that contrast the epic with the novel, and further posit the increasing obsolescence of the one in the shadow of the other. Thus, in Lukács' most famous pronouncement against the epic, *The Theory of the Novel* (1920), the epic is defined as an expression of a long-faded primitive existence, while the novel has emerged to express the views of the more complex, modern world. The former is defined by its naïve investment in an objective and hermeneutically sealed worldview, while the latter is characterised by multiple subjectivities and open-endedness: 'The epic gives form to a totality of life that is rounded from within; the novel seeks, by giving form, to uncover and construct the concealed totality of life.'[2] For this reason, according to Lukács, 'The novel is the art-form of virile maturity, in contrast to the normative childlikeness of the epic'.[3] Similarly, Bakhtin's theory of the novel, first expressed in 1941, contrasts the simplicity of the epic, which expresses a linear, stable 'absolute past', with the novel, which is able to capture the confusion and 'polyphony' of the present; Bakhtin's theory culminates in such remarks as this, that 'the novel should become for the contemporary world what the epic was for the ancient world'.[4] The ideas behind such pronouncements are further discernible in such mid-century studies of the epic as E. M. W. Tillyard's *The English Epic and Its Background* and C. M. Bowra's *Heroic Poetry*, whose magisterial historical surveys pointedly end by the late eighteenth century.[5]

None the less, more recent epic criticism has discerned a distinctive development in the epic form in the twentieth century. This is a phenomenon one critic has labelled the 'lyric epic', and another an increasingly 'encyclopaedic' trend in epic-writing.[6] Most strikingly, Franco Moretti has asserted the existence of what he calls the 'modern epic', which he defines as a text that struggles to express a modern worldview while maintaining a connection with previous epic tradition; that is, it reveals 'a discrepancy between the totalizing will of the epic and the subdivided reality of the modern world'.[7] This balance takes the form, in what will here be referred to as modernist epic, of an allusion to and reliance on the mythical wholeness promised by traditional epic, in order to show up the chaos and flux of the present day.

It is not, however, just any myth that lends itself to an exposition of the modernist view. Some myths over others yield a nostalgic promise of wholeness while presciently revealing the future instability of the twentieth century. Just such a myth is the Homeric narrative of Odysseus. The contrast inherent in the myth between instability and stability, between wandering and home, between adventure and *nostos*, captures the contradictions of the modern age – excitement at the dawn of a brave new world and a longing to return to a familiar past. W. B. Stanford's influential study, *The Ulysses Theme*, defines these opposing impulses as the centrifugal and centripetal aspects of the Odyssean myth respectively.[8] More recently, David Adams has updated Stanford's ideas to show how the Odysseus figure resonates particularly strongly for modernists in a colonial age.[9] Where home is increasingly identified as unstable and unsatisfying, the impulse arises to find satisfaction and understanding by travelling the world – particularly as that world was being made increasingly accessible through colonial expansion. The journey becomes a quest for self-discovery, for if home can bring about only confusion and instability, it is hoped that wandering, paradoxically, can restore a sense of self. The Odyssean quest therefore presents itself as an emblem for this journey, not just because of its narrative of *nostos* but because in its very status as an inaugural epic text it suggests a return to mythical origins. Adams usefully shows how the two impulses of the Odyssean myth correspond to two classicist postures in the modernist period – a celebratory progressivism that recognises the heroic potential of the new age and a cynical anti-progressivism that yearns for a mythical heroic wholeness.[10] Though Adams's analysis focuses on the modernist novel, especially on colonialist journeys in such novels, this duality is at the heart of those texts that identify themselves, in one way or another, as twentieth-century epics.

Hardy's *Dynasts*

Before dealing with the innovation of the modernist epic, however, it is worth examining briefly a text written in the first decade of the twentieth century, which bridges the traditional epic and the modernist epic. *The Dynasts*, subtitled an 'epic-drama', is a play of astonishing length and scope: three parts, 19 acts and 131 scenes.[11] It was not intended to be staged but, as Hardy himself put it, was meant for 'mental performance'.[12] Hardy probably intended the play to be read as an epic, for it deals with traditional epic material in the form of the Napoleonic Wars, and gives this an ostensibly nationalistic treatment, inasmuch as it presents the wars from a British perspective. Early on in its conception, indeed, Hardy imagined the play as a series of lyrics 'forming altogether an Iliad of Europe from 1789 to 1815'.[13] And like the *Iliad*, the play's action would eventually cover a span of ten years, from England's entry into the war against Napoleon to the Battle of Waterloo. It even introduces, as far as modern sensibilities would allow, supernatural machinery. These 'impersonated abstractions, or Intelligences, called Spirits', primarily the Spirit of the Years and the Spirit of Pities, oversee and comment on the human actions that unfold beneath them.[14]

Yet, while *The Dynasts* attempts the conventionally epic objective of narrating events of historical and military importance, it expresses the encroaching cynicism that would shape modernist literature. Hardy's epic has no hero; certainly not Napoleon, and not even Wellington or Nelson count as such. This is primarily because the play's actions and those who carry them out are beholden to an Immanent Will, and where there is no free will, there can be no heroes. As R. J. White puts it, the play expresses 'Hardy's notion of modern history, indeed modern life in general, as populated by automata and ghosts'.[15] Hardy himself, in responding to the criticism that met his play on its publication, stated in a letter to the *Times Literary Supplement*:

> The truth seems to be that the real offence of the *Dynasts* lies, not in its form as such, but in the philosophy which gave rise to the form. ... The philosophy of the *Dynasts*, under various titles, is almost as old as civilisation. Its fundamental principle, under the name of Predestination, was preached by St. Paul.[16]

What provoked unease, however, was not the concept of humankind's predestination in itself, but the fact that Hardy's version of the Immanent Will by which we are predestined is seemingly aimless. As defined in the first scene by the Spirit of the Years in response to questions from the other spirits, 'It works unconsciously':

> Hold what ye list, fond unbelieving Sprites,
> You cannot swerve the pulsion of the Byss,
> Which thinking on, yet weighing not Its thought,
> Unchecks Its clock-like laws.
>
> (Pt 1.I. fore-scene)

In such a universe, Napoleon is merely a man who can take no responsibility for either his deeds or misdeeds. As he confronts the soldiers he has killed, he asks, 'Why hold me master, if I be / Ruled by the pitiless Planet of Destiny?' (Pt 3.VI.iii).

In querying the self-assurance of we have seen in the Romantic and Victorian epics, Hardy's Napoleonic epic recalls Tolstoy's, written some fifty years earlier. Translated into English in 1889, *War and Peace* was one of countless books that Hardy read in his historical research for *The Dynasts*. Yet, Tolstoy rejected free will in the public sphere of battle only to embrace it in the private sphere of love and family. Hardy, however, grapples throughout his massive drama with the problem that no human action can be accounted for by human consciousness. As Glen Wickens has suggested, the drama that unfolds and the dialogue between the Spirits is essentially a debate, a plea for the possibility of human consciousness against the backdrop of the unconsciousness of the laws of the universe.[17] Hardy's desperate need to believe in the power of consciousness, coupled with his doubts in the plausibility of its existence, endows his epic with a sense of despair. Such despair, which Hardy elsewhere labelled the 'ache of modernism', is what drives the search for an alternative mode of epic and of heroism in succeeding twentieth-century literature.[18]

Joyce's *Ulysses*

James Joyce's *Ulysses* initially suggests itself as an entirely nostalgic and fossilising epic gesture. Yet it ultimately reveals, as we shall see, a renovative stance to epic form, for it contains a celebratory attitude to modern life and hopefulness in the existence of a modern heroism and a modern epic.

At the outset, it seems necessary to offer a description of Joyce's *Ulysses*, though near impossible to do so straightforwardly. Even a definition of the text as a novel is a risky way to begin. By dint of its radical stylistic and narrative technique, it evades both easy generic classification and brief synopsis. Beneath the layers of stylistic and formal experimentation, however, it is possible to summarise its plot as a day in the life – 16 June 1904, to be precise. The protagonist is Leopold Bloom, an advertising canvasser and an Irishman of Jewish extraction. Ostensibly carrying out a number of social and professional tasks, Bloom wanders about Dublin, reluctant to return home because he is aware that his wife, Molly, has arranged a meeting with her lover. In the course of the day, Bloom frequently bumps into Stephen Dedalus, the son of an acquaintance, and a character who had figured in Joyce's *Portrait of the Artist as a Young Man* as a semi-autobiographical version of himself.

This brief synopsis already signals the text's fraught relationship to the epic form. This is hardly, it would seem, a heroic tale. Yet, the text's epic intentions are signalled by its title, harking back to Odysseus through the Latin version of his name, and its length (the first edition of 1922 runs to 732 pages). In addition to this, the text's generic ambivalence actually makes feasible or at least possible its epic status. For if it sometimes seems too stylistically and narratologically baggy to be classified decisively as a novel, then epic arises to fill the ensuing generic vacancy. In any case, Joyce's decision to align his text with the *Odyssey* may be traced to a boyhood fascination with the story, particularly in Charles Lamb's retelling, *The Adventures of Ulysses*. Joyce recalled to his biographer Herbert Gorman that he had written about Odysseus/Ulysses in a schoolboy essay about his 'favourite hero'.[19] The inspiration to write a modern version of the *Odyssey* story, founded on this childhood interest, apparently came to Joyce while working on his collection of short stories, *Dubliners*:

> I was twelve years old when we dealt with the Trojan War at school; only the *Odyssey* stuck in my memory.... When I was writing *Dubliners*, I first wished to choose the title *Ulysses in Dublin*, but gave up the idea. In Rome, when I had finished about half of the *Portrait*, I realised that the *Odyssey* had to be the sequel, and I began to write *Ulysses*.[20]

Joyce's title advertises its text, then, as a kind of modern-day odyssey. His own alignment of the Homeric text with first *Dubliners* and then *Portrait* further suggests a parallel between Odysseus' adventures and a personalised, modern-day wander through Dublin.

On a reading of *Ulysses*, however, there seems nothing beyond the title that announces its epic intentions. Yet, Joyce apparently had in mind a schema of parallels between his text and the Homeric narrative at the levels of both plot and style. Two versions of this schema he provided to the would-be translator of his projected work *Exiles*, Carlo Linati, and his friend and critic Stuart Gilbert.[21] According to these schemata, each chapter of *Ulysses* corresponds to a Homeric episode. The most obvious correspondences have to do with the correlation between Bloom and Odysseus/Ulysses, Molly and Penelope, and Stephen and Telemachus. Hence, the three first chapters concerning Stephen correlate to the Telemachy, the penultimate chapter, in which Bloom finally returns home, is 'Ithaca', and the concluding chapter, Molly's monologue, is simply labelled 'Penelope'. But the connections are often more abstruse; for example, Bloom's meeting with the blustering newspapermen corresponds to Odysseus' encounter with Aeolus, guardian of the winds, and his run-in with a one-eyed anti-Semite is meant to echo Odysseus' fight with the Cyclops. More than this, Joyce intended for his chapters to correspond, for the most part, to hours of the day, colours, organs of the body and different narrative techniques, these alluding, for example, to classical rhetoric, catechism and the laws of logic. None the less, the seeming scientific rigour of the schema belies the artistic play involved in constructing and adhering to these parallels. One example will suffice to demonstrate this. The chapter designated by Joyce as the 'Oxen of the Sun' corresponds to the Homeric episode in which Odysseus' men land at Thrinakia and kill the sacred cattle of the sun god Helios, thus offending him and further delaying their homecoming. Joyce's chapter involves Bloom's visit to a friend in a maternity hospital, and his encounter with Stephen and a group of inebriated medical students. The Homeric allusion seems to arise entirely out of the juxtaposition of the young men's drunken disdain for the miracle of maternity, what Joyce called 'the crime committed against fecundity by sterilizing the act of coition'.[22] The action takes place at 10 pm; the chapter is associated with the colour white and the organ in question is the womb. Meanwhile, Joyce employs a narrative technique Linati calls 'Embryo-Foetus-Birth' and Gilbert 'embryonic development'.[23] In practice, this is an historically determined progress, paragraph by paragraph, through the English language, from alliterative Anglo-Saxon through up to contemporary American slang.

The careful planning behind the Homeric-inspired divisions of Joyce's text has inspired a school of equally careful scholarly criticism, what Bernard Benstock called a tradition of 'Applied Homerics', intent on tracing the provenance and significance of every Homeric parallel.[24] It is easy to concede, however, as A. Walton Litz does, that 'Invaluable to Joyce as a ready-made guide for the ordering of his material, the correspondences with the *Odyssey* do not provide a major level of meaning in the completed work'.[25] Yet, notwithstanding that an awareness of the Homeric parallels is superfluous to a reading of the text, their existence is paramount to an understanding of it as epic. As Litz puts it, 'it must be acknowledged that the "epic" proportions of *Ulysses* are absolutely dependent on the major Homeric analogues and, to a lesser extent, on the other ordering frames'.[26] This is so not only because they establish an epic self-consciousness but because they reveal directions in epic innovation; that is, they both signal Joyce's epic intentions for his text and reveal the modernist contours of these intentions.

The question arises, then, as to why Joyce desired to write a 'Ulysses in Dublin'. What, first, did Odysseus/Ulysses represent to Joyce and why, second, did he place him in contemporary Dublin? Of course, Odysseus resonates as the first questing hero of Western literature and therefore as a repository for the modernist drive to make sense of the world. Yet, Joyce seems to have been interested in the figure not as a way towards resolving confusion but in encompassing it. He described Odysseus to his friend Frank Budgen as the only 'complete all-round character presented by any writer...a complete man...a good man'.[27] To Joyce, who wanted to write an epic inasmuch as epic may be defined as a breadth of scope and vision, Odysseus served the extrinsic function of alluding to an inaugural epic text while intrinsically embodying and thus signalling the comprehensiveness of epic. It is not, then, just Odysseus' return home, but the scope afforded by his wandering, that defines him as a forebear of Joyce's hero.

By reducing Odysseus' quest to the story of one man's wanderings, Joyce therefore simultaneously turns his epic inwards and outwards. This apparent paradox is implicit in Joyce's description of his text and the elaborate system underpinning it as:

> the epic of two races (Israel-Ireland) and at the same time the cycle of the human body as well as a little story of a day (life)...It is also a kind of encyclopaedia. My intention is not only to render the myth *sub specie temporis nostri* but also to allow each adventure (that is, every hour, every organ, every art being interconnected and interrelated in the somatic scheme of the whole) to condition and even to create its own technique.[28]

Here, Joyce insists that, on the one hand, the text is epic because, like Ulysses himself, it presents a comprehensive encyclopaedic perspective, representing all aspects of the body and the mind in its various styles. On the other hand, Joyce suggests that the text is epic in its telling of nationhood; however, this telling is to be achieved by collapsing time and scale into a day in the life of one man. The two impulses are seemingly contradictory because one is macrocosmic, the other microcosmic. Joyce's epic intention, then, is dialectic. He insists that the universal is to be found in the personal, that what is epic is also everyday. What Joyce called the 'classical temper', in S. L. Goldberg's words, 'accepts the ordinary world of humanity as the primary object of its attention, and endeavours to see it and present it steadily and whole'.[29] These two impulses – the one enlarging, the other reductive – combine 'to evoke through a single coherent circumstance and with encyclopaedic intensity the quality and spirit of a nation and an epoch'.[30]

Importantly, when combined, the microcosmic impulse becomes more than a simple despair at the incoherence and fragmentation of modern life, and the macrocosmic turn does not entirely correspond with a naïve hope that classical mythology will provide a kind of hermeneutic wholeness. In other words, because it simultaneously celebrates and renovates Homeric heroism, *Ulysses* successfully synthesises the opposing classicist attitudes found in the modernist age – the cynical and the celebratory. As Goldberg remarks:

> The Homeric parallel, I believe, *is* centrally important in *Ulysses*...in so far as the parallel worlds do not meet, the result is a kind of mock-epic irony, an oblique criticism of the Bloomworld; in so far as they do, the result is a kind of *stasis*, a universalised vision of the life of modern man.[31]

The result, that is, is to reveal the heroic quality of modern life while showing it to be distinct from the equally heroic classical life.

But what makes Bloom heroic? Daniel Schwarz suggests that Bloom's heroism lies in an extrapolation of the less overtly heroic traits in Ulysses/ Odysseus. In the terms set up in our examination of the *Odyssey*, these aspects of Odysseus' heroism constituted an interrogation of the Homeric code, which had been established by the *kleos*-driven characteristics of prowess and courage in the field of battle. According to Schwarz, Joyce 'chose the *Odyssey* because it was the epic that stresses how an individual man uses his intelligence, judgment, and inner strength to overcome obstacles and, finally, to accomplish his goal'.[32] In focusing on these traits, the 'novel redefines the traditional concept of a hero to emphasize not only pacifism, but commitment to family ties, concern for the human needs of others, sense of self, tolerance, and decency'.[33] The term to set against Odysseus' adventures, after all, is *nostos*, a longing for home and therefore for domestic ties. Certainly, beneath the stylistic manoeuvres of Joyce's text, Bloom emerges as a thoughtful man, in both the contemplative and compassionate senses of the word. His gentle treatment of Molly, his fondness for his daughter, his soft-spoken demeanour among professional and personal acquaintances, his playful attitude to language, and, most memorably, his defence of the Jewish people in argument with the one-eyed Irish nationalist of the *Cyclops* episode – all this bespeaks a quietly heroic man.

At least one of Joyce's stylistic techniques helps rather than hinders Bloom's characterisation as heroic, at least heroic in these new quiet, thoughtful terms. This is Joyce's use of the 'stream of consciousness' technique. This phrase, more or less equivalent to the term 'interior monologue' (coined by Joyce himself), describes the unmediated representation of the unspoken, even half-conscious, thoughts of his characters, often a train of reverie provoked by a combination of thought-association and external stimuli. There is room for just one example here. In the chapter entitled 'Lestrygonians', Bloom's mind wanders as he muses over what to have for lunch, taking in everything from advertising slogans to a half-remembered song to cultural (including Jewish) attitudes to food:

> Sardines on the shelves. Almost taste them by looking. Sandwich? Ham and his descendants musterred and bred there. Potted meats. What is home without Plumtree's potted meat? Incomplete. What a stupid ad! Under the obituary notices they stuck it. All up a plumtree. Dignam's potted meat. Cannibals would with lemon and rice. White missionary too salty. Like pickled pork. Expect the chief consumes the parts of honour. Ought to be tough from exercise. His wives in a row to watch the effect. *There was a right royal old nigger. Who ate or something the somethings of the reverend Mr Mac Trigger.* With it an abode of bliss. Lord knows what concoction. Cauls mouldy tripes windpipes faked and minced up. Puzzle find the meat. Kosher. No meat and milk together. Hygiene that was what they call now. Yom kippur fast spring cleaning of inside. Peace and war depend on some fellow's digestion. Religions. Christmas turkeys and geese. Slaughter of innocents. Eat, drink and be merry. Then casual wards full after. Heads bandaged. Cheese digests all but itself. Mighty cheese.
> – Have you a cheese sandwich? (163)[34]

The narrative switches, as Bloom's mind does, from what he sees to what he thinks and what he says. Harry Blamires rendering of the scene in 'plain English' reminds us that the whole occurs as 'a quick sequence of thought' in one moment.[35] Through the medium of the stream of consciousness, or the interior monologue, Bloom is presented to us as a man of imagination and intelligence. This man of many thoughts is not too far off, of course, from Homer's 'man of many ways'.

Yet, whereas Odysseus/Ulysses puts his cunning to work to re-establish domestic order through a spectacular victory, or *aristeia*, Bloom regains his home and, it would seem, his wife, through no goal-directed action of his own. As a result, the long-awaited culmination of the *nostos* seems simply to be a matter of course. This has several important corollaries in considering the text as epic. First, it establishes Molly's agency in Bloom's heroic quest, for the homecoming is encapsulated in her reaffirmation of her love for Bloom, expressed in a magnificent repetition of 'yeses' as she reminisces about her acceptance of his proposal of marriage: 'and then he asked me would I yes to say yes my mountain flower and first I put my arms around him yes and drew him down to me so he could feel my breasts all perfume yes and his heart was going like mad and yes I said yes I will Yes' (732). Molly's epilogue, so often cited as an example of feminised writing, injects a female agency into the male-driven quest of the Homeric narrative – a masculinity that, as we have seen, the *Odyssey* only hints at with Penelope's very latent heroic potential.

Second, the ostensibly unheroic ending reminds us once again that Bloom's heroism, not just pacifist, is passive. Much of the book is concerned with Bloom's thoughts, and yet they do not actually achieve anything in terms of plot. If Bloom's imagination is what makes him heroic, this is no active heroism for it is imagination heroicised for its own sake. It is no wonder, then, that, as much as the text may be read as a heroicisation of Bloom, it is also a heroicisation of Joyce. As Schwarz remarks of Joyce's relentless Homeric schematising, 'there are moments when Joyce is less interested in what the correspondences signify than in his own ingenious performance of imagining the parallels'.[36] Joyce, in writing *Ulysses* as a *tour de force* of symbolic construction, replays the Romantics' discernment of the heroic capacity of the epic poet in Milton and their determination to display it themselves. Though the text pretends at a direct display of the subjectivities of its characters, it can never escape the fact that this display requires the craft of the writer. As Carl Jung famously put it: 'The ego of the creator of these figures is not to be found. It is as though it had dissolved into the countless figures of *Ulysses*. And yet, or rather for that very reason, all and everything, even the missing punctuation of the final chapter, is Joyce himself.'[37]

Finally, it problematises any question of resolution. The narrative of Bloom's wanderings is resolved inasmuch as he returns home, but it remains unresolved inasmuch as the kaleidoscopic nature of his vision and imagination is necessarily continuous. Bloom will awaken and start another day, and another and another, and all will be as chaotic, as full of possibility, and therefore as 'epic' as 16 June 1904. Joyce, positioning himself as the supremely imaginative – and therefore supremely epic – writer, produced a supreme celebration of the human imagination that was also therefore supreme epic, in its form (as a product of rigorous creative thinking), its style (as an expression of the workings of the mind) and its content (as the story of a profoundly thoughtful man). It is this exhaustive exposition of the labyrinthine inner workings of the human mind in direct encounter with the outer world that makes this text a modernist epic, for it is these inner workings that offered the modernists such an inexhaustible object of interest amidst the anarchy of the Great War.

Eliot's *Waste Land*

Eliot's reaction to *Ulysses* is telling, though more for what it reveals about Eliot's own epic intentions than for any elucidation of Joyce's text. Unlike Pound, Eliot saw the Homeric foundation of *Ulysses* as an important generic innovation. In an essay entitled 'Ulysses, Order and Myth' (1923), he declared the novel dead ('The novel ended with Flaubert and James') but did not go so far as to designate *Ulysses* as epic. Yet, Eliot identified the myth-based text, such as *Ulysses*, as the only possible narrative form for his age. For Eliot, *Ulysses* is 'the most important expression which the present age has found'.[38] According to Eliot, the Homeric parallels that Joyce used had all the importance of a new narrative method: 'In using the [Ulysses] myth, in manipulating a continuous parallel between contemporaneity and antiquity, Mr. Joyce is pursuing a method which others must pursue after him'.[39] Eliot went on to note of the Homeric foundation of Joyce's text:

> It is simply a way of controlling, of ordering, of giving a shape and a significance to the immense panorama of futility and anarchy which is contemporary history. ...Psychology (such as it is, and whether our reaction to it be comic or serious), ethnology, and *The Golden Bough* have concurred to make possible what was impossible even a few years ago. Instead of narrative method, we may now use the mythical method. It is, I seriously believe, a step towards making the modern world possible for art...[40]

According to Eliot, the Homeric narrative gave meaning to the modern world inhabited by Joyce's Bloom. It mattered not for Eliot that Joyce's text isolated only those heroic elements in Odysseus/Ulysses that could also be heroic in the twentieth century. It mattered not, either, that *Ulysses* encyclopaedically exposed modern life in all its chaos, and indeed used the controlling frame of myth to throw this chaos into relief. Eliot read Joyce's use of myth as a source of order, and, in his own long poem, *The Waste Land*, exploited myth to such ends. Whereas Joyce employs myth to show the gap between antiquity and contemporaneity, and to celebrate the heroic in each, Eliot employs it in order that antiquity and contemporaneity can be shown to be part of an overriding pattern. Where Joyce embraces 'the immense panorama of futility and anarchy which is contemporary history', Eliot can do so only once he has subordinated it to a meaningful order, an order justified by myth. Using such resources as the anthropological investigations of James Frazer's magisterial *Golden Bough*, Eliot imposes in *The Waste Land* a sense of order on chaos. It is Eliot's insistence on 'the mythical method' as the only generic alternative left to writers to reveal and explain modern life in all its complexity, and his subsequent employment of it in *The Waste Land*, that make this poem his claim to modernist epic.

The Waste Land consists of five books of just 434 lines. If one insisted on length as a prerequisite to epic status, the poem's brevity would certainly exclude it; however, as a follower in the footsteps of *Ulysses* (particularly after the pronouncements of '*Ulysses*, Order, and Myth') it cannot be overlooked in discussing the modernist epic. Indeed, Hugh Kenner states that because the poem was too short for 64 pages of print and too long for 32, Eliot expanded on a few brief notes in order to fill in the blank pages.[41] As we shall see, although these notes sometimes helpfully elaborate on Eliot's mythological sources, and much critical effort has been spent in examining them, they are probably best read as adjuncts to the text, which Eliot probably intended them to be. The temptation to rely on the notes, however, is strong, as the poem appears to consist of a series of disconnected allusions and statements, with no narrative rationale and logic.

None the less, the poem repays close reading as an example of Eliot's 'mythical method', particularly if that method is read as deriving from the mythological sources identified by the original brief notes. Eliot identifies both Jessie Weston's *From Ritual to Romance* (1920) and the Adonis, Attis and Osiris volumes of Frazer's *Golden Bough* (1890) as important sources.[42] Weston's book examines the role played in the Grail legends by the story of the Fisher King, which appears in several medieval *chansons*. Like Joyce, then, Eliot's poem has a basis in early heroic narrative. As collated by Weston, these *chansons* tell the tale of a king who suffers a wound that leads to drought and decay in his kingdom; both king and land are healed by a knight who undertakes to discover the Holy Grail. Weston's gloss on the story points out that the link between the rulers' health and the state of the land is found too in ancient spring celebrations of the Near East.[43] These, surveyed in those volumes of Frazer specified by Eliot, discuss rituals concerning the fertility gods known variously as Adonis, Tammuz, Osiris and Attis. These rituals, in which an effigy of the god is drowned and retrieved, represent the god's symbolic death and resurrection and allegorise the cycle of the seasons.[44] The two sources combine to demonstrate the poem's preoccupation with decay and resurrection – bodily, vegetative and spiritual. The Fisher King legend also allows Eliot to express the search for revivification as heroic wandering and quest, significantly that epic element which Joyce had alluded to in his use of the Odysseus figure.

The themes of decay and resurrection recur in the various images that are scattered throughout the poem. Yet, these themes are also set within a long view of history, a history that ends for Eliot with the despair following the Great War. Stephen Spender's personal reminiscence, indeed, establishes the profundity of the effects of the war on Eliot: 'Eliot – who tended to take a historic view of his work – once said to me that *The Waste Land* could not have been written at any moment except when it was written – a remark which, while biographically true in regard to his own life, is also true of the poem's time in European history after the First World War.'[45] The poem's epigraph – lines from the poet Petronius in which the Sybil, the mythical prophetess, yearns for death – suggests both history and the wishfulness for death that accompanies a knowledge of history. The first book, 'The Burial of the Dead', presents us with a series of images that together connect decay with the decadence that preceded the war and the loss of innocence and happiness that followed. Thus, the springtime of April is 'the cruellest month, breeding / Lilacs out of the dead land, mixing / Memory and desire' (1–3), containing a longing for peace that cannot be fulfilled, and the memories of Countess Marie, cousin of Archduke Ferdinand, mingle with the yearnings of sailors who have left behind their beloveds in Wagner's opera *Tristan und Isolde*. The clairvoyant Madame Sosostris can only warn her interlocutor to beware 'death by water', which, as in the ritual drowning of the fertility gods, will bring not the joy of spring but the despair of a spring without innocence. The images of decay culminate in a vignette of postwar London, an 'Unreal City' (60), whose inhabitants are recognisable as both oppressed city workers and war refugees: 'I had not thought death had undone so many. / Sighs, short and infrequent, were exhaled, / And each man fixed his eyes before his feet' (61–3). These speak, however, as soldiers in the ancient Punic battle at Mylae. Wars, both ancient and modern, are connected in this book with each other, as well as with a more general and eternal sense of loss, whether contemporary urban despair, operatic lost love, or the decay of the seasons.

The second book, 'A Game of Chess', begins an alignment of this sense of recurrent decay with sexual emptiness. It opens with an unnamed woman, whose baroque boudoir, with its 'laquearia' (92), 'coffered ceiling' (93) and dressing table littered with 'strange synthetic perfumes' (87), bespeaks both artificiality and artifice. It briefly mentions the legend of Philomel, 'by the barbarous king/So rudely forced' (99–100), who was turned into a nightingale after being mutilated and raped. The theme of sexual deceit continues from the seemingly aristocratic to the mythological to the everyday working classes, with the figure of Lil, whose sexual life is a litany of misery, from the necessity of pleasing a husband home from the war to the desperation of both raising and aborting unwanted children. Like the general decay that begins the poem, this sexual sterility too is eternalised. In the third book, 'The Fire Sermon', the theme of sexual decay continues, this time combined with the urban despair earlier foreshadowed. We return to the 'Unreal City' (207), through which flows the River Thames, associated with 'empty bottles, sandwich papers, / Silk handkerchiefs, cardboard boxes, cigarette ends' (177–8) and 'A rat cre[eping] softly through the vegetation/Dragging its slimy belly on the bank' (188–9). The city-dwellers include Mr Eugenides, 'the Smyrna merchant/Unshaven' (209–10), who propositions the narrator with 'a weekend at the Metropole' (213–14), and the typist and the clerk, whose love-making consists of 'unreproved, if undesired' (238) caresses and 'patronising' (247) kisses, of 'vanity' (241) on his side and 'indifference' (242) on hers. We learn that Tiresias, the double-sexed prophet of Homer's *Odyssey* and Ovid's *Metamorphoses* who watches the coupling, has 'foresuffered all' (243), and should not be surprised by this when we consider the poem's insistence that such fruitless activity has recurred throughout history.

Decay haunts the poem as a fact of history, but what of resurrection? If indeed the spring rite described by Frazer acts as an emblem for this poem, then that ritual's figuration of decay in the drowning and retrieval of a god into and out of water becomes highly resonant. Throughout the poem, both water and the lack of water become tropes of death and decay, and either might be evoked by the sense of 'waste' that pervades the poem and inhabits its title. The fourth book, 'Death by Water', then, is the poem's pivot, offering both a reiteration of decay as well as the possibility for renewal, just as the death by water of the ancient fertility god betokens both the harshness of winter and the eventual return of spring. This brief book – consisting of eight lines in all – carries with it a warning not to ignore the drowning of Phlebas, the Phoenician sailor: 'Gentile or Jew/O you who turn the wheel and look to windward, / Consider Phlebas, who was once handsome and tall as you' (319–21). We are reminded that death stalks us all, but perhaps so does the possibility for renewal. The poem ends, then, with this possibility. In the final book, 'What the Thunder Said', the themes of vegetative, bodily and spiritual want recur – the 'Dead mountain mouth of carious teeth that cannot spit' (339), the 'dry sterile thunder without rain' (342), a land in which 'there is no water' (358) – in a whirlwind of images. None the less, when the spectre of Christ is evoked – appearing as a 'third who always walks beside you' (359) – it is worth recalling that he is descended from the ancient fertility gods but emblematic more of redemption than its counterpart of decay. When we are presented with yet another waste landscape in the image of the chapel 'In the decayed hole among the mountains' (345), we might care to refer to Weston's versions of the Fisher King legend, in which the knight's quest to save the Fisher King culminates in the discovery of the grail in the Chapel Perilous. The quest for resurrection with which *The Waste Land* is concerned meets therefore with success. With 'a damp gust bringing rain' (393–4), the much longed-for water arrives. With it comes thunder, and what the thunder says is salutary: '*Datta*' (401), '*Dayadvham*' (411) and '*Damyata*' (418) being the Sanskrit for 'give', 'sympathise' and 'control'. As Kenner suggests, 'To sympathize is to give oneself; to control is to give governance'.[46] Having reminded us of the right relations both between ourselves and others and within ourselves, the poem ends with 'Shantih shantih shantih' (433), glossed by Eliot himself in his notes as 'the Peace which passeth understanding'.

The poem insists on death and despair as constants, indeed as historically recurrent. Yet, rebirth is offered as a counterpart to death, particularly by the poem's presiding myth of the Fisher King and its origins in spring rites. The result is a pattern of cyclical death and rebirth. This, then, is the order that Eliot's mythical method imposes on to the 'panorama of futility and anarchy' that is modern life. Hence, for Eliot, there is some hope. Though both myth and modernity appear chaotic in his poem, he reads out of this madness a method. The fragments that form his poem seem to mirror the fragments of which – the modernists realised – life is made. But the end result is a mosaic that gestures towards a unified picture. Joyce, in comparison, read method out of a classical – or, in Eliot's terms, mythical – text, and in the juxtaposition of this methodical mythical precursor with modern life, demonstrates and celebrates the chaos that ensues.

Yet, Eliot positioned himself as a practitioner of Joyce's mythic method. For, according to Eliot, there was only one way left to tell of life. Because he followed Joyce in insisting on representing both the age and the unrepresentable, Eliot's poem becomes part of a tradition that is both epic and modernist. The modernist epic is initiated by Joyce, who alludes to past epic so that we do not miss his gesture. It is consolidated by Eliot.

Pound's *Cantos*

Eliot showed drafts of *The Waste Land* to Pound in 1921; Pound's rigorous editing resulted in the brief and disjointed collection of images that the poem resembles in its final form. It is no surprise, then, that Pound's own attempt at modernist epic is the enigmatic *Cantos*, with its profusion of seemingly incoherent ideas and allusions. What might be surprising, considering the succinctness that Pound enforced on Eliot's lines, is that Pound's work is a sprawling collection of 117 cantos of free verse, possessing very little in the way of narrative. These, appearing separately, under such titles as *Cantos XXX*, the *Fifth Decad of Cantos* and the *Pisan Cantos*, were composed and published over a fifty-year period.[47]

Yet, Pound seems to have conceived of this disparate work as epic. The modernist epic, implicitly defined by Joyce and Eliot as representative of the spirit of the age, is explicitly described so by Pound. He variously defined epic as 'the speech of a nation through the mouth of one man' and as 'a poem including history'.[48] For Pound, as for Joyce, the Odysseus figure possesses talismanic properties in his epic-writing task. In a letter to his mother in 1909, he considered the *Odyssey* as the primary model for a modern epic.[49] 'From the beginning', notes Forrest Read, 'in his essays and reviews, he compares the modern experimental writer to an Odyssean adventurer into the unknown. In his poems the voyage with Homeric echoes of exile and discovery crops up incessantly.'[50] Pound therefore appropriates the questing hero for his own ends, as a figure for the poet's own search for success. As we shall see, this quest, like that of Eliot's Fisher King, is to find a resolution to contemporary confusion, to impose order on the modern awareness of chaos. Pound may have been acutely aware of the heady sense of flux that defined the age in which he lived, and he was appreciative of Joyce's success in representing that flux. Yet, he was also desirous that his poetry demonstrate 'form', that disparate images be allowed magically to come together to reveal a design, just like iron fillings ordered into shape by magnetic force: 'The *forma*, the immortal *concetto*, the concept, the dynamic form which is like the rose pattern driven into the dead iron fillings by the magnet, not by material contact with the magnet itself, but separate from the magnet.'[51]

A sense of flux is what emerges most forcefully on a first reading of the *Cantos*. If there is any coherence at all in the poem, it is in its despair at incoherence, at the vicissitudes of two world wars. The preponderance of images brings to mind Pound's early poetic vision of imagism, a vision which proved so influential on *The Waste Land*. Pound was, indeed, the unofficial spokesperson of the Imagist movement, whose famous doctrines, attributed to Pound, were published by F. S. Flint in 1913:

1. Direct treatment of the 'thing', whether subjective or objective.
2. To use absolutely no word that did not contribute to the presentation.
3. As regarding rhythm: to compose in sequence of the musical phrase, not in sequence of a metronome.[52]

Imagist poetry, in its essence, then, is the brief, succinct and precise description of an object, without recourse to its symbolic potential. The *Cantos* seem, therefore, to be a collection of imagist poems. Put another way, they are comparable to a series of Chinese ideograms, with which Pound was so preoccupied as compact expressions of both the visual and the linguistic. According to Albert Cook, 'the ideogram has been correctly regarded as the structural principle basic to the *Cantos*'.[53]

Yet, as Cook further points out, these imagist statements, or ideograms, possess a potential for coherence, of which Pound was aware but that he never fully realised. Each set of ideograms accumulate to become a *persona* – that is, in Pound's vocabulary, a recurring figure or idea. *Personae* such as Dionysus, Actaeon and of course Odysseus appear in the early cantos (indeed, after some revision, Odysseus was made to appear in the very first canto) and subsequently recur. As Cook explains:

> Each individual canto is made up of blocks of statement, and each block tends to centre in a visual perception (ideogram) or an event from someone's life (*persona*), or occasionally in something that possesses the dual character of ideogram and *persona*. ... Beyond the smaller blocks within cantos, each canto itself constitutes a larger block, usually a *persona*, which is set off against other blocks: the Odysseus-block of Canto I sets off a Sordello-block in Canto III the two set off a Cid-block; all set off a Dionysus-block, etc.[54]

None the less, it is one thing to read a pattern of recurrent and accumulative images and another to attribute to these an overall design. Tellingly, Pound described the recursive figures of the *Cantos* thus: 'The first cantos are preparation of the palette. I have to get down all the colours or elements I want for the poem. Some perhaps too enigmatically and abbreviatedly. I hope, heaven help me, to bring them into some sort of design and architecture later.'[55] That design never happened. The cumulative effect of the *Cantos*, then, is of the flux of modern life and, indeed, of that flux as it appears to the poet himself. For, as Cook reminds us, the only constant in the shifts that constitute the *Cantos* is the poet's self: 'Within the *Cantos*, the fact that Pound declares the sections to be sections of the same poem allows him to enlist for that poem the flux of the self.'[56]

The *Cantos*, adopting the stance of the newly established genre of modernist epic, sets off mythical allusions against modern polyvalence in order to express the age, an age seemingly descending further into moral anarchy with the events of the Second World War – the Holocaust and atomic bombings. Like Joyce, then, Pound seeks to employ myth as an organising principle against which the flux of modern life can be thrown into full relief. Unlike Eliot, he did not venture *a posteriori* to extract from myth any meaningful antidote to that chaos. No wonder, then, that, *pace* Eliot, he read Joyce's use of the Homeric myth as 'chiefly [Joyce's] own affair, a scaffold, a means of construction, justified by the result, and justifiable by it only'.[57] The Odyssean quest for home becomes the poet's quest for meaning, but, as in Joyce's text, resolution will always be deferred.

H. D.'s *Helen in Egypt*

H. D., or Hilda Doolittle, was Pound's contemporary, correspondent, friend and sometime lover. Their long association also included a shared poetics, particularly a shared investment in imagism early on in their careers. When H. D. completed her long poem *Helen in Egypt* in 1961, she explicitly construed it as a version of Pound's modernist epic. As Jacob Korg notes:

> With *Helen in Egypt*, her major work, H. D. resumed the poetic dialogue with Pound, for she referred to it as 'my Cantos', as though her poem were in some sense a reply to the *Pisan Cantos*. She said that it had been 'simmering' for three years, which was the period after she had seen the *Pisan Cantos*. Her enthusiasm for the *Cantos* wavered while she was writing *Helen in Egypt*, but she was always conscious of it.[58]

H. D.'s poem is both strikingly similar to and different from Pound's poem. Inspired by versions of the life of Helen of Troy told by the Greek dramatist Euripedes and the Greek poet Stesichorus, H. D. recounts, in a series of lyrics that could be described as imagist, how Helen was never in Troy, having been replaced by a phantom by Zeus and spirited away to Egypt instead. The story is profoundly ironic, since it posits that the prime cause of the historic watershed that is the Trojan War was false. It is also rich in potential, since it allows H. D. to explore Helen's character more fully. Like Pound, then,

H. D. employs a Homeric allusion and a series of ostensibly disconnected images and *personae* in order to produce a text that is both self-consciously epic yet intentionally fragmented, that is, she situates herself in the emerging modernist epic tradition. However, a sense of coherence is latent within her text, not only because there is a palpable – if difficult – narrative, but also because its images and events are all imagined, perceived or remembered by a central protagonist, Homer's Helen. As Korg states, 'the whole *Cantos*, with its wide-ranging visits to all sorts and conditions of men, has a broad ethical dimension that contrasts with the interior monologue that occupies most of *Helen in Egypt*'.[59] Moreover, H. D.'s utilisation of classical epic is not as a source of inspiration or point of departure but as a text to be rewritten and reimagined. H. D.'s epic possesses, then, a concrete and consistent aim – the revisioning of a key Homeric figure and hence of Homeric epic. In repositioning the central female figure of this epic, H. D. presents a feminist rewriting of classical epic, positing what Susan Stanford Friedman calls a 'women's mythology'.[60] None the less, the poem is ultimately irresolute, and its conclusion – in keeping with modernist sentiments – seems to be that there can be no conclusion. As Claire Buck argues, incoherence is the ultimate aim of the poem inasmuch as it ends by 'defining the knowledge of woman as something you can know only by knowing that you do not know it'.[61]

Helen in Egypt proceeds in three parts. Each part is divided into six or seven books, with each book further comprising eight lyrics, and each lyric composed of a series of mostly unrhymed tercets. The first part, the 'Pallinode' (literally, a 'writing against'), depicts Helen in Egypt, where, alone in the temple of the Egyptian god Amen, she encounters Achilles, or, possibly, the ghost of Achilles. In the second, 'Leuké', Helen finds herself back in Greece, on the island of Leuké, where Paris had lived as a shepherd before he had been recognised as one of the princes of Troy. Helen encounters not only Paris but her first lover, Theseus, and sifts through, with Theseus' help, the memories and meaning of her life. In the final part, the 'Eidolon', Helen is in Egypt again, where, in a dreamlike state, she seems to reconcile the various demands on her life posited by her various lovers, and to find some sort of resolution in bearing Achilles' son.

This primary opposition of the two Helens – of Troy and of Egypt – becomes the basis of a dichotomy that runs through the poem. This dichotomy is that which, according to Friedman's analysis of H. D., divides war from love, masculinity from femininity, the external and power-driven from the internal and psychological.[62] Significantly, H. D. also distinguishes patriarchal Greek myth from Egyptian hermeneutics, which she reads as feminised and maternalised, and as expressive of an earlier phase in human history of goddess worship.[63] In making these distinctions, H. D. therefore draws on Freud's identification of the two drives that underpin human psychology – the love-drive of Eros and the death-drive of Thanatos – and explicitly genders this. According to Friedman, however, H. D. 'depart[ed] radically from Freud's presentation' and 'associated Eros with the woman's world and Thanatos with the man's world'.[64] This juxtaposition is expressed alternately within the poem as the split between Eros and Eris – the gods of love and strife respectively – or between the forces of 'L'Amour' and 'La Mort'. Additionally, Achilles seems initially to represent the masculine, martial impulse, whereas Paris carries with him connotations of femininity and love. Their enmity across the battlefields of Troy and the death of Achilles from an arrow fired by Paris thus replay the schism at the heart of H. D.'s epic. The poem therefore revises the impulses at the heart of the Homeric heroic code. Masculinity and war as told by the Greek tradition are marginalised; in its place is a story of femininity and love located in the older, less knowable civilisation of Egypt. It matters not whether Helen of Troy was a phantom and whether the Helen we meet in Egypt is distinct and real. What the initial division between these two Helens achieves is a space in which the figure of Helen can be depicted outside the confines of the epic tradition. Within the Greek tradition, Helen is reviled and misunderstood. Where she is acknowledged as a victim of the fates, she is seen as the silent pawn of masculine ambition and desire and, paradoxically, where she is granted volition, she is construed as sexually deviant and destructive. As the poem opens, however, she finds herself, finally, in a place where she can define herself: 'here there is peace / for Helena, Helen hated of all Greece' (*Pallinode* I.1).[65]

Helen's questioning of the masculine code and her discovery of an alternative feminine wisdom express themselves in the poem's symbolic vocabulary, which posits the base elements of weaponry – flint, steel, and iron – against less tangible aspects of nature – the stars and the sea, embodied by their presiding goddesses Astarte, Thetis, Ishtar and Isis. This dichotomy recurs too in the many events that unfold or that Helen recalls. First, Helen's union with Achilles is a clash of her love for him and his famous bellicose wrath. Achilles in his guise as Greek warrior is one of a council of bearers of masculine honour, 'the iron ring of war or the death cult' (*Leuke* VII.4) that also includes Agamemnon and Odysseus. Achilles' and Helen's consummation is then figured first by his attempt to strangle her 'with his fingers' remorseless steel' when he discovers her identity and then by the '*star in the night*' that shines over them (*Pallinode* I.8). Achilles' own development, we are reminded later in the poem, was marked by a turn from femininity and passivity to manhood and martiality. His mother's plans for him to live in peace, which included disguising him as a girl and placing him on the island of Scyros, were firmly rejected and forgotten when he embraced war at Odysseus' goading: 'He forgot his mother/when the heroes mocked/at the half-god hidden in Scyros' (*Eidolon* VI.3). It is only after his union with Helen and reconciliation with the feminine alternative she represents that Achilles can recall his mother's wishes:

> hers was a simple wish
>
> that he learn to rule a kingdom,
> but he had forgotten Scyros,
> forgotten his vows of allegiance
>
> to the king, forgotten his marriage-vows
> to the king's daughter;
> he had followed the lure of war,
>
> and there was never a braver,
> a better among the heroes,
> but he stared and stared
>
> through the smoke and the glowing embers,
> and wondered why he forgot
> and why he just now remembered.
>
> (*Eidolon* V.8)

In the poem's most important subtext, Helen's recurring preoccupation with the fate of her sister Clytaemnestra, wife of Agamemnon, the schism between love and strife is explicitly replayed as women's oppression at the hands of men. Clytaemnestra and her lover famously killed Agamemnon on his return from the Trojan War. Yet, Clytaemnestra, like Helen, is transformed by this poem from a figure of hate and betrayal into a defender of feminised love against the masculinised demands of war and strife. As Friedman states, 'Deep in family history...Helen finds Clytaemnestra's motivations to be her defense of the woman's world. ...In contrast to the metallic world of war, [the woman's world] is characterized by the ascendance of peace and harmony'.[66] The reasons for Clytaemnestra's murder of Agamemnon are located in his sacrifice of their daughter Iphigenia to appease the goddess Artemis and enable his ships to set sail for war. Though we are told that "Clytaemnestra's problem or Clytaemnestra's 'war' is not Helen's", we do learn that 'her Lord Agamemnon and Achilles do have the iron-ring of the war or the death-cult in common' (*Pallinode* VII.4). Clytaemnestra's revenge of her daughter is emblematised by love and purity. Both mother and daughter are linked through bridal innocence and floral beauty, for Iphigenia, sacrificed at what she thought was her bridal altar, resembles Clytaemnestra on her own wedding day. Helen remembers:

> She was a bride, my sister,
> with a bride's innocence,
> she was a lover of flowers
>
> and she wound in her hair,
> the same simple weeds
> that Iphigenia wore . . .

But this love is marred by masculinist, martial strife:

> it was a moment
>
> of infinite beauty,
> but a war-Lord
> blighted that peace.
>
> (*Pallinode* V.6)

Clytaemnestra's revenge is specifically a woman's revenge; a revenge against warfare, symbolised here by its steel weaponry; a revenge seemingly approved by Astarte, ancient goddess of fertility, whose name also associates her with the stars:

> if a woman fights
> she must fight by stealth,
>
> with invisible gear;
> no sword, no dagger, no spear
> in a woman's hands
>
> can make wrong, right;
> . . .
> she is not Nemesis, as you named her,
> nor Nepenthys, but perhaps Astarte
>
> will re-call her ultimately . . .
>
> (*Pallinode* VII.3)

With these two opposite terms marking Helen's progress, the poem moves tentatively towards a resolution that will somehow unite them. Assisted by Theseus, who unites the roles of lover, father and analyst, Helen gropes her way towards an understanding of her disparate selves. Friedman has pointed out how Helen moves through three phases in the poem, phases associated with the three manifestations of the goddess identified by Robert Graves, whose book *White Goddess* greatly interested H. D. H. D.'s own notes for the poem state: 'the New Moon is the white goddess of birth and growth; the Full Moon, the red goddess of love and battle; the old Moon, the black goddess of death and divination'.[67] According to Friedman, Helen similarly moves from a phase of youthful love with Paris; to a mature, almost maternalised relationship with Achilles, particularly in her identification with Thetis; to a repositioning of herself as a figure not unlike Persephone, bride of the god of the underworld, whose marriage symbolises seasonal rebirth. For Helen's union with Achilles is, ultimately, the fusion of feminised love with masculinised war and strife. 'The essence of H. D.'s pallinode', writes Friedman, 'is the growing understanding and acceptance of power and values in a woman's world'.[68]

In her epic about Homer's Helen, then, H. D. actively questions the values that underpin Homeric epic. The 'numberless / tender kisses, the soft caresses' that mark Helen's life according to H. D. had no role in the traditional epics – 'none of these / came into the story, / it was epic, heroic' (*Eidolon* VII.1). Her poem is not just a simple retelling of Helen's story, but an active reclamation of epic territory in order that it may include a feminine principle of love and an acknowledgement of female power. In this, it differs significantly from the male-authored modernist epics that precede it. The epic is linked by H. D. to the dominance of masculinist values of war over the feminised principle of love. Thus, the mythical foundation to H. D.'s poem can offer no foil to the troubles of the modern world, when it is itself a source of those troubles.

In telling the story of a woman marginalised by epic tradition, H. D. attempts also to tell her story as a poet – just as Pound's fragmentary visions in the *Cantos* were indicative of his poetic quest to transcend confusion in a united artistic vision. Helen is readable on one level as a version of H. D., for the men in Helen's life correspond to those in H. D.'s, most notably Achilles with H. D.'s lover, Lord Dowding, and Theseus with Freud.[69] According to Friedman, the relationship between Helen and Theseus echoes H. D.'s own experiences under treatment with Freud, and encapsulates her very real desire for resolution 'in the epic as well as in her life'.[70] Helen's quest for integration as a woman, then, is also interpretable as her poet's quest for wholeness and resolution as a woman poet.

None the less, H. D.'s poem is also a modernist epic, and, like Pound's epic, it eschews any readily available resolution, for either poet or protagonist. The fruit of Helen's union with Achilles is not presented in the poem, only prefigured. Moreover, the child, Euphorion, possesses a dual identity, reflecting the dichotomy that splits the worlds his parents inhabit. Euphorion, remarks Friedman, 'is the androgynous One that incorporates both the archetypal polarity of mother and father and the dualities within each of them'.[71] Helen states, 'If I think of a child of Achilles', it is both 'the child in Chiron's cave' and 'a child that stared/at a stranger' (*Eidolon* VII.1); that is, it is both the boy Achilles and the girl Helen. The two principles of love and war come together in H. D.'s epic, but they do not fuse. For Buck, this duality is, indeed, part of the poem's feminist message: 'H. D.'s formulation of the woman and her knowledge in *Helen in Egypt* provides a model for the representation of femininity which moves beyond the opposition of wholeness and lack, unity and division'.[72] The result is a feminist modernist epic: a feminist appropriation of Homeric epic and a modernist celebration of the flux that is life specifically identified as feminine.

Walcott's *Omeros*

In what we have labelled the modernist epic, the myth of quest and resolution – usually explicitly identified as Odyssean – offers, through illusion and allusion, a way to highlight the restlessness and irresolution of the modern world. H. D. alone of the modernist epic poets, however, interrogates that myth and the wholeness it promises, since that wholeness is unavailable to a feminist poetics. Similarly, Derek Walcott does not simply allude to the Homeric epic, but actively challenges it as inadequate to the demands of a postcolonial society and a postcolonial poet. In aligning Walcott with H. D. in this way, it is important to beware the risks of ghettoising gender and race issues together under the convenient banner of the 'subaltern' or marginalised; yet it is worth noting that both H. D. and Walcott demonstrate a way to renovate the epic tradition beyond its dead white maleness.

Omeros is comprised of seven books of verse, each book divided into 64 chapters, each chapter comprising three cantos of mostly unrhymed tercets. Set on Walcott's home of the island of St Lucia, its primary plot deals with the conflict between two fishermen, Achille and Hector, over a beautiful housemaid, Helen. The lives of Helen's employers, the British expatriate Dennis and Maud Plunkett, provide a subplot, which is concerned largely with Dennis's interest in the history of the island and Maud's homesickness. Interspersing these plots are the narrator's experiences, which echo

Walcott's own – his memories of his father, his residence in the United States and his return to the West Indies. All this is framed by the figure of Omeros, whose name echoes the original Greek for Homer; he is identifiable mainly as a local itinerant poet nicknamed 'Seven Seas' but also metamorphoses into a destitute man on the streets of London and finally into a talking statue of Homer.

As this summary suggests, Walcott resituates Homeric motifs into a postcolonial context, specifically to the West Indian island of St Lucia. In the colonial context, the alienation felt at home that renders the Odyssean theme so poignant is easily imagined in modernist texts such as Joseph Conrad's *Heart of Darkness* and E. M. Forster's *Passage to India*, as the impulse to travel to far-flung, colonised, 'otherised' lands. But, as Adams suggests, such quests are ill-fated, as alienation inheres in the traveller himself.[73] In the postcolonial world of Walcott's text, the colonial journey is inverted: the West Indian poet must travel to the old centres of colonial power in order to make sense of his postcolonial self and society. Certainly, the colonial quest is present in the character of Dennis Plunkett, the English army major who retires with his Irish wife to St Lucia. Thus, the former colonial Plunkett, and his increasing sense of dislocation from Britain, offer a mirror against which to read the postcolonial poet's migration to the United States. But the poet's journey is circular, and suggests a way of understanding oneself by integrating the worlds in which one has lived, rather than by simply polarising them. This theme of identity as a mosaic of one's wanderings is at the heart of Walcott's epic.

Walcott's use of Homeric epic – and most importantly of the Odyssean theme – is therefore central to the question of shaping identity in a postcolonial world. But it is not simply about recognising Walcott's inversion of the quest motif into a trope for postcolonial identity. For Walcott's very position as epic poet is fraught with issues of race and language, because he has inherited the Homeric epic through an English literary canon. Walcott's oft-quoted poem, 'A Far Cry from Africa', articulates the West Indian poet's split loyalties:

> I who am poisoned with the blood of both,
> Where shall I turn, divided to the vein?
> I who have cursed
> The drunken officer of British rule, how choose
> Between this Africa and the English tongue I love?
> Betray them both, or give back what they give?
> How can I face such slaughter and be cool?
> How can I turn from Africa and live?[74]

Walcott's dilemma is that, by writing in English, he risks turning his back on his African origins. For he then inscribes himself within an English literary heritage and aligns himself with a culture that he sees as a hated oppressor. The nub of the problem is, however, that Walcott's heritage is a dual one – for one thing, his West Indian bloodlines are both English and African; for another, he loves the language and literature of England as much as he may identify himself as a descendant of Africa. 'With respect to the assessment of postcolonial literature', Joseph Farrell warns in his discussion of *Omeros*, 'the critical discourse of epic poetry acquires a racist tinge'.[75] To go on to frame the epic status of *Omeros* within the poet's earlier identification of his dual racial and cultural heritage is to recognise that Walcott's poem must treat traditional Western epic with a mix of suspicion and veneration.

The position of *Omeros* in relation to that later manifestation of the epic form – the modernist epic – is slightly different. Walcott has explicitly sought to dissociate *Omeros* from traditional epic, and has been quoted as saying, 'I do not think of it as epic. Certainly not in the sense of epic design. Where are the battles? There are a few, I suppose. But "epic" makes people think of great wars and warriors.'[76] None the less, the sparseness of wars and warriors would not, it would seem, preclude his poem from ranking as a modernist epic. Walcott himself describes *Ulysses* as an epic on strikingly non-martial grounds: '*Ulysses* is an epic because it breathes. It's an urban epic, which is remarkable in a small city. ...The subject is a matter of a reflective man, not a man of action, but a sort of wandering Jew.'[77] If *Ulysses* counts as epic because it is a believable recreation of one man's thoughtfulness and restlessness, then *Omeros*, which deals very much with the same attributes in a number of characters, is not to be discounted either. Moreover, Walcott had suggested early in his career that he shares with Joyce, or rather with Joyce's fictional alter-ego, Stephen Dedalus, a love-hate affair with English culture: 'Like Stephen...I was a knot of paradoxes: hating the Church and loving her rituals, learning to hate England as I worshipped her language.'[78] Unsurprisingly, Joyce figures in *Omeros* as 'our age's Omeros' (200).[79] Although he might abjure the traditional Homeric epic mode as representative of a monolithic English heritage, Walcott, it seems, would be happy to place his poem within an explicitly modernist epic lineage under the aegis of Joyce's *Ulysses*, which signals instead the fragmentation and uncertainty of identity of which Walcott himself writes.

It would be too simple, however, to read Walcott's poem as a modernist epic in the Joycean vein, in which Homeric parallels show up an everyday heroism by means of both convergence and divergence between myth and modernity. Certainly, there are moments in the poem that allow such a reading, and much can be made of the Homeric echoes in *Omeros*.[80] The conflict between Achille and Hector over Helen, initially a quarrel over a tin can, recalls the greater clash between their Achaean and Trojan namesakes, while the two quarrels can be said to display the same elemental passion and jealousy. Even fleeting images constitute allusions to the Homeric texts: the swift that leads Achille to Africa recalls Homeric Achilles' epithet of 'swift-footed', and the recurring horse motifs surrounding Hector's death remind us of Hector's description in Homer as 'breaker of horses'. Additionally, Ma Kilman's healing of Philoctetes' wound in *Omeros*, when read against the Homeric counterpart (which enables the Achaean victory over the Trojans), becomes interpretable as a triumphant assertion of the St Lucians' African heritage. And Achille's dream return to Africa, when read as an epic descent to the underworld in the footsteps of Odysseus and Aeneas, becomes a heroic reclamation of the past in order to achieve victory in the present. Most significantly, then, the struggles of the inhabitants of St Lucia in making their way in a postcolonial world may be read with particular resonance as an epic quest on a par with the heroics of Homer's warriors. This is the message, it would seem, in Walcott's evocation of the St Lucians' slave forebears, who lived through the notorious Middle Passage from Africa to the Caribbean: 'But they crossed, they survived. There is the epical splendour' (149).

Yet, the reason why such a positioning of *Omeros* as modernist epic would be too simple is, although Walcott responds positively to Joyce's epic, that *Omeros* does not participate in the modernist epic programme in precisely the same way as *Ulysses* does. Joyce, after all, invests heavily in the heroism at the centre of his Homeric precursor; it is imperative that he does so in order to establish his own protagonist as quietly heroic. Walcott, on the other hand, sees a different Homer altogether. In the interview in which he points out that '"epic" makes people think of great wars and great warriors', Walcott continues, 'that isn't the Homer I was thinking of; I was thinking of Homer the poet of the seven seas'.[81] Walcott, stripping Homer of battles and heroes, evokes the elements of desire and restlessness that are the prime movers of Homeric conflict, and then embodies these in the itinerant Omeros. A nomadic spirit finally come home to rest, Omeros is – like Blind Billy Blue, the bard of Walcott's stage adaptation of the *Odyssey* – a character in his own right.[82]

We are further reminded that the theme of fragmented identity is what makes Homer relevant to a West Indian context when the poem aligns Greece with the West Indies on the basis of geography. For Walcott, the archipelagic nature of the West Indies emblematises its shifting subjectivity: 'Antillean art is this restoration of our shattered histories, our shards of vocabulary, our archipelago becoming a synonym for pieces broken off from the original continent.'[83] Thus, in Odysseus' only appearance in the poem, his ship metamorphoses from Greek to West Indian, his crew transformed into African slaves whose sense of dislocation is exacerbated by the fact that they have found themselves amidst the fragmented geography of the archipelago: 'Island after island passing. Still we ain't home' (203). The Homeric hero's wandering and the Homeric poet's itinerancy make up the core constituents of the Homeric legacy for Walcott's postcolonial epic.

It is because Walcott refuses to equate Homeric with heroic that his poem warns against any easy epical reading of his setting and characters. Walcott has stated elsewhere that 'One reason I don't like talking about an epic is that I think it is wrong to try to ennoble people'.[84] Indeed, this is precisely the mistake made in the poem by both Plunkett and the poet. Initially, Plunkett seeks to confirm local history in assigning St Lucia a pivotal role in the Anglo-French battle for supremacy in the Caribbean and thus confirm the island's nickname, 'Helen of the West Indies': 'none noticed the Homeric repetition / of details, their prophecy. That was the difference. / He saw coincidence, they saw superstition' (97). Details such as the surrender of a French vessel to the British commander, Admiral Rodney, in the pivotal Battle of the Saints offer themselves up for a Homeric rewriting of the island's history. Having 'found his Homeric coincidence', Plunkett excitedly points out to Maud:

> 'Look, love, for instance,
> near sunset, on April 12, hear this, the *Ville de Paris*
>
> struck her colours to Rodney. Surrendered. Is this chance
> or an echo? Paris gives the golden apple, a war is
> fought for an island named Helen?' – clapping conclusive hands.
>
> (100)

For Plunkett, however, the alignment of West Indian history with ancient Greek myth takes on special significance when he comes across their housemaid, Helen, the local beauty, trying on Maud's jewellery:

> the passionless books
> did not contain smell, eyes, the long black arm, or his
>
> knowledge that the island's beauty was in her looks,
> the wild heights of its splendour and arrogance.
>
> (97)

Having made this imaginative leap, Plunkett now reads Helen as a carrier of a West Indian triumph over its history of oppression. At first, this reading is based on his desire for her, and he imagines that the triumph could be attained by her bearing his child. Then, having discovered that one of the casualties of the battle was a young midshipman named Plunkett, he locates Helen's triumph in the fact that a British youth – whom he sentimentally claims as both ancestor and son – died for her island:

> He remembered the flash of illumination
> in the empty bar – that the island was Helen,
> and how it darkened the deep humiliation
>
> he suffered for her and her yellow frock. Back then,
> lightning could lance him with historic regret
> as he watched the island through the slanted monsoon
>
> that wrecked then refreshed her. Well, he had paid the debt.
> The breakers had threshed her name with the very sound
> the midshipman heard. He had given her a son.

(103)

For Plunkett, that the British too suffered and died for the island annuls his own part in any collective guilt that might be felt. Because this guilt had been specifically experienced by Plunkett as an embarrassed lust for his housemaid, it is further absolved by holding her somehow responsible for the childless state of his marriage. Thus, in a leap of bad logic and of bad faith, Helen is transformed into Helen of Troy, prime cause of Plunkett's battle-inflicted metaphorical impotence – his inability to father a child.

If it is not already evident, the dubiousness of any attempt to epicise Helen is unmistakeable by the end of the poem. After Maud's death and his miraculous recovery from his head wound, Plunkett learns to accept Helen for what she is, 'not a cause or a cloud, only a name/for a local wonder' (309). Significantly, the narrator-poet, in writing *Omeros*, has repeated Plunkett's error; fortunately, he also shares Plunkett's epiphany. Of Helen and of the parallels between his poem and Homer's, the poet finally realises:

> She walked on this parapet in a stolen dress,
>
> she stood in a tilted shack with its open door.
> Who gives her the palm? Did sulking Achille grapple
> with Hector to repeat themselves? Exchange a spear

for a cutlass; and when Paris tosses the apple
from his palm to Venus, make it a *pomme-Cythère*,
make all those parallels pointless. Names are not oars

that have to be laid side by side, nor are legends;
slowly the foaming clouds have forgotten ours.
You were never in Troy, and, between two Helens,

yours is here and alive; their classic features
were turned into silhouettes from the lightning bolt
of a glance. These Helens are different creatures,

one marble, one ebony.

(312–13)

As Robert Hamner points out, this is an important aspect of the poem's dénouement: 'Both [the poet] and Major Plunkett have attempted to impose alien dimensions on Helen and their island. Upon discovering their common error, Walcott ultimately repudiates classical aspirations for his black heroine, and Dennis Plunkett learns humbly to accept St. Lucia's Helen for the remarkable woman she is without reference to external models.'[85]

Significantly, the poet makes this recognition after he has encountered Omeros as a statue of Homer come to life. The Homeric poet himself confesses that his *Iliad* was about a real, living Helen rather than the impersonality of conflict and conquest: 'A girl smells better than a book. I remember Helen's/ smell. The sun on her flesh. The light's coins on my eyes. That ten years' war was nothing, an epic's excuse' (284). In other words, Omeros reminds the poet how to appreciate the island and its people for themselves, and not for their epic potential. Appropriately enough, in a scene that recalls Virgil's guidance of Dante's *Divina Commedia*, Omeros and the poet board a boat that takes them to an underworld peopled by rapacious colonisers and hypocritical, superficial poets alike. The poet awakens from this nightmare just as he is being pulled into the hellish pit of the poets, and thus escapes the charge of writing pretentious and disingenuous poetry.

Most importantly of all, what the poet learns from Omeros is to integrate his fragmented experiences of both the coloniser's world and his once colonised home:

...there are two journeys
in every odyssey, one on worried water,

the other crouched and motionless, without noise.
For both, the 'I' is a mast; a desk is a raft
for one, foaming with paper, and dipping the beak

of a pen in its foam, while an actual craft
carries the other to cities where people speak
a different language, or look at him differently,

while the sun rises from the other direction
with its unsettling shadows, but the right journey
is motionless; as the sea moves round an island

that appears to be moving, love moves round the heart –
with encircling salt, and the slowly travelling hand
knows it returns to the port from which it must start.

(291)

The poet learns not only that the itinerant poet must return home, but
that, while journeying, he must never forget home. Thus, he must occupy
two positions simultaneously – that of the restless self who travels the
world and the restful self who writes of and at home. For Walcott in
relation to the epic tradition, this has special poignancy. He learns both to
appreciate his Homeric forebear and to resituate him in his own West
Indian context.

In order to understand the debt that *Omeros* owes to Homeric epic, then,
it is important to understand the special way in which Walcott defines the
Homeric epic. For Walcott, it is identifiable primarily by the themes of
wandering and fragmentation. He rejects outright an alignment of the
Homeric with the heroic, particularly with the bellicose heroic. In Gregson
Davis's words, Walcott appears to disavow epic only to embrace it on its
own terms.[86] In *Omeros* he redefines the idea of epic by removing it from its
canonical trappings and placing it under the image of the sea – that symbol
of restlessness and flux:

The ocean had

no memory of the wanderings of Gilgamesh,
or whose sword severed whose head in the *Iliad*.
It was an epic where every line was erased

yet freshly written in sheets of exploding surf . . .

. . .

however one read it, not as our defeat or
our victory; it drenched every survivor

with blessing.

(296)

Fittingly, then, the poem ends with that never-ending epic that is the ocean:
'the sea was still going on' (325)

Coda: Paulin's *Invasion Handbook*

Whither the epic in the twenty-first century? Just over a decade after Walcott's
poem, that fragmentary, encyclopaedic mode of literary expression that we
have called the modernist epic seems still to be a tenable art-form. One
notable example is *The Invasion Handbook* by Tom Paulin, the first of a
projected three volumes of lyrical images narrating events of the Second
World War.[87] The poem's epic agenda is immediately evident, as is its epic
pedigree. The title refers to the name of an early Irish saga that recounts
how the Celts settled in Ireland. In content – the events leading up to and
surrounding a single war, narrated in three instalments – it recalls Hardy's
Dynasts, to which Paulin as a Hardy scholar would be no stranger.[88] In
form – a series of images differing in style from largely free verse to rhymed
metre to prose, in mode from the dramatic to the narrative to the documentary –
it recalls the modernist epic. It consciously alludes to, for example, Eliot and
Joyce, in what one reviewer has labelled 'longish bits of Joycery and
word-quibbles'.[89] The poet himself refers in the poem to his 'looseleaf
epic' and 'epic in cento'. Reviewers have largely agreed on its epic status,
describing it variously as an 'epic poetic history of the Second World War'
and a 'bitty epic'.[90] Though the critical jury is, it would seem, still out on the
merits of Paulin's poem, it is at least possible to say that the allusive,
fragmentary modernist epic lives on in the publication of this initial
volume and the anticipated appearance of two more volumes.

Of course, the other expression of the epic impulse shows no sign of
abating. The epic film, as we shall see in the next chapter, emerges soon
after the birth of film itself, enjoys its apotheosis in the 1950s and 1960s,
but has undergone something of a revival in recent years. It is this uniquely
modern offshoot of epic with which our history of the epic ends.

6
The Twentieth and Twenty-first Centuries: Epic Film

With the popularity of the word as a simple adjective of scale at the end of the twentieth century, the term 'epic' has been applied loosely in cinema to describe films of either great duration or spectacular effects or both. The epic film, however, is more than just a blockbuster and, although we will investigate the links between the special effects blockbuster and the epic film, we will be concerned in this chapter with tracing the fortunes of that genre of film that has come to be referred to as epic and with establishing what characteristics accrued to this genre. We will also keep in mind the question of how epic film relates to the literary tradition whose name it borrows.

In discussing epic film as opposed to epic literature, the ways in which genre operates in film need first to be addressed. Steve Neale's influential work in the area suggests that genre in film, as in literature, is primarily about communication between filmmakers and audiences.[1] Tom Ryall's early investigation into film and genre adopts an attitude similar to structuralist theories of genre in literature. Ryall suggests that:

> The master image for genre criticism is a triangle composed of artist/film/audience. Genres may be defined as patterns/forms/styles/structures which transcend individual films, and which supervise both their construction by the film maker, and their reading by an audience.[2]

In its simplest form, Ryall suggests, film genre operates, like literary genre, as a set of conventions of which both filmmaker and audience are aware, and which may be manipulated to enhance audience enjoyment and critical appreciation. This would be the case particularly for independent filmmaking and, to some extent, the *auteur* process associated with European 'art' cinema, in which the filmmaker is seen as the text's primary artistic controller. One could argue, however, that the communication process between filmmaker and audience is not always a straightforward one, particularly since external sources of funding – most commonly, the film studio – may interfere with artistic and generic decisions. The financial demands of the filmmaking process (as opposed to the literary text, in which composition is relatively cheap and often author-funded) can mean that profitability becomes key. As Walter Benjamin, as well as Theodor Adorno and Max Horkheimer, warned early on in the history of film, in the age of easy technological reproduction the critical determiner of a text's success is its mass appeal.[3] In an effort to ensure popularity and profitability, mainstream studio films can seem generically conservative, even formulaic. For this reason, as Neale points out, questions of genre are often seen as antithetical to *auteur* cinema, in practice and theory.[4] None the less, Neale maintains that all film, like all literature, is produced under considerations of genre, whether these are adhered to or actively avoided. Furthermore, it must be borne in mind that literature does not operate all that differently, for literary genre is not immune from financial constraints and demands of marketability. It is simply important, as Neale suggests, to recognise of both literature and film that some genres, more than others, are constructed by maintaining generic markers in an effort to secure audience recognition and appeal.[5] It is often the case, after all, that studio-funded big-budget films adhere to generic conventions. Such films are often labelled 'genre films' (although Neale recommends the epithet 'generically-marked film' in acknowledgement that all film is, strictly speaking, generic) and include the Western, the gangster film and the epic film.[6]

What is epic film?

As with discussing the epic in general, the problem in discussing epic film is the circular one of how to proceed from a discussion of definition to identifying examples, when that definition is itself derived from examples. The circuit has to be broken at some point, and that point, in this case, is the common-place among film scholars that the 'epic film' refers to a significant number of films produced mostly in Hollywood in the 1950s and 1960s.[7] These films, referred to often and consistently in their own time as epic, are characterised by their substantial length, spectacular effects and restricted setting – either biblical or Roman. The links with traditional literary epic are immediately evident: Derek Elley's discussion of epic film, while it overlooks the obvious shared traits of length and historical content, emphasises how epic film has appropriated the epic tendency towards nationalistic ideology, which we have traced in Chapter 1 to Virgil.[8] As we delineate the history of epic film, we will consider the connections being forged – or forced, as the case may be – between epic film and epic literature.

As a film genre, the epic film traces its roots to the very origins of cinema. This chapter will not only examine the apotheosis of epic film in the mid-twentieth century, but will also look at its rise in the very earliest of films. The interest in historical narrative was evident first in Italy and then in the US, most famously in D. W. Griffith's pioneering *Birth of a Nation* (1915). The combination of spectacle and history seen in Griffith's films was consolidated into a genre by Cecil B. DeMille, who made several grand historical films in the 1920s and 1930s, each supposedly possessing his trademark 'cast of thousands'. These include *Joan the Woman* (1916), *The Ten Commandments* (1923), *The King of Kings* (1927), *The Sign of the Cross* (1933) and *Cleopatra* (1934). Already evident in DeMille's work at this stage is an interest in biblical and classical content that emerges in full force in the 1950s and 1960s.

As we go on to survey the corpus of the epic film genre – the 'classic' Hollywood epics of the 1950s and 1960s – we find that DeMille's influence on the rise of the form is incalculable. The appetite for large-scale biblical and classical narrative among postwar audiences was instigated, as Neale suggests, by the successful re-release of *The Sign of the Cross* in 1944. Moreover, a combination of Cold War ideology and advances in technology contributed to this phenomenal outpouring of DeMillesque movies. Bruce Babington and Peter Evans posit at least two major types of Hollywood epic – the Old Testament epic and the Roman Christian epic – may be traced to such DeMille films as *The Ten Commandments* and *Cleopatra*.[9] Moreover, DeMille's *The Sign of the Cross*, which tells of a love affair between a young Christian woman and a Roman soldier in the reign of Nero, heralds the two overriding themes of mid-twentieth-century Hollywood epic: the rise of Christianity and the imperial power of Rome. This chapter will discuss such Old Testament epics as DeMille's remake of *The Ten Commandments* (1956) and *The Bible* (1966), and the Roman Christian films *The Robe* (1953) and *Ben Hur* (1959), as well as a film that Babington and Evans describe as 'on the margins of Roman-Christian epic', *Spartacus* (1960).[10] This substantial 'corpus' allows us to establish what filmmakers, studios and audiences agreed to be the defining markers of the genre, and the ways in which these relate to literary epic. Interestingly, the use of ancient narrative as a way of addressing contemporary issues, already evident in DeMille's early work, offers itself as an important, though not always overt, generic trait, as early Christianity and imperialist power acquired special resonance in a jittery Cold War society.

The demise of the classic epic film by the 1970s allows the history of epic film a pause, as Hollywood engendered and encountered first a taste for domestic psychological dramas and then entered towards the end of the decade the age of the ubiquitous 'special effects' blockbuster. The chapter ends, however, on a resurgent note, with the apparent re-emergence of the classic Hollywood epic film at the turn of the millennium. This revival has been attributed primarily to *Gladiator* (1998), heralded by film critics as the first example of the genre in fifty years, and consolidated by *Troy* (2004), the film version of Homer's *Iliad*.

Our discussion of epic film from the early twentieth century to its zenith in the middle of the century and on to the twenty-first century will demonstrate that, from its beginnings, film has attempted to represent history on a grand scale, and thus to marry statements of historical verisimilitude with extravagant display. This was, as we shall see, part of an effort to secure middle-class respectability for the new medium, by bringing together didactic value and aesthetic pleasure, and ultimately conspicuous consumption. Accordingly, then, a bourgeois ideology of conservative politics and aspirational consumerism lies at the heart of epic film. This positioning of epic film as a populist form of entertainment and instruction ensured a broad appeal and thus its firm entrenchment in the mid-twentieth century as a film genre.

Our analysis will also indicate that the two moments in which epic film finds itself popular – the 1920s and 1930s, and the 1950s – are both postwar eras. Thus, the epic film demonstrates a comparable, but ultimately opposite, tendency to modernist epic. Both forms involve a turn to a mythical past to shore up doubts about the stability and coherence of the present. But where the despair engendered by the First World War resulted, for literary epic, in fragmented narratives that pointed the way towards incoherence as the only way to proceed, epic film evinces a completely nostalgic embrace of an utterly coherent past. Biblical and Roman worlds offer, in epic film, a myth of completeness and wisdom, one a hermetically sealed realm in which God's word is law and the other an ancient empire whose philosophies and policies are time-honoured and therefore venerable.

This raises the question, moreover, of the way in which epic film defines itself in relation to literary epic. Epic film does not refer to the tradition of literary epic directly, consulting instead the Bible and relatively modern fictions about ancient Rome. Though, as has been suggested in Chapter 1, the Bible may be read as sharing some of the qualities of Homeric epic, it does not itself participate in the epic tradition; yet, as Milton showed in *Paradise Lost*, it has potential as – and indeed superiority to – epic, because it has been the presiding mythology of the modern Western world. But biblical epic film does not recreate literary epic; it simply alludes to it. Similarly, the texts on which many of Hollywood's Roman epic films are based, such as Lew Wallace's *Ben Hur* (1880) and Lloyd C. Douglas's *The Robe* (1942), are relatively modern novels. Even the story of *Spartacus*, though ultimately derived from the true story of the revolt led by the Thracian slave Spartacus against Rome, comes to us via Raffaello Giovagneli's 1874 novel, *Spartaco* and Howard Fast's 1951 novel, *Spartacus*.[11] The epic films which these works have inspired merely invoke the world of classical Roman epic, but do not explicitly refer to it. Thus, epic film associates itself with literary epic by one remove, sometimes more. Instead, its epic claims are made with more directness in terms of scale and length, as well as spectacle – which, as Elley remarks, 'is merely the cinema's own transformation of the literary epic's taste for the grandiose'.[12]

Early historical film

Historicity has defined filmmaking from the outset. 'Early attempts', suggests Elley, 'evolved from a natural desire to use the medium's power to evoke past ages'.[13] This is evident in the first instance in Italy, where colonial expansion coincided with an interest in ancient Italian – that is, Roman – history.[14] Furthermore, Maria Wyke points out, Italy's ambitions to establish itself as a cultural and economic power meant advances in film technology, and, 'as a result of capital investment, industrial competition, and the economic and aesthetic need to increase the artistic status and range of motion pictures, Italian films rapidly increased in length'.[15] Film technology thus matched the desire for historical story-telling, for not only did Italians want to produce and view history on a grand scale, they had developed the uninterrupted, feature-length, multi-reel format with which to do it. *Quo Vadis?* (1913) and *Cabiria* (1914), both set at the height of the Roman Empire's power, enjoyed sensational success, due in no small part to their reception as both authentic and accessible history. One critic of *Cabiria*, for example, described the film's enormous emotional impact on audiences, and in doing so conveyed his own considerable excitement:

An intense emotion grasped the entire audience, the emotion of the incomparable spectacle which, through a set-designer's tenacious effort, revived the people of the third century [BC] and flung them into tremendous struggles before the steep walls of a city, into the burning waves of a flaming sea, at the feet of an idol crimson with fire. . . . On their feet, on all sides of the theatre, the crowd shouted with enthusiasm and joy. A genuine, sincere, unrestrained frenzy accompanied the majestic film from beginning to end. . . . *Cabiria* is something that will last. It will last because at that instant the vulgar art of cinema ceases and history succeeds.[16]

Obviously, the spectacle of historical film played no small part in lending film a degree of prestige, particularly as a cultural descendant of literary representations of history. According to Wyke:

Feature-length film narratives such as *Quo Vadis?* (1913) and *Cabiria* (1914), formed part of a strategy to win over the bourgeoisie to the new cinematic art-form by bestowing on the modern medium a grandiose register and an educative justification. Such films borrowed from the whole spectrum of nineteenth-century modes of historical representation (literary, dramatic, and pictorial) in pursuit of authenticity and authority for cinema as a mode of high culture . . .[17]

From the outset, then, filmmaking sought to establish itself on a continuum from literature. Yet, as Wyke's remarks remind us, the historical film's objective of verisimilitude meant that – notwithstanding the overtly classical content of early Italian film – its most obvious literary influences were not the epic but the novel and theatre. Early historical film utilised scale and spectacle to establish itself as a respectable cultural medium. Most importantly, however, the demands for historical filmmaking arose out of contemporary social and political concerns – in the case of Italy, imperialist pride combined with capitalist ambitiousness. This use of history as a vehicle of contemporary ideology is part of historical film from its very beginning, and becomes an abiding characteristic of epic film.

The Italian combination of historical spectacles and feature formats made a substantial impact on American filmmaking, enjoying box-office success in the US.[18] They transformed the way in which films were made and screened, from shorter single-reels in tiny nickelodeon theatres to feature-length multi-reels that were 'road-shown' to cities and towns and screened in large theatres and halls.[19] The combination of the new feature format with historical narrative is no more evident in early American cinema than in the work of D. W. Griffith. Griffith's interest in history prior to the influence of Italian cinema may be seen in the films he made with the Biograph company from 1908 to 1914. These were mostly single- and double-reel narratives about the Civil War, but also include his first significant feature, *Judith of Bethulia* (1914), a biblically inspired story.[20] In the light of the immense popularity of Italian historical features, Griffith made his most important feature-length historical film. This, running at twelve reels and lasting three hours, was *The Birth of a Nation* (1915). This demonstrated unequivocally the popularity of the long, feature-length historical film, particularly when spectacular effects and large-scale casts and sets were employed.

Based on the 1905 novel *The Clansman*, by Thomas Dixon, the film deals with events during and after the American Civil War, concentrating on the period of Reconstruction in the South. It tells of the friendship between two families, the Southern Camerons and the Northern Stonemans, whose patriarch, Austin Stoneman, was modelled on the radical abolitionist Thaddeus Stevens. The film's first half deals with the Civil War and the hardships it imposes on the Camerons. The second half narrates events after the war, when romance develops between the Camerons' eldest son, Ben, and Stoneman's daughter, Elsie, but is jeopardised when Stoneman leads a policy of destruction against the South. Stoneman seeks to undermine the South by enfranchising and empowering the Blacks, 'crush[ing] the White South under the heel of the Black South'. The Blacks, depicted as a simple people easily manipulated by Stoneman and his mulatto crony, Silas Lynch, eventually take to rioting and rapine (though a few 'faithful souls', such as the Camerons' servants, remain loyal). The besieged Whites, under the leadership of Ben Cameron, form the Ku Klux Klan to protect their property and women. The film ends with Lynch's persecution of the Cameron family, as well as his attempt at forcing a marriage with Elsie Stoneman. In a triumphant attack by Ben Cameron and his fellow Klansmen on the town's rioting Black population, Elsie and the Camerons are saved and Elsie and Ben finally marry.

From the outset, Griffith felt that his historical film would strike a chord with its audience. So enthused was Griffith by making a film version of Dixon's popular novel that he swore his cast to secrecy to ensure the idea was not poached by other filmmakers.[21] A Kentuckyan by birth, he was apparently immediately drawn to the subject matter; he would later state that when the idea for the film was first suggested to him 'it hit me hard; I hoped at once that it could be done, for the story of the South had been absorbed into the very fibre of my being'.[22] Of real significance to Griffith was the story's central – and, for many, inflammatory and racist – narrative of the rise of the Ku Klux Klan, which he saw as the story of the birth of a people, one that would have particular impact because 'it had all the deep incisive emotionalism of the highest patriotic sentiment'.[23] For him, the struggle of the South to define itself both against the North and against its former slaves was the story of the forging of American nationhood. In an interview given in 1915, Griffith insisted, 'The Civil War was fought fifty years ago. But the real nation has only existed the last fifteen or twenty years, for there can exist no union without sympathy and oneness of sentiment. ... The birth of a nation began, according to one authority, with the Ku Klux Klans ... '[24] The underlying rationale for Griffith's film, then, was one of ultra-conservative patriotism. And, though it screened at theatres for a costly $2 a seat, it was vastly popular, running for 45 weeks in New York alone and becoming the first film to be shown at the White House.[25]

Another important part of the film's appeal, of course, is its spectacular scale and effects. The costs and numbers involved were unprecedented – by Griffith's own reckoning, he employed some 30,000 to 35,000 actors and spent $250,000.[26] Griffith's technical innovations were legion and most would be lasting: for example, his use of night and soft-focus photography, and the juxtapositioning and cross-cutting of differing camera angles and shot-lengths, both to build a narrative rhythm and to bring out symbolic contrasts. Griffith's cross-cutting technique – 'the intercutting of parallel scenes occurring at different locations in space, but at the same location in time, each of which has a bearing upon the other, with the meanings of both carefully inter-woven, and with the tensions of either relieved only when the two are finally brought together' – is a staple of cinematic suspense now, but was innovative and extremely effective when it was employed in *Birth of a Nation*.[27]

The acclaim which met Griffith's film went hand in hand with its posi-tioning of itself as authentic history. Griffith faithfully reproduced his film sets in accordance with historical sources: titles preceding 'historical' scenes such as Abraham Lincoln's assassination and the surrender of Robert E. Lee to Ulysses S. Grant proclaimed the veracity of the sets as 'facsimiles' of actual sites as described in history books.[28] After the film's release, boosted by such remarks as President Woodrow Wilson's announcement on viewing the film that 'it teaches history by lightning', Griffith emphasised the cultural and didactic value of filmmaking as a medium. In one interview given shortly after the film's release, he referred explicitly to President's Wilson's remarks, stating:

The foremost educators of the country ... have told us repeatedly that the motion picture can impress upon a people as much of the truth of history in an evening as many months of study will accomplish. As one eminent divine said of pictures, 'They teach history by lightning!'[29]

In another, he remarked:

If I had a growing son I should be willing to let him see motion pictures as he liked, because I believe they would be an invaluable aid to his

education. They would stimulate his imagination, without which no one
would go far. They would also give him a fund of knowledge, history and
otherwise, and all good.[30]

For Griffith, as for many others, *The Birth of a Nation* had legitimised film as
a cultural medium, its supposed historical accuracy adding to its spectacle in
order to achieve both popularity and respectability.

Griffith's position, then, is as a pioneer and an enabler of the genre of epic
film, although the label 'epic' was not readily applied at the time to his own
output, nor was the great spectacular historical narrative of *The Birth of a Nation*
linked by contemporary critics in any obvious way to literary epic. Indeed,
in developing the historical film for an American audience, he supplanted
the ancient Roman subject matter of Italian films with the recent American
history. In this respect, then, Griffith's most obvious literary antecedent is the
nineteenth-century novel. The Soviet director Sergei Eisenstein would later
note that Griffith's films – in their use of romance as well as cause and effect,
which would become crucial elements in classic Hollywood narrative – show
the influence of such realist novelists as Dickens, and it is only through
Dickens that Griffith embodies the aims and techniques of epic literature:

> Let Dickens and the whole ancestral array, going back as far as the Greeks
> and Shakespeare, be superfluous reminders that both Griffith and our
> cinema prove our origins to be not solely as of Edison and his fellow
> inventors, but as based on an enormous cultural past . . .[31]

Griffith's film is a milestone in the history of epic film because it articulated,
for future filmmakers, the potency of the mix that was historically 'authentic'
narrative, multi-reel length, and, most importantly, impressive scope and
effects. It 'helped found a tradition of large-scale, high-cost spectacles'.[32] It
offered itself for consolidation into a genre defined by historical documenta-
tion and the cultural credence that attended it, combined with emotionality
in impact and grandeur in scale. It was, in other words, ready to provide the
foundations for a genre whose development would be overseen by one
director in particular. That genre was the classic Hollywood epic; the director
was Cecil B. DeMille.

DeMille and early epic

DeMille's filmmaking trademark was spectacle, evident across all the genres
in which he worked: comedy, romance and history. It was in combining
spectacle with historical narrative, however, that DeMille achieved his greatest

successes. These include *Joan the Woman* (1916), *The Ten Commandments* (1923), *The King of Kings* (1927), *The Sign of the Cross* (1932), *Cleopatra* (1934), *Samson and Delilah* (1949) and his biggest hit, a remake of *The Ten Commandments* (1956).

DeMille's personal agenda, and that of his production company, Lasky Players, was to augment film's connection with high culture by cultivating a middle-class audience and consolidating conservative social values. Spectacle played a crucial part in this agenda. As Sumiko Higashi has shown, in the minds of early twentieth-century audiences, spectacle was already associated with civic theatre pageants designed to inculcate patriotic values and responsible citizenship.[33] Thus, in his first historical film, *Joan the Woman*, a version of the life of Joan of Arc, DeMille's aim was lavish spectacle from production to distribution, in order to create a grand visual display that would unite the public in a time of war. A telegram from his lawyer and business associate Arthur Friend, for example, underlines the importance of spectacle even in the film's marketing: 'We...will make the exploitation of your first big picture the most lavish and impressed exploitation of anything offered to the theatres in this country.'[34] As Higashi points out, such sentiments were followed up by theatre lobby displays of 'suits of armour, historical costumes, colourful banners, and murals framed by drapery embroidered with fleur-de-lys'.[35] The ultimate intention was to present the film as patriotic propaganda. One advertisement announced that 'This picture...may become a great shaping force in this remarkable era. .... Patriotism and religious fervour...will sweep all Europe after the war. ... the motion picture will outdo the mightiest work ever accomplished by a free press.'[36]

The film, however, was a box-office failure, a result Higashi attributes to the film's proto-feminist tendencies.[37] With his next historical film, *The Ten Commandments*, DeMille did not repeat his mistake. He realised that a biblical narrative would work more effectively to forge morally conservative values, and knew too that such a narrative would also afford scope for spectacle. The two tendencies – moral and spectacular – were a heady combination. In a telegram sent during the making of the film, DeMille assured his business associate Adolph Zukor, 'it will be the biggest picture ever made, not only from the standpoint of spectacle but from the standpoint of humaness [*sic*], dramatic power, and the great good it will do'.[38] The moral resonance of a biblical narrative, particularly in a post-war society, is made clear in the opening title of the film:

Our modern world defined God as a 'religious complex' and laughed at the Ten Commandments as OLD-FASHIONED.

Then, through the laughter, came the shattering thunder of the world war.

And now a blood-drenched, bitter world – no longer laughing – cries for a way out.

There is but one way out. It existed before it was engraven upon Tablets of Stone. It will exist when stone has crumbled. The Ten Commandments are not rules to obey as a personal favor to God. They are the fundamental principles without which mankind cannot live together.

They are not laws – they are the LAW.

And, in case the intended relevance of the biblical narrative was lost on his audience, DeMille divided his narrative into two – the 'prologue' telling of Moses' delivery of his people and his prophetic reception of the Ten Commandments and the modern-day 'story' exemplifying the biblical teachings. The events of the modern story take up most of the film's running time, yet it is the 45-minute biblical prologue, starring Theodore Roberts as Moses and Estelle Taylor as Miriam, for which the film is best remembered. Although DeMille was not the first filmmaker to attempt a biblical narrative – early biblical films include *Moses and the Exodus from Egypt* (1907), *The Way of the Cross* (1909) and Griffith's *Judith of Bethulia* – he was the first to combine such large-scale spectacle with a major biblical story. The film employed technical experimentation, special effects and, of course, colossal sets. Thus the opening action takes place in a monumental Egyptian city, complete with massive statues flanking the city walls and a giant wheeled Sphinx on which the Pharaoh sits enthroned. The exodus from Egypt, using new colourising techniques, is comprised of a sensational chase scene in which the Egyptians' horse-drawn chariots plunge down steep dunes, and a dramatic parting of the Red Sea. In order to achieve such a spectacle, DeMille's set and location facilities assumed unheard-of proportions: a 'tent city' took up 24 square miles, housed 2,500 people and 3,000 animals, and possessed its own water, electrical and telecommunications supplies.[39] Such off-screen excesses were well publicised by DeMille in industry magazines and even the film's souvenir programme, for they were as important as onscreen extravagance in establishing the film's status as consumerist spectacle.

The powerful potential of the biblical epic may be seen in the film's reception. Though it was a resounding box-office success, critics disliked the modern story, a sentimental narrative about two brothers, one who obeys the Ten Commandments and the other who breaks them. It was, according to critics, the 'amazing and overpowering', 'wonderful spectacle' of the biblical sequence that deserved acclaim.[40] No small wonder, then, that DeMille went on to reproduce his success by focusing on the biblical element in subsequent films. The film-going public's appetite for historical and biblical narrative had already been demonstrated by the popular success enjoyed by Fred Niblo's *Ben-Hur* (1925). DeMille therefore rejected his screenwriter Jeannie MacPherson's suggestion that he insert a modern story in *The King of Kings*.[41] The result is a narrative of the life of Christ that proceeds as a series of rich tableaux reminiscent of biblical paintings, allowing for DeMille's customary spectacle in sets such as Pontius Pilate's grand palace. In insisting on a purely biblical narrative, as Elley puts it, 'DeMille advanced the historical epic film from adolescence to adulthood'.[42]

Though DeMille followed up his efforts in the 1930s with the Roman Christian and Egyptian stories of *The Sign of the Cross* and *Cleopatra*, the advent of synchronised sound fed an interest in psychological interior dramas as well as vibrant musicals, and shifted attention away from the epic's heavily visual element. It would take new technological advances in the 1950s – in 'Technicolor' and widescreen – to renew audience demand for the epic film.

Classic Hollywood epic

In 1944, DeMille re-released *The Sign of the Cross*. So popular did it prove that he followed it up with *Samson and Delilah* in 1949. But DeMille's most important decision was to remake *The Ten Commandments* into a 1956 feature lasting 220 minutes, in the latest colour and widescreen technology – 'Technicolor' and 'Vistavision'. Shot on location in Egypt at the cost of $13.5 million, it was, unsurprisingly, the most expensive film of its time. DeMille, in effect, expanded the biblical prologue of his original film to tell the life-story of Moses. Billed as the 'greatest motion picture event of all time', the film is defined by its spectacle, a trait that would be reiterated in subsequent biblical films of the period. In the absence of a modern story, the film's most obvious large-scale sequence – the exodus, followed by the reception of the Ten Commandments – becomes its centrepiece. Filmed in colour and with the benefit of relatively sophisticated technology, such scenes as the chariot chase, the parting of the Red Sea and the orgiastic worship of the Golden Calf at the foot of Mount Sinai were presented with even greater impressiveness, and won the film an Academy Award for Best Effects.

What is also important, however, is that, while the biblical story is expanded temporally and spatially, its narrative is distilled to a conflict between Moses and the Pharaoh Rameses, played by Charlton Heston and Yul Brynner respectively, particularly to Moses' struggle to free the Jews from their enslavement by Egypt. In this, too, the film sets a precedent for subsequent Hollywood epics, transforming the battle between good and evil into an heroic struggle against a cruel regime. As Babington and Evans remark, epic 'protagonists are old-style heroes, each embodying good over evil'.[43] One important corollary of this is that the epic film adheres to the Hollywood convention of hero-driven narrative, a convention that had seen the creation of the star system, which, tautologically, has become a factor in maintaining Hollywood's preoccupation with heroes. But what is also important is that the epic film particularises its hero's struggle as a fight against tyranny. Certainly, the heroicisation of Christianity is no stranger to the epic form, being a staple of the Renaissance romance epic, but, while these chivalric narratives portray moral conflict as a conquest over various temptations ultimately derived from the devil, the Hollywood epic film, from *The Ten Commandments* onwards, locates evil in political oppression. Thus, DeMille, who had narrated *Samson and Delilah* against the backdrop of a guerrilla struggle by the Jews against the Philistines, depicts in *The Ten Commandments* the Jews' liberation from Egyptian tyranny.

In translating Judaeo-Christian ideology as contemporary democracy, DeMille implicitly aligns the anti-Christian forces in his films with the threat of communism felt by many Americans during the Cold War. Indeed, he inserted a prologue to *The Ten Commandments*, in which, in a speech made directly to camera, he states:

> The theme of this picture is whether men ought to be ruled by God's law or whether they are to be ruled by the whims of a dictator like Rameses. Are men the property of the state or are they free souls under God? This same battle continues throughout the world today.

For DeMille, the heroic struggle undergirded by the Ten Commandments, once relevant to the cynical postwar world of the 1920s, was particularly apposite in the context of the Cold War. A quotation attributed to DeMille in his posthumously published autobiography of 1959 reiterates this:

> The Bible story was timeless. It was also timely. It is a story of slavery and liberation, two words that the world's experience since 1923 had saturated with more vivid meaning, with more real fear and more anxious hope. When Moses stood before Pharaoh, voicing the divine demand, 'Let my people go!', the same two forces faced that confront one another today in a world divided between tyranny and freedom.[44]

Both *Samson and Delilah* and *The Ten Commandments*, as Babington and Evans suggest, 'clearly articulate the allegory of America: Democracy; Russia: Slavery'.⁴⁵ What is more, slavery becomes 'shorthand', in DeMille's epic films and after, for 'the whole nexus of autocracy, atheism, state control and social programming seen as the communist alternative to American democracy'.⁴⁶ Christianity offers itself to a movie-going public in the 1950s as part of a uniquely American heritage.

The tendency to retell biblical narrative in Cold War terms is even more apparent in Roman Christian films, such as *The Robe* and *Ben Hur*. Based on a popular 1942 novel by Lloyd C. Douglas, a Congregational minister, *The Robe*, directed by Henry Koster, tells the story of a Roman soldier, Marcellus Gallio (played by Richard Burton), who oversees the crucifixion of Christ. Marcellus wins Christ's robe when he and his men gamble over it at the foot of the Cross. Tortured by remorse brought on by the robe's godly powers, he eventually converts to Christianity, and, with the help of the Apostle Paul, travels through the Roman Empire as a teacher of Christ. All this occurs as the Emperor Caligula, viewing the rise of Christianity as a threat, decides to persecute Christians. The climax of the film is Marcellus' return to Rome at the risk of losing his life as well as his love, Diana (Jean Simmons). In a majestic trial scene at Caligula's palace, Marcellus refuses to renounce his faith and is condemned to death. Diana, in a gesture of true love, joins him in embracing Christianity and asks to die with him.

The depictions of *The Robe* of imperial splendour in full Technicolor gave it the effect of luxury and lavishness, enhanced for audiences by the first ever use of widescreen. According to Wyke, such splendour was just as important as political resonance in establishing the film's popularity: 'in its production, distribution, and reception as much (if not more) attention was paid to its technical virtuosity as to its political parallels with the present'.⁴⁷ One contemporary review in *Time*, for example, raved about the 'spectacular movie murals of slave markets, imperial cities, grandiose palaces and panoramic landscapes that are neither distorted nor require the use of polarized glasses'.⁴⁸

As with DeMille's epics, *The Robe* also demonstrates a readiness to juxtapose Christianity against tyranny in power. Its opening scene is set in a slave market, voiced over by Burton as Marcellus, who reminds us that the Roman Empire is built on slavery, for 'The people of thirty lands send us tribute and their proudest sons to be our slaves. We have reached the point where there are more slaves in Rome than citizens'. Throughout the film, Roman imperialism is associated with enslavement and brutality; thus, Marcellus' slave, Demetrius, a Christian convert, taunts him: 'Masters of the world, you call yourselves. Thieves! Murderers!' and the ageing Emperor Tiberius describes Christianity as 'man's desire to be free'.

What this suggests, however, is a possible contradiction: the visual celebration of imperial majesty is set against the narrative's rejection of its politics. For this reason, Michael Wood comments that lavish historical films 'invite our sympathy for the oppressed, of course.... But then the movies, themselves, as costly studio productions, plainly take the other side.'[49] Yet, the apparent paradox is easily resolved if we consider the larger ideological picture, that of the bourgeois celebration of both economic stability and freedom discernible in epic film's visual excesses from the outset.

In other words, the political motivation behind epic spectacle is consonant with an investment in American bourgeoisie morality. The combination of special effects extravagance and moralistic story-telling is only ostensibly self-contradictory. The publicity machines that surround these films are unselfconscious about this apparent inconsistency. The tagline for *The Robe*, for example, trumpets it as 'The Greatest Story of Love, Faith, and Overwhelming Spectacle'. The problem of reconciling visual excess with moral conservatism is no longer a problem when one considers that, in a staunchly capitalist society, marketability can be construed as accessibility, and accessibility, where a moral message is concerned, as proselytisation. Epic films, therefore, 'communicate as paradigms of a highly secularised society's dramatising of its religious foundations through mechanisms on which secular values have had a profound impact'.[50]

Another corollary of the drive to moralise within a very specific context of commodification and saleability is the epic film's use of a tried-and-tested film convention – romance. Though the biblical epics are impeded in their narrative choices by their scriptural sources, the Roman Christian epics experience no such problems. Romantic interests are a consistent feature of such films, and indeed become a central part of the hero's assumption of a Christian moral system. In *The Robe*, Diana, though initially suspicious of her lover's new faith, comes to support him in this and indeed to offer him the inner strength to martyr himself to it. Thus, a pattern in which 'the pure Christian (or proto-Christian) maiden who becomes the male protagonist's redeemer' emerges in Hollywood epic.[51] This pattern is very much in keeping, of course, with audience expectations of Hollywood film in general.

The primary concern underlying Hollywood epic film, it must therefore be remembered, is the profit motive. Such a motive acquired new urgency in the 1950s, when television emerged as a competitor for audience attention. The widescreen spectacle of the Hollywood epic betrays studio anxieties about the threat of television. Spectacle represents the most obvious weapon in Hollywood's artillery, as this *Time* review of *The Robe* makes clear: 'Obviously, Hollywood has finally found something louder, more colourful and breathtakingly bigger than anything likely to be seen on a home TV screen for years to come.'[52] Thus, the proliferation of such films suggests a simplistic desire to replicate success and subsequently to increase profits. This desire fuels the generic process, as studios and filmmakers seek to emulate success by imitating conventions and hence to produce bigger and better epics. The simplicity with which this motive operates is evident in the follow-up to *The Robe*, a sequel called *Demetrius and the Gladiators* (1954), filmed almost simultaneously as its predecessor and clearly designed to 'cash in' on its appeal.

The desire to replicate a successful formula occurs at its most spectacular in *Ben-Hur*. Its director, William Wyler, would state later that he agreed to direct the film because he 'wanted to make a Cecil B. DeMille picture'.[53] If DeMille's biblical epics and such Christian Roman narratives as *The Robe* established a successful combination of visual spectacle underpinned by biblical text and Cold War subtext, *Ben-Hur* perfected it. Subtitled 'A Tale of the Christ', and set during Christ's lifetime, *Ben-Hur* tells the story of a Jewish prince, Judah Ben-Hur (Charlton Heston), betrayed by his childhood friend, Messala (Stephen Boyd), a high-ranking Roman and representative of the governor in Jerusalem. Judah is wrongfully condemned by Messala when he refuses to turn informant against the Jews, and endures slavery in the galleys of Roman battleships before rising to a position of influence in Rome. The film's climax is its famous chariot race, in which Judah and Messala take part, Judah winning and Messala losing his life.

The conflict between the two is troped from the outset as a conflict between an oppressed society and its imperial coloniser. The men's first meeting since childhood, for example, demonstrates Judah's concern for his people and Messala's Roman bigotry. The reunion between friends (some have suggested lovers) quickly turns into a heated exchange. When Judah reminds Messala, 'I'm a Jew!' Messala responds, 'You're a Roman! What do you have in common with the rabble that makes trouble here?' To this Judah answers, 'Rabble? They're my people – I'm one of them!' Judah's strong Jewish faith is what sustains him through his three years of slavery in the galleys. Moreover, his victory over Messala in the arena is explicitly a victory for the Jews; he is crowned by Pontius Pilate not just as the winner but, in Pilate's words, the 'people's true god'.

But Judah's victory is not solely his or that of the Jews: it is a Christian triumph over tyranny. Judah is not his people's true god, for that epithet rightly belongs to another – Christ. It is important that Judah's lifetime occurs during Christ's; indeed, the parallel between the two is made explicit when Judah is almost mistaken for Christ by Balthasar, one of the three wise men, who has come back to look for the Messiah. Significantly, Judah's fight against Roman tyranny is also a Christian struggle against brutality in general. The film's prologue informs us that:

> In the year of our Lord, Judea, for nearly a century, had lain under the mastery of Rome. ... Even while they obeyed the will of Caesar, the people clung proudly to their ancient heritage, always remembering the promise of their prophets that one day would be born among them a redeemer to bring them salvation and perfect freedom.

Most importantly, Judah has fateful encounters with Christ throughout his life and finally is converted to Christ's teachings. Crucially, he must cross the line between simple vindictiveness, aligned with Roman tyranny, and forgiveness, presented as the basis of Christianity. Esther, the one-time slave whom Judah loves, conveys advice she has heard directly from Christ – 'Love your enemy. Do good to those who despitefully use you' – before warning him, 'Hatred is turning you to stone. It's as though you had become Messala. I've lost you, Judah.' Thus, Judah's true victory over Rome is not his defeat of Messala but his forgiveness of him. If the first half of the film is concerned with the former, the second half and dénouement must complete Judah's Christianised quest by dealing with the latter. Although the film underplays the conversion scene as it had been presented in both the 1925 version and Wallace's novel, its narrative is still driven purposively by Judah's assumption of a new faith in exchange for revenge, and looks forward, at the conclusion, to Christianity supplanting Roman imperialism, troped as a brutal programme of power and force giving way to an ideology of forgiveness and hope.

   None the less, it is the visual excess of *Ben-Hur* that proved a crucial element in the film's success. After all, the film's narrative structure, as Elley points out, is 'little more than a refinement' of its 1925 predecessor.[54] The 1925 film had transformed the original novel by Lew Wallace, as well as the long-running theatrical production it inspired, into an effective series of tightly focused dramatic actions, which Wyler's version reproduces to a great extent. Spectacle too had been an important part of this early film. Scenes such as the naval battle and the chariot race – on which Wyler had worked as an assistant director – had been shot on a massive scale and to magnificent effect. The entire film had cost $4 million to make. Yet, Wyler's version, 24 years later, possessed 'all the added resources of 70mm colour photography [and] stereo sound'.[55] The set in Rome was DeMillesque in proportions – 40,000 cubic feet of timber, 1 million pounds of plaster and 215 miles of metal tubing were used to build it. The battle at sea was shot on a manmade lake using substantially sized miniatures.[56] The chariot race that is now remembered as the film's centrepiece surpassed previous film attempts at visual spectacle in terms of cost, technical resources and skill, although, shot by shot, it adheres closely to the chariot sequence in the 1925 version. The scene's stunts took a year's preparation, which included training the actors to ride the chariots themselves. However, the more thrilling spills – such as the jump by Judah's chariot and horses over a crashed chariot – had to be carefully planned and carried out by stuntmen. Wyler utilised several 65 mm cameras, each a costly and technologically innovative piece of equipment at the time, to achieve the widest shots possible. The set for the Circus Maximus, in which the race takes place, was built on the outskirts of Rome and contained thousands of extras; the suggestion of scale and multitude was enhanced by matte paintings applied after filming. None the less, the eventual production cost, estimated at $15 million, was more than recouped by receipts of some $80 million.[57] The film also won a record eleven Academy Awards, and has been credited with rescuing its studio, Metro-Goldwyn-Mayer, from the brink of bankruptcy.

The epic film genre may be considered to have gained its zenith at the end of the 1950s, particularly if we consider one other major epic film, *Spartacus*. Once more a moralising narrative is set against a backdrop of visual excess – elaborate sets, a long and stately running time, and a climactic battle scene memorable largely for its long shot of carefully chore-ographed troop formations which required the direction of thousands of extras against a vast landscape.

However, what is of primary interest is the way in which the narrative, like earlier epic film, was adapted and pressed into the service of a pro-American Cold War ideology. As Wyke shows, the narrative originally possessed a subversive Marxist thread. The film is based not only on the novel by Giovagnelli but on a more recent book by Howard Fast. Fast had been blacklisted and imprisoned in the McCarthy era, in which hundreds of Americans were persecuted and arrested for supposed communist tendencies and activities. He had published his novel in protest against such political oppression, as he explained in film publicity in 1960:

I wrote this novel because I considered it an important story for the times in which we live. Not in the mechanical sense of historical parallels, but because there is hope and strength to be taken from such a story about the age-old fight for freedom – and because Spartacus lived not for one time of man, but for all times of man.[58]

Fast's novel tells of Spartacus, a third-generation slave who, forced to become a gladiator, escapes and leads an army of slaves against Rome; although their revolt is unsuccessful, their example is tragically inspiring. The novel questions various modes of political oppression, throwing its support behind both women's rights by playing up the role of the slave-women in the gladiators' escape, and civil rights, by including a black character, Draba, and framing the discourse of slavery within a racial context.[59]

The film, it would seem, continued the novel's anti-government agenda and distanced itself from the conservative values of the Hollywood epic. Stanley Kubrick, the director, identified his influences as Soviet film directors rather than DeMille and Wyler, and the film was marketed as a 'thinking man's epic'.[60] Certainly, as Wyke points out, the film 'partially preserves or adapts for screen the defense of American political activism and the investigation of labor which had been encoded in Fast's novel'.[61] Its portrayal of the slaves' revolt contains traces of communist ideals of worker solidarity. Slaves stand up for each other, as when Draba (Woody Strode) refuses to kill Spartacus (Kirk Douglas) when the two are commanded to fight to the death. Most strikingly, after the decisive battle, the defeated army is threatened with death unless Spartacus gives himself up. Spartacus valiantly does so, rising and declaring, 'I am Spartacus'; yet, his men deny him this, one after another naming himself as Spartacus and confounding the Romans' attempt to identify the slave leader. The issues of race and gender equality, too, are foregrounded, in the retention of the character of Draba and in the slave army's commitment to including women in its camp.

As if to confirm its potential for protest and subversion, Kirk Douglas as executive producer hired Dalton Trumbo, a blacklisted scriptwriter, to adapt the novel for the screen. However, as Carl Hoffman suggests, Trumbo and Douglas played a central role in inscribing the film within a conservative ideology: 'Douglas and his team ... revised Fast's idealized proletarian gladiator into a populist hero whose character and conflicts are designed to speak to the mass American audience of the early 1960s.'[62] Trumbo's revisions substantially diluted Fast's Marxist connotations, rewriting references to 'revolution' and speeches to 'comrades'.[63] As a result, the solidarity of the slaves and the tyranny of Rome are easily read in the terms set by earlier epics. The slaves as a peace-loving people besieged by a mean militaristic machine may be compared to American defiance in the face of the threat of war from the communist world. Thus, the community spirit of the slave camp, which, in Wyke's words, appears as a 'utopian, proto-Communist society peopled by whole families who share their work and meager possessions' also, according to Hoffman, conveys the message that 'these happy, self-sufficient people could create independent lives for themselves if only the power-obsessed Romans would leave them alone'.[64] There are generic markers that further align *Spartacus* with its morally conventional predecessors. For one thing, *Spartacus* adheres to the 'aural paradigm set by Cecil B. DeMille's historical epics' and found too in *Ben-Hur*, whereby heroes are played by Americans and villains speak in upper-class English accents. Although, as some of the film's commentators have pointed out, the casting of the English Jean Simmons as Varinia, Spartacus' love interest, complicates this, the film adheres largely to this 'earlier analogical device', not just with Kirk Douglas playing Spartacus, but with Tony Curtis playing the young slave-singer Antoninus, and Lawrence Olivier the Roman general Crassus. All this aligns Rome with a more recent imperial force that is particularly relevant to American history – the British Empire.[65] Most importantly, the film explicitly describes Roman tyranny as anti-Christian. In a gesture that repeats the conventional openings of epics such as *Samson and Delilah*, *The Ten Commandments* and *The Robe*, the film begins with a solemnly intoned prologue. It informs the audience that the action of *Spartacus* takes place three centuries before the coming of Christ, who was 'destined to overthrow the pagan tyranny of Rome and bring about a new society'. That Spartacus himself might be aligned with Christ is suggested by the film's closing scene, which sees him crucified on a Roman road. Unsurprisingly, then, the film, despite its dubious provenance, was easily appropriated by right-wing politics. One critic remarked:

> Although it deals with a revolt by slaves against the Roman Empire, the desire for freedom from oppression that motivates Spartacus has its modern counterpart today in areas of the world that struggle under Communist tyranny, and it stands as a sharp reminder for all mankind that there can be no truly peaceful sleep whilst would-be conquering legions stand poised to suppress.[66]

It also recouped for Universal Studios its $12 million production costs, proving to be both a box-office hit and a critical success.[67]

For all its right-wing appropriation, however, *Spartacus* did herald an age in which conservative ideology was loosening its grip on Hollywood epics, and Cold War anxieties were increasingly set aside. Released in 1966, John Huston's *The Bible* suggests a turn away from overtly political messages to a simple re-rendering of scripture. The film takes its viewers through a series of vignettes, beginning with Genesis and including the stories of Noah and of Abraham. Though not lacking in impressive settings and effects, such as a stunning Tower of Babel and a convincing Ark and flood, the film does not convey the moralistic fervour of its generic predecessors. As Elley states, 'The filmmakers placed no orthodox religious interpretation on the material; Huston treated it as the "emergence out of myth and legend"'.[68] At two and a half hours, it is also shorter than the major epics of the previous decade, and lacks the drive towards a visually spectacular climax that characterises the films that had come to dominate the epic genre, *The Ten Commandments*, *Ben-Hur* and *Spartacus*.

The Bible demonstrates a significant trend in Hollywood movie-making: that is, the increasing rejection of historical spectacle in film. Two last-ditch attempts at returning to the heyday of Hollywood epic – *Cleopatra* (1963) and *The Fall of the Roman Empire* (1964) – proved to be financially disastrous, their bloated production costs meeting with apathy at the box-office. The genre suffered, for one thing, from its own success, having been reproduced so efficiently that it was now an identifiable commodity and in danger of appearing formulaic. This was particularly so as audience demographics shifted from families and adults to an increasingly younger audience. Thus, the epic was easily seen as old-fashioned by a new generation of filmgoers, mostly teenagers who favoured shorter, modern narratives.

Epic in the age of the blockbuster

The release of George Lucas's *Star Wars* (1977) heralded the age of the blockbuster. In its powerful mix of special effects spectacle, pervasive publicity and merchandising spin-offs, it recalls the epic film. As a staple of Hollywood cinema since the late 1970s, however, it superseded the epic of the 1950s and 1960s as motion picture 'event'. In many ways, these films represent a distinct generic development; yet, it seems worthwhile to consider briefly one trend in the Hollywood blockbuster on account of its generic similarities to the earlier epic. This is the science fiction blockbuster, which employs spectacle, now thoroughly defined as 'special effects', to depict fantasy worlds, and to give Hollywood epic heroics a mythical dimension. Thus, the first *Star Wars* trilogy (including *The Empire Strikes Back* [1980] and *The Return of the Jedi* [1983]) retains the Hollywood epic's central heroic battle between good and evil, but relocates it to a futuristic world (although the prologue insists that the action takes place 'long, long ago, in a galaxy far, far away'). Indeed, as Martin Winkler has suggested,

Lucas's depiction of the Empire echoes earlier film representations of the Roman Empire in *The Fall of the Roman Empire*.[69] These early *Star Wars* films, moreover, hark back to classical epic in their creation of an alternative universe and a presiding mythology, in which supernatural machinery is represented by 'the Force' and its evil counterpart, the Empire. A comparable text, albeit not as far-reaching in its cultural influence, is the *Superman* trilogy (1978, 1980, 1983), based on the comic series. Although in these the focus seems to be on the struggles between the eponymous hero and various 'bad guys', these struggles are always played out as a conflict between universal good and universal evil. Superman's alien origins establish him as a mythical saviour of humankind, who fights evil in both terrestrial and extra-terrestrial guides. Thanks to special effects, all Superman's battles are fought in marvellous fashion, and include not just running 'faster than a speeding bullet' and leaping 'tall buildings in a single bound', but, ludicrously, the ability to turn back time by rotating the earth backwards. In the 1990s, Hollywood's capacity for fantasy spectacle has increased exponentially with the introduction of computer-generated images (CGI). *The Lord of the Rings* trilogy (2001, 2002, 2003), directed by Peter Jackson, like *Star Wars*, depicts moral warfare in an otherworld, the mythical possibilities set up by J. R. R. Tolkien's novels now spectacularly enhanced. The second *Star Wars* trilogy (*The Phantom Menace* [1999], *The Attack of the Clones* [2002], *The Revenge of the Sith* [2005]) has also clearly demonstrated the considerable impact of updated technology on the science-fiction blockbuster. Along with such CGI disaster films as *Independence Day* (1996) and *The Day After Tomorrow* (2004), a distinct genre has developed, marked by heroic action in defence of good played out in an imaginary world depicted on an astonishing scale.

The special effects science-fiction blockbuster is significant because it demonstrates not just the spectacle but the moral heroism that marked classic Hollywood epic. Indeed, as Geoff King astutely points out, these films often require their viewers to tread a thin line between feeling for the gritty moral dilemmas they portray and looking on in awe at spectacular effects. King suggests that blockbusters such as *Independence Day* and *Star Wars* ultimately yoke their large-scale spectacles to human-sized action.[70] As we have seen with classic Hollywood epic, a similar tension between marvelling at the lavish Romanised settings and appreciating the heroism of oppressed Christianity may occur. Yet, the stakes set by spectacle can be very high. Such is the case with *Titanic* (1997), supposedly the most expensive film ever made, at a reported $200 million. Although, as King's analysis suggests, the narrative drive is as important to the film's appeal as its special effects, the publicity surrounding the film both during and after production consistently paid more attention to the latter.[71] As a milestone in the story of epic film, *Titanic* demonstrates the triumph of spectacle over heroism. What confuses the story even more, however, is that *Titanic* has consistently been labelled epic, apparently on the strength not just of its running time (three hours) but its excesses in both budget and special effects. Thanks in large part to *Titanic*, then, it is mere extravagance – in both the spectacular and financial senses of the word – that became a byword for epic in the 1990s.

None the less, *Titanic* was also an important generic landmark because it demonstrated the possibilities of computer-generated effects not for establishing a world of pure fantasy but for recreating an historical event on an incredible scale. Though itself ambiguous in its treatment of the epic formula, it enabled the re-emergence of the classic Hollywood epic as a genre. In 1998, the head of the Dreamworks studio, Walter Parkes, 'noted a trend in the box-office success of recent "classic" films like James Cameron's *Titanic* and thought it was time for a rebirth of the toga film'.[72] Dreamworks eventually persuaded Ridley Scott to direct what would become *Gladiator* (2000). Scott was no stranger to science fiction spectacle, having directed *Alien* (1979) and *Blade Runner* (1982), but was apparently initially reluctant to make a Roman epic.[73] In the end, however, he agreed, as he put it, to 'revisit the genre'.[74]

Unlike its predecessors, *Gladiator* is based on an original screenplay. It tells the fictional story of a powerful Roman general, Maximus Decimus Meridias, favourite of the Emperor Marcus Aurelius. On the emperor's death, his jealous and corrupt son and successor Commodus kills Maximus' family and orders his death. Though he escapes his executors, Maximus is captured and sold into slavery as a gladiator, but his success in the arena means that he eventually performs in Rome and comes to the young emperor's attention. In the film's climax – a gladiatorial recreation of the Battle of Carthage at the Colosseum – Maximus kills the emperor, but is himself slain in the attempt. Nevertheless, by the end of the film, Maximus has fulfilled Marcus Aurelius' last wish, by having helped in a plot to return power to the Roman senate and establish Rome as a republic.

In both narrative and visual display, the film reiterates the conventions established by mid-century epic film. Its spectacles include an opening battle-scene and an impressive parade by Commodus through Rome, and the climactic fight in a magnificently depicted Colosseum. Indeed, in a neat metaphor for *Gladiator*'s updating of the kind of spectacle to be found in *Ben-Hur*, the Circus Maximus of the earlier film and the Colosseum of the later one were built in very much the same way, with the bottom tiers constructed at full scale and the top added at the post-production stage;

only what had once been achieved by matte painting could now be done with computers.[75] Of course, it is not just in its splendid depictions of Roman architecture, pageantry and battle that *Gladiator* establishes itself as Hollywood epic. Its plot trajectory of a powerful man fighting his way back from gladiatorial slavery clearly echoes both *Ben-Hur* and *Spartacus*, and its narrative's concerns with the corruption wrought by the Emperor Commodus recalls *The Fall of the Roman Empire*, whose story, notes Martin Winkler, 'it lifts wholesale, if with some variations'.[76] More generally, the film replays the genre's overall concern with heroism in the face of oppression.

Yet, the film lacks the Cold War context that made earlier epic film so politically reverberant. Certainly, as a hero for an increasingly secular society, Maximus' heroism could not contain the religious overtones of that of Judah Ben-Hur or even of Spartacus. Indeed, he was intended, according to David Franzoni, the film's screenwriter, to be 'a character who is deeply moral, but who's not traditionally religious'.[77] However, as Monica Cyrino suggests, the immense popular and critical acclaim that met the film did none the less stem from its appropriateness to the times.[78] What defines Maximus as a hero is, first, his status as a fighter against the odds, in the face of political machination and corruption, a heroic archetype that Winkler sees re-emerging in late twentieth-century film.[79] Cyrino sees this brand of heroism as apposite for an audience disenchanted with and suspicious of America's worldwide political dominance:

> as the first Roman epic made after the end of the Cold War, *Gladiator* arrived in an altogether different social and political world. . . . Its prologue, set against a sepia-toned background and with haunting female vocals as its only accompaniment, informs us rather portentously that Rome is at 'the height of its power'. The American spectators in the year 2000, supremely confident and unencumbered by doubts about their country's geo-political dominance, experience not an indecisive tug or a double-sided connection with ancient Rome but rather a shock of recognition. The Romans depicted in *Gladiator* undeniably stand in for us; the film is 'a meditation on the perplexity of the world's sole surviving superpower'.[80]

Although Cyrino describes the American perspective, concerns about America's unchecked economic and political influence are, of course, internationally relevant. Second, Maximus is, quite literally, down to earth; he is a farmer-turned-general, who wants nothing more than to return to his farm and his family. When offered any reward by Marcus Aurelius after his success in battle, he answers simply, 'Let me go home'. Before every battle, even those fought as a gladiator, he picks up a handful of sand with which to dust his hands. The hero who struggles against a morally decayed imperial power must be a steady, rock-like individual, whose priorities are personal, not political. He distances himself from Roman values: when he scrapes off his imperial tattoo, he does so in a gesture not just of self-preservation but of disillusionment. The overall effect is of a juxtaposition between corrupt politics and 'back-to-basics' morality. Franzoni has been quoted as remarking, 'We're stewing in self-indulgent mediocrity, and here's a noble figure who's almost swallowed up by the Roman equivalent, and he endures.'[81] The central Hollywood epic conflict of the 1950s and 1960s, then, is rewritten by *Gladiator* thus:

> Earlier films traditionally made Rome the imperialistic oppressor of implausibly virtuous and racially harmonious groups, the most common narrative formula being the subjugation of Christians, Hebrews, or slaves. ... But *Gladiator* presents an imaginative new development by casting the Roman Empire as the oppressor of its true self, the Republic.[82]

In doing so, evil is relocated and remodelled, inwardly and psychologically, so that it is no longer manifest in brute force but in decadence.

Strikingly, the tension between indulging in Rome's visual pomp on the one hand and sympathising with its victims on the other is also revisioned in *Gladiator*. It would seem that turning an awestruck gaze on Rome's excesses and debauches would be appropriate to a film that seeks to undermine them. Yet, the film rejects such a celebration; perhaps precisely because such extravagance is ultimately undermined it cannot be displayed too ostentatiously in the first place. Instead, Rome is depicted in sombre shadows and its buildings appear cold and blue. Though the expansive landscapes and architectural wonders such as the Colosseum are still available as awe-inspiring spectacles, much of the audience's fascination, as Arthur Pomeroy suggests, is reserved for the ultra-violence of the combat scenes.[83] Quick editing, tense music and crystal-clear aural effects (enhancing, for example, the sound of steel slicing into flesh and blood) combine to produce realistic depictions of mutilation. A somewhat different sort of hypocritical scopophilia emerges, then – one that curiously inverts that of 1950s epic film. Instead of guiltily gazing at Roman luxuriance yet shaking one's head at its brutality, the spectator of *Gladiator* enjoys the thrill of combat while denouncing Roman debauchery.

There is no denying, then, that *Gladiator* successfully updates the Hollywood epic, drawing on contemporary political concerns and catering to modern audience expectations. It was widely and critically proclaimed as a 'reinvention of the genre'.[84] In a review subtitled, 'Ridley Scott's exhilarating and impressive *Gladiator* brings the epic back to life', one critic declared, 'the movie is at once gloomy and exciting, oppressive and exhilarating.... . Its Rome is as grand as that of past movies, but a harder, harsher place, and the succession of battles in the arena are electrifyingly staged, imaginatively varied and increasingly ferocious.'[85] It takes more than one text, however, to revive a genre. More recently, *Gladiator* has been credited with inspiring a new wave of epic films, from *Troy* (2004) to two films on Alexander the Great – Oliver Stone's *Alexander* (2005) and Baz Luhrmann's forthcoming biopic.[86]

Coda: epic film versus epic literature

The recent release of Wolfgang Petersen's *Troy* (2004) would seem to have consolidated the epic film as a contemporary genre at the start of the twenty-first century. Identifying itself as a film adaptation of the *Iliad*, the film also allows a comparison of epic film and epic literature.

The film's debt to Hollywood epic film is obvious enough. Its concern with ancient Greek rather than Roman history is a small divergence from the standard Hollywood epic; after all, Greek settings were not unknown to such Hollywood epics as *Alexander the Great* (1956). Its use of Hollywood epic conventions in continuation of *Gladiator* is self-evident, moreover, in its computer-generated spectacles, for example, the depiction of the Greek fleet at sea, a series of shots seen from above which increasingly widen back to reveal thousands upon thousands of ships at sail. The epic hero's struggle is now locatable in a tradition particularly crystrallised by Hollywood epic heroes. When Cyrino suggests that *Gladiator*'s disillusioned Maximus is part of a 'whole history of insulted heroes from Achilles in Homer's *Iliad* to Mad Max in George Miller's apocalyptic film trilogy', she reminds us that the film hero who rises up against oppression is just as recognisable to modern audiences as Homer's tragic young warrior, if not more so. Brad Pitt's Achilles, then, owes as much to Hollywood heroic conventions as to the Homeric heroic code. Indeed, Pitt as Achilles could resonate with an audience attuned to the Hollywood star system as a throwback to the actor's first notable onscreen appearance as a James Dean-like cowboy in Ridley Scott's *Thelma and Louise* (1991).

So much does the film adhere to Hollywood codes over Homeric ones that it modifies the *Iliad* in accordance with these. Thus, the film provides Achilles with a romantic love interest, an inescapable marker of earlier epic films and, therefore, Briseis becomes much more than a simple piece of chattel, or *geras*, and is fought over not for pride but for love. Furthermore, the Hollywood epic's ambivalence towards homoeroticism – seen, for example, in Wyler's and Heston's denial of a homosexual subtext in *Ben-Hur* and the cutting of a scene depicting Crassus' attempted seduction of Antoninus from *Spartacus* – emerges here in the film's treatment of the relationship between Achilles and Patroclus.[87] With the two depicted in *Troy* as kinsmen, the men's love for each other is rendered safely readable as cousinly rather than erotic.

This ambitious conjunction of traditional epic with epic film, however, has impressed neither scholars nor critics. According to Peter Green, '*Troy* revamps Homer's narrative in *simpliste*, and flatly modern, moral terms'.[88] Reviews of the film were mixed, and particularly disapproving of what was construed as a confusing of the two traditions. Thus, for example, one review has noted that 'This version of the Trojan war tries – in the way of the stolid Fifties Hollywood epics from which it's descended – to provide something for everyone', while another announced in its headline, 'Well, the horse is great... and Brad looks pretty, but the action-packed epic, *Troy*, does not do justice to the ultimate war story'. This critic goes on to complain of 'the dubious meddling with established legend for dramatic effect'.[89] There has emerged, it would seem, a cultural cringe about forcing the links between epic film and epic poetry.

Notwithstanding the plethora of complaints over its inaccuracies, however, *Troy* valuably demonstrates the ways in which the epic film differs from the epic poem. Rather than quibbling over its points of divergence from the text, then, perhaps it is worth appreciating it for revealing the gulf between the inaugurating text of the epic tradition and one of its latest manifestations, for it simply reminds us of how rich and varied the history of the epic has been.

Notes

Introduction

1. A twenty-first-century example comes from the trial of the man accused of murdering British journalist Jill Dando. His lawyer described the case as an 'epic occasion', similar to other 'epic occasions' such as the death of the Princess of Wales and the bombing of Kosovo; Jason Bennetto, 'Dando jurors urged to put sympathies aside', *The Independent* (22 June 2001).
2. Gérard Genette, *The Architext: An Introduction*, 1979, trans. Jane E. Lewin (Berkeley: University of California Press, 1992).
3. Genette, 1–58. See also Daniel Javitch, 'The Emergence of Poetic Genre Theory in the Sixteenth Century', *Modern Language Quarterly* 59 (1998): 139–69.
4. Jean-Marie Schaeffer, 'Literary Genres and Textual Genericity', *The Future of Literary Theory*, ed. Ralph Cohen (New York: Routledge, 1989) 168–72.
5. Schaeffer, 172. See also Genette's discussion of how the labels epic, lyric and drama came to be seen by Romantics such as Goethe as 'natural forms' in a generic sense rather than a modal one; that is, as fixed forms determined by a range of criteria including theme and milieu rather than by simple mode of delivery, Genette, 60–7.
6. Jacques Derrida, 'The Law of Genre', *Glyph* 7 (1980): 203.
7. Derrida, 213.
8. David Duff, Introduction, *Modern Genre Theory*, ed. David Duff (Harlow: Longman, 2000) 11.
9. Tzvetan Todorov, *Genres in Discourse*, trans. Catherine Porter (Cambridge: Cambridge University Press, 1990) esp. 17–18.
10. E. D. Hirsch, Jr., *Validity in Interpretation* (New Haven, CT: Yale University Press, 1967) 71–89.
11. See Hegel's lectures on poetry in G. W. F. Hegel, *Aesthetics: Lectures on Fine Art*, 1835, trans. T. M. Knox (Oxford: Clarendon Press, 1975) vol. 2, 959–1237, in which Hegel's organicist approach is evident throughout. His discussion of epic poetry, for example, refers repeatedly to the existence of the 'epic proper' and the 'genuine epic', and his survey of the history of the epic suggests that the epic form attained perfection with the Greeks and has since developed into the romance, 1040–110.
12. Northrop Frye, *Anatomy of Criticism: Four Essays* (Princeton, NJ: Princeton University Press, 1957).
13. Alastair Fowler, 'The Life and Death of Literary Forms', *New Directions in Literary History*, ed. Ralph Cohen (Baltimore, MD: Johns Hopkins University Press, 1974) 77–94; see also Fowler, *Kinds of Literature: An Introduction to the Theory of Genres and Modes* (Oxford: Clarendon Press, 1982) 170–83.
14. Hans Robert Jauss, *Toward an Aesthetic of Reception*, trans. Timothy Bahti (Brighton: Harvester, 1982) 93.
15. Ralph Cohen, 'History and Genre', *New Literary History* 17 (1986): 210.

16. Derrida, 204.
17. Hirsch, 70–71 and Jauss, 80. Though he does not invoke Wittgenstein, Jauss does state that 'literary genres are to be understood not as *genera* (classes) in the logical senses, but rather as *groups* or *historical families*' (original emphasis).
18. Schaeffer, 175.
19. For Jauss, a genre is shaped by 'the interaction between author and society, the audience's expectations and the literary event', and, therefore, to 'inquire into such entanglements is indispensable if one is to be serious about the historicisation of genre poetics and the temporalisation of the concept of form' (90).
20. C. M. Bowra, *Heroic Poetry* (London: Macmillan, 1952) and E. M. W. Tillyard, *The English Epic and Its Background* (London: Chatto and Windus, 1954).
21. Tillyard, 530.
22. Georg Lukács, *The Theory of the Novel: A Historico-Philosophical Essay on the Forms of Great Epic Literature*, trans. Anna Bostock (1920; London: Merlin Press, 1978) and Mikhail Bakhtin, 'Epic and Novel', *The Dialogic Imagination: Four Essays*, ed. Michael Holquist, trans. Caryl Emerson and Michael Holquist (Austin: University of Texas Press, 1981).
23. Thomas M. Greene, *The Descent from Heaven: A Study in Epic Continuity* (New Haven, CT: Yale University Press, 1963) and Thomas Vogler, *Preludes to Vision: The Epic Venture in Blake, Wordsworth, Keats and Hart Crane* (Berkeley: University of California Press, 1971).
24. David Quint, *Epic and Empire: Politics and Generic Form from Virgil to Milton* (Princeton, NJ: Princeton University Press, 1993) and Colin Burrow, *Epic Romance: Homer to Milton* (Oxford: Clarendon Press, 1993).
25. Susanne Lindgren Wofford, *The Choice of Achilles: The Ideology of Figure in the Epic* (Stanford, CA: Stanford University Press, 1992) and D. C. Feeney, *Poets and Critics of the Classical Tradition* (New York: Oxford University Press, 1993); see also Feeney, 'Epic Hero and Epic Fable', *Comparative Literature* 38 (1986): 137–58.
26. John Kevin Newman, *The Classical Epic Tradition* (Madison: University of Wisconsin Press, 1986) and Paul Merchant, *The Epic* (London: Methuen, 1971).
27. This is the inherent flaw in all generic analyses that Adena Rosmarin so forcefully identifies in *The Power of Genre* (Minneapolis: University of Minnesota Press, 1985) 35.

Chapter 1

1. Walter J. Ong, *Orality and Literacy* (London: Methuen, 1982) 70.
2. For more on the textual history of *Gilgamesh*, see Benjamin Caleb Ray, 'The Gilgamesh Epic: Myth and Meaning', *Myth and Method*, ed. Laurie L. Patton and Wendy Doniger (Charlottesville: University Press of Virginia, 1996) 304–6 and Andrew George, Introduction, *The Epic of Gilgamesh*, ed. George (London: Penguin, 1999) xiii–lii.
3. George, xxviii and Ray, 306.
4. Johannes Haubold, 'Greek Epic: A Near Eastern Genre?', *Proceedings of the Cambridge Philological Society* 48 (2002): 8.
5. As opposed to earlier readings of *Gilgamesh* as the result of a single poetic vision, particularly of conscious innovations by Babylonian, or Akkadian, poets on

Sumerian material, see Charles G. Zug, 'From Sumer to Babylon: The Evolution of the *Gilgamesh* Epic', *Genre* 5 (1972): 217–34.

6. *The Epic of Gilgamesh*, ed. George; references are to tablet and line numbers. Italics indicate words that have been difficult to decipher with certainty, square brackets indicate missing words that have been restored with certainty from context, while italics in square brackets indicate missing words that are simply conjectural.

7. Ray, 306.

8. Donald H. Mills, *The Hero and the Sea: Patterns of Chaos in Ancient Myth* (Wauconda, IL: Bolchazy-Carducci, 2003) 46.

9. Mills, 46.

10. Ray, 307.

11. Ray, 320.

12. Haubold, 7.

13. Sarah Morris, 'Homer and the Near East', *A New Companion to Homer*, ed. Ian Morris and Barry Powell (Leiden: Brill, 1997) 606–7; Charles Rowan Beye, *The Iliad, the* Odyssey, *and the Epic Tradition* (London: Macmillan, 1968) 16.

14. Beye, 16–17. The spelling convention adopted in this chapter is that used by Richmond Lattimore, as all citations to Homer are from Lattimore's translations, *The Odyssey of Homer*, trans. Richmond Lattimore (New York: Harper Collins, 1965) and *The Iliad of Homer*, trans. Richmond Lattimore (Chicago: University of Chicago Press, 1951). References are to book and line numbers.

15. Haubold, 3.

16. Morris, 601.

17. J. B. Hainsworth, *The Idea of Epic* (Berkeley: University of California Press, 1991) 11–12.

18. Andrew Ford, *Homer: The Poetry of the Past* (Ithaca, NY: Cornell University Press, 1992) 41.

19. See Ford's discussion of the words *oimê*, which indicates both the theme of an epic and a path in a landscape, and *metabainô*, suggesting both the poet's progression from one *oimê* to another and a physical passing from one place to another; *Homer*, 42–4.

20. Ford, *Homer*, 46.

21. Charles Segal, *Singers, Heroes, and Gods in the* Odyssey (Ithaca, NY: Cornell University Press, 1994) 113–41.

22. Segal, 142–63.

23. Barry B. Powell, 'Homer and Writing', *A New Companion to Homer*, ed. Morris and Powell, 26–8.

24. Ong, 31–77.

25. Milman Parry, 'Studies in the Epic Technique of Oral Verse-Making. I. Homer and Homeric Style'; *Harvard Studies in Classical Philology* 41 (1930): 73–147; rpt. in *The Making of Homeric Verse: The Collected Papers of Milman Parry*, ed. Adam Parry (Oxford: Clarendon Press, 1971) 272.

26. Ong, 59.

27. Beye, 97.

28. Ford, *Homer*, 31–2.

29. Ford, *Homer*, 31–9.

30. Segal, 140.
31. Ong, 40.
32. Beye, 104–5.
33. Parry, 'The Traditional Epithet in Homer'; 1928; rpt. in *The Making of Homeric Verse* 6.
34. Beye, 14.
35. Gregory Nagy, *The Best of the Achaeans: Concepts of the Hero in Archaic Greek Poetry* (1979; Baltimore, MD: Johns Hopkins University Press, 1999) rev. edn, 3.
36. For a detailed discussion of this, see Barbara Graziosi, *Inventing Homer: The Early Reception of Epic* (Cambridge: Cambridge University Press, 2002) esp. 51–89.
37. Ford, *Homer*, 128–9; Richard Rutherford, *Homer* (Oxford: Oxford University Press, 1996) 58–9.
38. Nagy, *Best of the Achaeans*, 42–3.
39. William G. Thalmann, *Conventions of Form and Thought in Early Greek Epic Poetry* (Baltimore, MD: Johns Hopkins University Press, 1984).
40. Ford, *Homer*, 29.
41. Ford, *Homer*, 17.
42. Ford, *Homer*, 30–1.
43. Ford, 'Epic as Genre', *A New Companion to Homer*, ed. Morris and Powell, 410–11.
44. Nagy, *Comparative Studies in Greek and Indic Meter* (Cambridge, MA: Harvard University Press, 1974) 248; see also Segal, 88–9.
45. Segal, 85.
46. Seth L. Schein, *The Mortal Hero: An Introduction to Homer's* Iliad (Berkeley: University of California Press, 1984) 92.
47. Nagy, *Best of the Achaeans*, 29.
48. Schein, 70.
49. Richard Seaford, *Reciprocity and Ritual: Homer and Tragedy in the Developing City-State* (Oxford: Clarendon Press, 1994) 7.
50. Schein, 120.
51. Nagy, *Best of the Achaeans*, 32.
52. Beye, 21, 140–1.
53. Schein, 103.
54. Nagy, *Best of the Achaeans*, 49.
55. Nagy, *Best of the Achaeans*, 35.
56. Susanne Lindgren Wofford, *The Choice of Achilles: The Ideology of Figure in the Epic* (Stanford, CA: Stanford University Press, 1992).
57. Eric A. Havelock, *Preface to Plato* (Oxford: Blackwell, 1963) 61–85.
58. Ong, 70, a point also made by Havelock, 47.
59. Graziosi, 21–30.
60. Graziosi, 23.
61. Hainsworth, 43.
62. Robert Lamberton, 'Homer in Antiquity', *A New Companion to Homer*, ed. Morris and Powell, 34.
63. Xenophanes fr. 1 and 11, qtd. in G. M. A. Grube, *The Greek and Roman Critics* (London: Methuen, 1965) 8.
64. For helpful discussion of Plato, see Grube, 46–65 and Havelock, 3–19.
65. H. T. Swedenberg, *The Theory of the Epic in England 1650–1800* (Berkeley: University of California Press, 1944) 8.

66. Aristotle, *Poetics* 49b10, trans. Malcolm Heath (London: Penguin, 1996) 9.
67. Aristotle, 55b81, trans Heath, 28.
68. Aristotle, 59b35, trans. Heath, 39.
69. Aristotle, 59b35, trans. Heath, 39.
70. Stephen Halliwell, *Aristotle's Poetics* (London: Duckworth, 1986) 276.
71. Hainsworth, 33.
72. *Hipp. Min.* 363b; qtd. in Rutherford, 59.
73. *On the Sublime*, trans. W. Rhys Roberts (Cambridge: Cambridge University Press, 1935) 2nd edn, 67.
74. Hainsworth, 72.
75. For more on these poems, see Hainsworth, 76–87.
76. Hainsworth, 80; Duncan F. Kennedy, 'Virgilian Epic', *The Cambridge Companion to Virgil*, ed. Charles Martindale (Cambridge: Cambridge University Press, 1997) 145.
77. Richard Heinze, *Virgil's Epic Technique*, trans. Hazel and David Harvey (London: Bristol Classical Press, 1993) 202.
78. Hainsworth, 100.
79. Don Fowler, 'The Virgil Commentary of Servius', *The Cambridge Companion to Virgil*, ed. Martindale, 73–8
80. Virgil, *The Aeneid*, trans. C. Day Lewis (Oxford: Oxford University Press, 1986); references are to book and line numbers.
81. Colin Burrow, *Epic Romance: Homer to Milton* (Oxford: Clarendon Press, 1993) 38–9.
82. Cicero, *De re publica* 6.16, qtd. in Burrow, 39.
83. Burrow, 39.
84. Hainsworth, 104.
85. David Quint, *Epic and Empire: Politics and Generic Form from Virgil to Milton* (Princeton, NJ: Princeton University Press, 1993) 83.
86. Gian Biagio Conte, *The Rhetoric of Imagination: Genre and Poetic Memory in Virgil and Other Latin Poets*, ed. Charles Segal (Ithaca: Cornell University Press, 1986) 141–85.
87. Propertius 2.34.66, qtd. in R. J. Tarrant, 'Aspect of Virgil's Reception in Antiquity', *The Cambridge Companion to Virgil*, ed. Martindale, 56.
88. Ovid, *Metamorphoses*, trans. A. D. Melville (Oxford: Oxford University Press, 1986); references are to book and line numbers.
89. Hainsworth, 116–17.
90. Susan H. Braund, introduction, *Civil War* by Lucan (Oxford: Oxford University Press, 1992) xiii–xvi.
91. Lucan, *Civil War*, ed. Braund (Oxford: Oxford University Press, 1992); references are to book and line numbers.
92. Quint, esp. Ch. 4.

Chapter 2

1. Howard Clarke, *Homer's Readers: A Historical Introduction to the* Iliad *and the* Odyssey (London: Associated University Presses, 1981) ch. 3.
2. Hans Robert Jauss, *Toward an Aesthetic of Reception*, trans. Timothy Bahti (Brighton: Harvester, 1982) 96.
3. Christopher Baswell, *Virgil in Medieval England: Figuring the* Aeneid *from the Twelfth Century to Chaucer* (Cambridge: Cambridge University Press, 1995) 18.

4. Don Fowler, 'The Virgil Commentary of Servius', *The Cambridge Companion to Virgil*, ed. Charles Martindale (Cambridge: Cambridge University Press, 1997) 73–8.
5. Baswell, 17.
6. Baswell, 10.
7. Baswell, 10.
8. Baswell, 10.
9. Baswell, 11.
10. Colin Burrow, *Epic Romance: Homer to Milton* (Oxford: Clarendon Press, 1993) esp. 58–9; also Burrow, 'Virgils, from Dante to Milton', *Cambridge Companion to Virgil*, ed. Martindale, 83.
11. Julius Caesar Scaliger, *Poetices libri septem* (Lyons, 1561) 92.
12. H. T. Swedenberg, *Theory of the Epic in England 1650–1800* (Berkeley: University of California Press, 1944) 8.
13. Qtd. in Swedenberg, 11.
14. Daniel Javitch, 'The Emergence of Poetic Genre Theory in the Sixteenth Century', *Modern Language Quarterly* 59 (1998): 139–69.
15. Qtd. in Swedenberg, 10.
16. Baswell, 11.
17. Swedenber, 9.
18. Torquato Tasso, *Discourses on the Heroic Poem*, trans. Mariella Cavalchini and Irene Samuel (Oxford: Clarendon Press, 1973) 34.
19. Tasso, *Discourses*, 38.
20. Tasso, *Discourses*, 39.
21. *Beowulf*, trans. Seamus Heaney (New York: Norton, 2002). References are to line numbers.
22. Roberta Frank, 'The *Beowulf* Poet's Sense of History', *The Wisdom of Poetry: Essays in Early English Literature in Honor of Morton W. Bloomfield*, ed. Larry D. Benson and Siegfried Wenzel (Kalamazoo: Medieval Institute Publications, 1982) 53–65.
23. Thomas D. Hill, 'The Christian Language and Theme of *Beowulf*', *Companion to Old English Poetry*, ed. Henk Aertsen and Rolf H. Bremmer, Jr. (Amsterdam: VU University Press, 1994) 71.
24. Mindele Anne Treip, *Allegorical Poetics and the Epic: The Renaissance Tradition to Paradise Lost* (Lexington: University Press of Kentucky, 1994) 7–14.
25. Treip, 6.
26. Dante Alighieri, Letter to Cangrande della Scala, *Dante: The Critical Heritage 1314 (?) to 1870*, ed. Michael Caesar (London: Routledge, 1989) 93; see also Triep, 14–15.
27. Dante, Letter to Cangrande, 94.
28. Dante Alighieri, *The Divine Comedy*, trans. C. H. Sisson (Oxford: Oxford University Press, 1993); references are to canto and line numbers.
29. Dante, Letter to Cangrande, 96.
30. *The Song of Roland*, trans. Glyn Burgess (London: Penguin, 1990); references are to line numbers.
31. Ludovico Ariosto, *Orlando Furioso*, trans. Guido Waldman (Oxford: Oxford University Press, 1983); references are to canto and line numbers.
32. As Colin Burrow remarks, 'The priority of love as motive is the most obvious and important fact about *Orlando Furioso*', 55.
33. Patricia A. Parker, *Inescapable Romance: Studies in the Poetics of a Mode* (Princeton: Princeton University Press, 1979) 4.

34. Burrow, 53.
35. Andrew Fichter, *Poets Historical: Dynastic Epic in the Renaissance* (New Haven: Yale University Press, 1982) 91–7.
36. Fichter, 97.
37. Tasso, *Discourses*, 151–2.
38. Tasso, *Discourses*, 32.
39. Treip, 257–62.
40. Tasso, 'Allegory of the Poem', *Jerusalem Delivered*, trans. Anthony M. Esolen (Baltimore: Johns Hopkins University Press, 2000) 415.
41. Tasso, 'Allegory', 416
42. Tasso, 'Allegory', 416.
43. Tasso, 'Allegory', 416.
44. Tasso, 'Allegory', 416.
45. Tasso, *Jerusalem Delivered*, ed. Esolen; references are to canto and stanza numbers.
46. Tasso, 'Allegory', 418.
47. Tasso, 'Discourses', 47.
48. Tasso, 'Discourses', 47.
49. Treip, 267–74.
50. Treip, 96.
51. Spenser, *The Works of Edmund Spenser: A Variorum Edition*, ed. E. Greenlaw *et al.* (Baltimore, MD: Johns Hopkins University Press, 1932–49) X, 471.
52. Spenser, 'A Letter of the Authors Expounding His Whole Intention in the Course of the Worke', *The Faerie Queene*, ed. Thomas P. Roche (London: Penguin, 1978) 15–16.
53. Spenser, 'A Letter of the Authors', 15.
54. Spenser, 'A Letter of the Authors', 15.
55. Spenser, 'A Letter of the Authors', 16.
56. Spenser, 'A Letter of the Authors', 16.
57. Spenser, 'A Letter of the Authors', 16.
58. John Milton, *The Reason of Church Government Urged Against Prelaty* (1642), in *Paradise Lost*, ed. Scott Elledge (New York: Norton, 1975) 293.
59. John Dryden, *The Poems of John Dryden*, ed. James Kinsley (Oxford: Oxford University Press, 1958) 1445.
60. The phrase is Charles Martindale's: see *John Milton and the Transformation of Ancient Epic* (1986; London: Bristol Classical Press, 2002) 29.
61. Martindale, 33.
62. Martindale, 21.
63. Milton, *Paradise Lost*, ed. Elledge, 4.
64. F. T. Prince, *The Italian Element in Milton's Verse* (Oxford: Clarendon Press, 1954).
65. Martindale, 29.
66. Milton, *Paradise Lost*, ed. Elledge; references are to book and line numbers.
67. Martindale, 34.
68. Martindale, 38.
69. Northrop Frye, *The Return of Eden: Five Essays on Milton's Epics* (Toronto: University of Toronto Press, 1965) 25.
70. See Frye for a discussion of 'demonic' heroism in *Paradise Lost*, 27–30.
71. Milton, *An Apology Against a Pamphlet Called 'A Modest Confutation of the Animadversions upon the Remonstrant Against Smectymnuus'* (1642), *Paradise Lost*, ed. Elledge, 297–8.

72. Milton, *Aeropagitica* (1644), *Paradise Lost*, ed. Elledge, 291.
73. For this and the ideas that follow, I am indebted to conversations with Charlie Nicholls.
74. Martindale, 60.
75. C. S. Lewis, *A Preface to Paradise Lost* (Oxford: Oxford University Press, 1942) 132.
76. Milton, *An Apology, Paradise Lost*, ed. Elledge, 297.
77. Miguel de Cervantes Saavedra, *Don Quixote de la Mancha*, 1605 and 1615, trans. John Rutherford (London: Penguin, 2000); references are to page numbers.
78. Anthony Close, *The Romantic Approach to 'Don Quixote': A Critical History of the Romantic Tradition in 'Quixote' Criticism* (Cambridge: Cambridge University Press, 1977) 22.
79. For a discussion of Cervantes's understanding of contemporary and Renaissance debates on epic, romance and Ariosto, see Marina Scordilis Brownlee, 'Cervantes as Reader of Ariosto', *Romance: Generic Transformation from Chrétien de Troyes to Cervantes*, ed. Kevin Brownlee and Marina Scordilis Brownlee (Hanover, NH: University Press, of New England, 1985) 220–37.
80. Michael D. McGaha, 'Cervantes and Virgil', *Cervantes and the Renaissance*, ed. McGaha (Easton, PA: Juan de la Cuesta, 1980) 50.
81. L. A. Murillo, '*Don Quixote* as Renaissance Epic', *Cervantes and the Renaissance*, ed. McGaha, 58.
82. See, for example, the point made by Maria DiBattista, '*Don Quixote*', *Homer to Brecht: The European Epic and Dramatic Traditions*, ed. Michael Seidel and Edward Mendelson (New Haven: Yale University Press, 1977) 113: 'Sancho, in insisting on the performance of natural functions purely as natural functions, threatens to lift the heroic world off its idealized hinges'.
83. Richard L. Predmore, for example, elucidates this carefully as a clash between illusions and reality, with enchantment as a third term, offered by Quixote himself, to explain the gap between illusions and reality; see his *The World of Don Quixote* (Cambridge, MA: Harvard University Press, 1967).
84. DiBattista, 111.
85. Félix Martínez-Bonati, Don Quixote *and the Poetics of the Novel*, trans. Dian Fox (Ithaca: Cornell University Press, 1992). For an opposing view, insisting on the 'reality' of Quixote's world, see Diana de Armas Wilson, 'Where Does the Novel Rise? Cultural Hybrids and Cervantine Heresies', *Cervantes and His Postmodern Constituencies*, ed. Anne J. Cruz and Carroll B. Johnson (New York: Garland Publishing, 1999) 43–67.
86. Martinez-Bonati, 121.

Chapter 3

1. Stuart Curran, Introduction, *Le Bossu and Voltaire on the Epic* (Gainesville, FL: Scholars' Facsimiles and Reprintings, 1970) vi.
2. René Le Bossu, *Treatise of the Epick Poem* (1695), rpt. in *Le Bossu and Voltaire on the Epic*.
3. For Le Bossu's influence on Dryden, see Richard Thomas, *Virgil and the Augustan Reception* (Cambridge: Cambridge University Press, 2001) 134 ff.; for his influence on Pope, see Frederick M. Keener, 'Pope, *The Dunciad*, Virgil, and the New Historicism of Le Bossu', *Eighteenth-Century Life* 15 (1991): 35–57.

4. Joseph M. Levine, *The Battle of the Books: History and Literature in the Augustan Age* (Ithaca, NY: Cornell University Press, 1991) 1.
5. Levine, 1–2.
6. Joseph Addison, 'Notes upon the Twelve Books of *Paradise Lost*', *Spectator*, no. 267 (5 January 1712).
7. Dryden's epigram appears beneath the portrait in the 4th edition of *Paradise Lost*, published by Tonson (London, 1688), rpt. in John T. Shawcross, *The Critical Heritage: John Milton* (London: Routledge, 1972) I, 97.
8. Levine, 183ff.
9. Levine, 188.
10. Dryden, Dedication, *The Satires of Decimus Junius Juvenalis, Translated into English Verse . . . To Which is Prefixed, a Discourse Concerning the Original and Progress of Satire* (London: Jacob Tonson, 1697) xi.
11. Dryden, Dedication, *Satires*, xiii.
12. Dryden, Dedication, *Satires*.
13. Pope, Preface, *Poems* (1717), *The Poems of Alexander Pope*, ed. John Butt *et al.* (New Haven: Yale University Press, 1939–69) I, 6–7.
14. Pope, Preface, *The Iliad of Homer*, ed. Steven Shankman (London: Penguin, 1996) 3.
15. Kirsti Simonsuuri, *Homer's Original Genius: Eighteenth-Century Notions of the Early Greek Epic (1688–1798)* (Cambridge: Cambridge University Press, 1979) 62–3.
16. Pope, Preface, *The Iliad*, 4.
17. Pope, Preface, *The Iliad*, 4.
18. For more on previous English translations of the *Aeneid*, see L. Proudfoot, *Dryden's Aeneid and Its Seventeenth-Century Predecessors* (Manchester: Manchester University Press, 1960).
19. Dryden, Preface to *Ovid's Epistles* (1680), *John Dryden: Of Dramatic Poesy and Other Critical Essays*, ed. George Watson (London: J. M. Dent, 1962) I, 262–73.
20. Thomas, 125.
21. Dryden, Preface to *Ovid's Epistles*, 272.
22. Dryden, Preface, *The Aeneid, The Poems of John Dryden*, ed. James Kinsley (Oxford: Oxford University Press, 1958) 1015.
23. Le Bossu, 27.
24. Dryden, Preface, *The Aeneid*, 1015.
25. Dryden, Preface, *The Aeneid*, 1014.
26. Paul Hammond, *Dryden and the Traces of Classical Rome* (Oxford: Oxford University Press, 1999) 220–1.
27. Proudfoot 199ff.
28. Virgil, *The Aeneid*, trans. C. Day Lewis (Oxford: Oxford University Press, 1982); references are to book and line numbers.
29. Dryden, *The Aeneid, The Poems of John Dryden*, ed. Kinsley; references are to book and line numbers.
30. Proudfoot, 199.
31. Thomas, 132.
32. Thomas, 132, Proudfoot, 202.
33. Dryden, Preface, *The Aeneid*, 1018.
34. Dryden, Preface, *The Aeneid*, 1021.
35. Hammond, 226.

36. Hammond, 225.
37. Proudfoot, 204.
38. Pope, Preface, *The Iliad*, ed. Shankman, 20.
39. Simonsuuri, 55.
40. Simonsuuri, 51.
41. Pope, Preface, *The Iliad*, ed. Shankman, 12–13.
42. Pope, Preface, *The Iliad*, ed. Shankman 20.
43. Pope, Preface, *The Iliad*, ed. Shankman, 23.
44. Pope, Preface, *Poems* (1717), *The Poems of Alexander Pope*, ed. Butt, VIII, 557–8.
45. Levine, 209.
46. Peter J. Connelly, 'The Ideology of Pope's *Iliad*', *Comparative Literature* 40 (1988): 358–83.
47. *The Iliad of Homer*, trans. Richmond Lattimore (Chicago: University of Chicago Press, 1951).
48. Pope, *The Iliad*, ed. Shankman; references are to book and line numbers.
49. Connelly, 371.
50. Kathryn L. Lynch, 'Homer's *Iliad* and Pope's Vile Forgery', *Comparative Literature* 34 (1982) 7.
51. William Bowman Piper, *The Heroic Couplet* (Cleveland: The Press of Case Western Reserve University, 1969) 127–50.
52. Lynch, 7–8.
53. Piper, 102. It is of interest that, for both Pope and Dryden, the heroic couplet contributes to the ideologies at bottom of their translations – politeness for Pope and political critique for Dryden – which, as we have seen, ultimately come to reflect an awareness of the gulf between classical epic and modern conditions. For both poets, indeed, their heroic couplets could be read as a gesture against Milton's use of blank verse, which Dryden attributed to the simple fact that 'rhyme was not his talent'. As evidence of their ambivalence toward the possibility of modern epic signified by Milton, Pope's and Dryden's heroic couplets contain, interestingly enough, their acknowledgement of the irrelevance of ancient epic in the modern age.
54. Pope, 'A Receit to make an Epick Poem', *The Guardian* 78 (10 June 1713).
55. Pope, *The Rape of the Lock*, ed. Geoffrey Tillotson (London: Routledge, 1971); references are to canto and line numbers.
56. See, for example, Ian Jack, *Augustan Satire: Intention and Idiom in English Poetry 1660–1750* (London: Oxford University Press, 1952) 78ff.
57. Howard D. Weinbrot, '*The Rape of the Lock* and the Contexts of Warfare', *The Enduring Legacy: Alexander Pope Tercentenary Essays*, ed. G. S. Rousseau and Pat Rogers (Cambridge: Cambridge University Press, 1988) 21–48.
58. Fénelon, letter to Father LeTellier (1710), in *Oeuvres de Fénelon* (1835 edn), III, 653–54, qtd. in Patrick Riley, Introduction, *Telemachus* by Fénelon (Cambridge: Cambridge University Press, 1994) xviii.
59. Fénelon, *Lettre sur les occupations de l'Academie Française* in *Oeuvres de Fénelon*, III 249–50, qtd. in Riley, xvi.
60. Lewis M. Knapp, 'Smollett's Translation of Fenelon's *Télémaque*', *Philological Quarterly* 44 (1965): 405–7.
61. Pope, Preface, *The Iliad*, ed. Shankman, 20.
62. Henry Fielding, Preface, *Joseph Andrews*, ed. R. F. Brissenden (London: Penguin, 1985) 25.

63. Knapp, 405.

64. *An Essay on the New Species of Writing Founded by Mr. Fielding* (London: W. Owen, 1751) 46. The work was published anonymously but has been attributed to Francis Coventry.

65. Fielding, Preface, *Joseph Andrews*, ed. Brissenden, 25.

66. Fielding, Preface, *Joseph Andrews*, ed. Brissenden, 26.

67. Fielding, Preface, *Joseph Andrews*, ed. Brissenden, 28.

68. Fielding, Preface, *Joseph Andrews*, ed. Brissenden, 30.

69. Michael McKeon, *The Origins of the English Novel 1600–1740* (Baltimore, MD: Johns Hopkins University Press, 1987).

70. McKeon, 382–409.

71. Lennard J. Davis, *Factual Fictions: The Origins of the English Novel* (New York: Columbia University Press, 1983) 198.

72. Anthony Close, *The Romantic Approach to 'Don Quixote': A Critical History of the Romantic Tradition in 'Quixote' Criticism* (Cambridge: Cambridge University Press, 1977).

73. Ronald Paulson, *Don Quixote in England: The Aesthetics of Laughter* (Baltimore, MD: Johns Hopkins University Press, 1998), in particular 20–31.

74. Fielding, *Don Quixote in England: A Comedy* (London: J. Watts, 1734) 64.

75. Fielding, *Joseph Andrews*, ed. Brissenden; references are to page numbers.

76. Fielding, Preface, *Joseph Andrews*, ed. Brissenden, 28–9.

77. Paulson, *Don Quixote in England*, 78.

78. Paulson, 'The Pilgrimage and the Family: Structures in the Novels of Fielding and Smollett', *Tobias Smollett: Bicentennial Essays Presented to Lewis M. Knapp*, ed. G. S. Rousseau and Paul-Gabriel Boucé (Oxford: Oxford University Press, 1971) 57–78.

79. Fielding, *Tom Jones*, ed. John Bender and Simon Stern (Oxford: Oxford University Press, 1996); references are to page numbers.

80. John Richetti, 'The Old Order and the New Novel of the Mid-Eighteenth Century: Narrative Authority in Fielding and Smollett', *Eighteenth-Century Fiction* 2 (1990): 183–96.

81. Ian Watt, *The Rise of the Novel* (1957; London: Pimlico, 2000).

82. See G. W. F. Hegel, *Aesthetics: Lectures on Fine Arts*, trans. T. M. Knox (1835; Oxford: Clarendon Press, 1975), 2 vols, esp. Vol. II.

83. Georg Lukács, *The Theory of the Novel: A Historico-Philosophical Essay on the Forms of Great Epic Literature*, trans. Anna Bostock (London: Merlin Press, 1978); Mikhail Bakhtin, 'Epic and Novel', *The Dialogic Imagination: Four Essays*, ed. Michael Holquist, trans. Caryl Emerson and Holquist (Austin: University of Texas Press, 1981). For an enlightening comparison of Lukács and Bakhtin, see Michel Aucouturier, 'The Theory of the Novel in Russia in the 1930s: Lukács and Bakhtin', *The Russian Novel from Pushkin to Pasternak*, ed. John Garrard (New Haven, CT: Yale University Press, 1983) 227–40.

84. Klopstock, *The Messiah Attempted from the German of Mr. Klopstock*, trans. Mary Collyer and Joseph Collyer (London: Dodsley, 1763).

85. Joseph Collyer, 'The Translator's Preface', *The Messiah*, x–xi.

86. Robert M. Browning, *German Poetry in the Age of Enlightenment: From Brockes to Klopstock* (University Park: Pennsylvania State University Press, 1978) 199.

Chapter 4

1. Joseph Anthony Wittreich, Introduction, *The Romantics on Milton: Formal Essays and Critical Asides* (Cleveland: The Press of Case Western Reserve University, 1970) 13.
2. Samuel Johnson, 'Milton', *Lives of the English Poets*, ed. George Birkbeck Hill (Oxford: Clarendon Press, 1905) I, 156.
3. Wittreich, 10.
4. John Keats, *The Letters of John Keats*, ed. Hyder E. Rollins (Cambridge, MA: Harvard University Press, 1958) I, 170.
5. William Hayley, *An Essay on Epick Poetry*, ed. M. Celeste Williamson (1782; Gainesville, FL: Scholars' Fascimiles and Reprints, 1968) I, 261–4.
6. Hayley, *Essay on Epick Poetry* I, 242 and I, 231.
7. Qtd. in W. Macneile Dixon, *English Epic and Heroic Poetry* (London: J. M. Dent, 1912) 2.
8. James Beattie, 'On Fable and Romance', *Dissertations Moral and Critical* (London: W. Strahan, T. Cadell, and W. Creech, 1783) 573.
9. Clara Reeve, *The Progress of Romance and the History of Charoba, Queen of Aegypt* (1785; New York: Facsimile Text Society, 1930) I, 17.
10. Donald M. Foerster, *The Fortunes of Epic Poetry* (Washington, DC: Catholic University of America Press, 1965) 56–82.
11. See Brian Wilkie, *Romantic Poets and Epic Tradition* (Madison: University of Wisconsin Press, 1965) 30–58; as Byron suggested disdainfully, one could expect 'an epic from Bob Southey every spring' *Don Juan* III, 97.
12. Stuart Curran, *Poetic Form and British Romanticism* (Oxford: Oxford University Press, 1986).
13. Northrop Frye, 'Notes for a Commentary on Milton', *The Divine Vision: Studies in the Poetry and Art of William Blake*, ed. Vivian de Sola Pinto (London: Victor Gollancz, 1957) 102.
14. Wittreich, *Angel of the Apocalypse: Blake's Idea of Milton* (Madison: University of Wisconsin Press, 1975) 5.
15. Hayley, *Life of Milton*, ed. Joseph Wittreich (1796; Gainesville, FL: Scholars' Facsimiles and Reprints, 1970) xvii.
16. Wittreich, *Angel of the Apocalypse*, 5–6.
17. Lucy Newlyn, *Paradise Lost and the Romantic Reader* (1993; Oxford: Oxford University Press, 2004) 257–78.
18. Wittreich, *Angel of the Apocalypse*, 144.
19. David Riede, 'Blake's *Milton*: On Membership of Church Paul', *Re-membering Milton: Essays on the Texts and Tradition*, ed. M. Nyquist and M. W. Ferguson (New York: 1988), 259.
20. Blake, *Milton*, ed. Kay Parkhurst Easson and Roger R. Easson (London: Thames and Hudson, 1978); references are to plate and line numbers.
21. Blake, *Milton*, ed. Easson and Easson, 11–55.
22. Blake, *Milton*, ed. Easson and Easson, 61.
23. Wordsworth, '*The Prelude* of 1850', *The Prelude 1799, 1805, 1850*, ed. Jonathan Wordsworth, M. H. Abrams, and Stephen Gill (New York: Norton, 1979); references are to book and line numbers.
24. De Selincourt, Ernest. *The Letters of William and Dorothy Wordsworth: The Middle Years* (Oxford: Oxford University Press, 1937) II, 633.

25. Wordsworth, 'Prospectus to *The Recluse'*, line 1, *Norton Anthology of English Literature*, ed. Abrams *et al*. (New York: Norton, 1986) vol. 2, 5th edn.

26. Jonathan Wordsworth, 'Revision as Making: *The Prelude* and its Peers', *Romantic Revisions*, ed. Robert Brinkley and Keith Hanley (Cambridge: Cambridge University Press, 1992) 18–42.

27. Jonathan Wordsworth, 18–42.

28. This is what Geoffrey H. Hartman has termed the *via naturaliter negativa*, or the 'naturally negative way', of the poet's development in *The Prelude*; see Hartman, 'A Poet's Progress, 'A Poet's Progress: Wordsworth and the *Via Naturaliter Negativa*', *Modern Philology* 59 (1962): 214–24.

29. Mary Jacobus, 'The Writing on the Wall: Autobiography and Self-Inscription in *The Prelude'*, *Romanticism, Writing, and Sexual Difference: Essays on* The Prelude (Oxford: Clarendon Press, 1989) 8.

30. Indeed, Jacobus reads this enforced grandeur as Wordsworth's somewhat strained attempt at aligning his epic with Milton's; Jacobus, 9–12.

31. Hence Richard Bourke's insistence that Wordsworth's poetic programme be read as the appropriation of authority by the literary away from the political and financial, and thus as the poet's elevation of himself above ideology and beyond accountability; see Bourke, *Romantic Discourses and Political Modernity: Wordsworth, the Intellectual and Cultural Critique* (New York: Harvester Wheatsheaf, 1993).

32. Bourke, 243.

33. For more on how this crisis phase is constructed as a lapse into picturesque poetry, see Hugh Sykes Davies, *Wordsworth and the Worth of Words* (Cambridge: Cambridge University Press, 1986) 189–260 and Tim Fulford, *Landscape, Liberty and Authority: Poetry, Criticism and Politics from Thomson to Wordsworth* (Cambridge: Cambridge University Press, 1996) 157–213.

34. Stuart M. Sperry, *Keats the Poet* (Princeton, NJ: Princeton University Press, 1973) 182.

35. Sperry, 182.

36. Sperry, 313.

37. Jonathan Bate, 'Keats's Two *Hyperions* and the Problem of Milton', *Romantic Revisions*, ed. Robert Brinkley and Keith Hanley (Cambridge: Cambridge University Press, 1992) 336–7.

38. Keats, *The Poetical Works and Other Writings of John Keats*, ed. H. Buxton Forman (New York: Scribners, 1939) vol 5, 303–4.

39. Keats, 'Hyperion. A Fragment', *John Keats: The Complete Poems*, ed. John Barnard (London: Penguin, 1988) 3rd edn; references are to book and line numbers.

40. Michael O'Neill, 'When this Warm Scribe My Hand': Writing and History in *Hyperion* and *The Fall of Hyperion'*, *Keats and History*, ed. Nicholas Roe (Cambridge: Cambridge University Press, 1995) 154.

41. Bate, 334.

42. Keats, 'The Fall of Hyperion. A Dream', *Complete Poems*, ed. Barnard; references are to canto and line numbers.

43. See O'Neill, as well as Mark Sandy, ' "To See as a God Sees": The Potential *Übermensch* in Keats's *Hyperion* Fragments', *Romanticism* 4 (1998): 212–23, and Christoph Bode, '*Hyperion, The Fall of Hyperion* and Keats's Poetics', *Wordsworth Circle* 31 (2000): 31–7.

44. Bode, 37.

45. O'Neill, 154.

46. Bode, 37.
47. Carol L. Bernstein, 'Subjectivity as Critique and the Critique of Subjectivity in Keats's *Hyperion*', *After the Future: Postmodern Times and Places*, ed. Gary Shapiro (Albany, NY: SUNY Press, 1990) 42; Bernstein's case is weakened, however, by being restricted to the first *Hyperion*, which means that her coherent knowing subject is not the poet of *The Fall of Hyperion* but Apollo in *Hyperion*, who, it seems, is inadequate to the task of carrying the burden of her argument.
48. Thomas Medwin, *Journal of the Conversations of Lord Byron: Noted During a Residence with His Lordship at Pisa in the Years 1821 and 1822* (London: Henry Colburn, 1824) 164.
49. Byron, *Don Juan*, ed. T. G. Steffan, E. Steffan and W. W. Pratt (London: Penguin, 1993), rev. edn; references are to canto and stanza numbers.
50. Jerome J. McGann, Don Juan *in Context* (London: John Murray, 1976) xii.
51. Harold Bloom, *The Visionary Company: A Reading of English Romantic Poetry* (Oxford, 1963) 258; for a more recent discussion of nihilism in *Don Juan*, see Charles LaChance, '*Don Juan*, "a Problem, Like All Things"', *Papers on Language and Literature* 34 (1998): 273–300.
52. Donald H. Reiman, '*Don Juan* in Epic Context', *Studies in Romanticism* 16 (1977): 587–94.
53. Wilkie, 188–226 and George deForest Lord, *Trials of the Self: Heroic Ordeals in the Epic Tradition* (Hamden, CT: Archon Books, 1983) 133–56.
54. Frederick Garber, 'Self and the Language of Satire in *Don Juan*', *Thalia: Studies in Literary Humor* 5 (1982): 37.
55. McGann, *Towards a Literature of Knowledge* (Oxford: Clarendon Press, 1989) 50.
56. McGann, *Towards a Literature of Knowledge*, 51.
57. For a good discussion of the difference between heteroglossia and polyphony, see Sue Vice, *Introducing Bakhtin* (Manchester: Manchester University Press, 1997) 112.
58. Bakhtin, 'Discourse in the Novel', *The Dialogic Imagination: Four Essays*, ed. Michael Holquist, trans. Caryl Emerson and Holquist (Austin: University of Texas Press, 1981).
59. It is because Romantic epics imbricate the reader as the endpoint of their narratives that Tilottama Rajan has labelled them 'transactional'; see 'The Other Reading: Transactional Epic in Milton, Blake, and Wordsworth', *Milton, the Metaphysicals, and Romanticism*, ed. Lisa Low and Anthony John Harding (Cambridge: Cambridge University Press, 1994) 20–46.
60. Bakhtin, 'Epic and Novel', *The Dialogic Imagination: Four Essays*.
61. As Simon Dentith notes, irony and parody 'can in fact be the local forms of discourse in which monologism is secured'; see *Bakhtinian Thought: An Introductory Reader* (London: Routledge, 1995) 48.
62. See, particularly, Marjorie Stone, *Elizabeth Barrett Browning* (Basingstoke: Macmillian, 1995) ch. 2.
63. Kathleen Blake, 'Elizabeth Barrett Browning and Wordsworth: The Romantic Poet as a Woman', *Victorian Poetry* 24.4 (1986): 387–98.
64. Elizabeth Barrett Browning, *The Greek Christian Poets and the English Poets* (London: Chapman and Hall, 1863) 201, 198; the essay first appeared in *The Athenaeum* in 1842.

65. Barrett Browning, *The Greek Christian Poets and the English Poets*, 206.
66. Meredith B. Raymond and Mary Rose Sullivan, eds, *The Letters of Elizabeth Barrett Browning to Mary Russell Mitford 1836–1854*, (Winfield, KA: Wedgestone Press, 1983) III, 49.
67. Barrett Browning, *The Greek Christian Poets and the English Poets*, 197.
68. Elvan Kintner, ed., *The Letters of Robert Browning and Elizabeth Barrett Barrett 1845–1846* (Cambridge, MA: Belknap Press, 1969) I, 31.
69. Holly A. Laird, '*Aurora Leigh*: An Epical *Ars Poetica*', *Writing the Woman Artist: Essays on Poetics, Politics, and Portraiture*, ed. Suzanne W. Jones (Philadelphia: University of Pennsylvania Press, 1991) 353–70.
70. Barrett Browning, *Aurora Leigh*, ed. Kerry McSweeney (Oxford: Oxford University Press, 1993); references are to book and line numbers.
71. Laird, 360.
72. Beverly Taylor, ' "School-Miss Alfred" and "Materfamilias": Female Sexuality and Poetic Voice in *The Princess* and *Aurora Leigh*', *Gender and Discourse in Victorian Art and Literature*, ed. Antony H. Harrison and Beverly Taylor (Dekalb: Northern Illinois University Press, 1992) 24.
73. Angela Leighton, *Elizabeth Barrett Browning* (Brighton: Harvester, 1986) 141–57.
74. Dorothy Mermin, *Elizabeth Barrett Browning: The Origins of a New Poetry* (Chicago: University of Chicago Press, 1989) 212.
75. Kathleen Blake, 397.
76. Kathleen Blake, 398.
77. Taylor, 23.
78. Kintner, I, 31.
79. Frederick G. Kenyon, *The Letters of Robert Browning and Elizabeth Barrett Barrett* (New York: Macmillan, 1897) II, 228.
80. See Stone, 141.
81. See, for example, Franco Moretti, *The Way of the World: The* Bildungsroman *in European Culture*, trans. Albert Sbragia (1987; London: Verso, 2000) and Lorna Ellis, *Appearing to Diminish: Female Development and the British* Bildungsroman *1750–1850* (Lewisburg: Associated University Press, 2001).
82. For more on this, see Herbert F. Tucker, '*Aurora Leigh*: Epic Solutions to Novel Ends', *Famous Last Words: Changes in Gender and Narrative Closure*, ed. Alison Booth (Charlottesville: University Press of Virginia, 1993) 62–83.
83. See, for example, L. D. Opul'skaya, *Roman-èpopoeia L. N. Tolstogo 'Voina i mir'* (*Tolstoy's Epic-Novel, 'War and Peace'*), (Moscow: Prosveshchenie, 1987) and the discussion of Opul'skaya in Rimvydas Silbajoris, *War and Peace: Tolstoy's Mirror of the World* (New York: Twayne, 1995) 110; Maksim Gorky, 'Leo Tolstoy', *Sobranie Sochinenij* (Collected Works) (Moscow: State Belles Lettres Publishing House, 1963), 18.80, qtd. in Silbajoris, 110.
84. Leo Tolstoy, *War and Peace*, ed. Henry Gifford, trans. Louise and Alymer Maude (Oxford: Oxford University Press, 1991); references are to page numbers.
85. Ernest J. Simmons, *Tolstoy* (London: Routledge and Kegan Paul, 1973) 87.
86. Silbajoris, 113.
87. John Bayley, *Tolstoy and the Novel* (London: Chatto and Windus, 1966) 78.
88. Gary Saul Morson, '*War and Peace*', *The Cambridge Companion to Tolstoy*, ed. Donna Tussing Orwin (Cambridge: Cambridge University Press, 2002) 74.

89. Silbajoris, 120.
90. Bayley, 124.
91. Simmons, 90.
92. As Bayley points out, the Russian word for 'peace' – *mir* – also means 'both universe and community. The association of the two words has wider and more metaphysical implications than can be rendered in English'; Bayley, 136.
93. Bayley, 136; for a discussion of Tolstoy's attitude to French-speaking Russians and to France, see R. F. Christian, *Tolstoy* (Cambridge: Cambridge University Press, 1969) 120–2, 147–8.
94. For more on this, see Christian, 116–29.
95. Silbajoris, 118.
96. N. N. Strakhov, 'Statyi o *Voine i Mire*', *Zarya* ('Articles on *War and Peace*', *Dawn*) 1869–1870; qtd. in Simmons, 92. For commentary on Tolstoy and epic, see, for example, Harry J. Mooney, *Tolstoy's Epic Vision: A Study of* War and Peace *and* Anna Karenina (Tulsa, FL: University of Tulsa, 1968).
97. Tolstoy, *Polnoe Sobranie Sochinenii* (Complete Works), ed. V. G. Chertkov *et al.* (Moscow, 1928–58), 13.55, qtd. in Christian, 103.
98. Andrew Baruch Wachtel, *An Obsession with History: Russian Writers Confront the Past* (Stanford, CA: Stanford University Press, 1994) 88–122.
99. See Bayley, 158: 'Tolstoy takes for granted and conveys with overwhelming assurance the authenticity of the individual vision. *All* his characters see reality as it really is.'
100. Morson, *Hidden in Plain View: Narrative and Creative Potentials in 'War and Peace'* (Stanford, CA: Stanford University Press, 1987) 186, 9–36; see also Isaiah Berlin's classic study, *The Hedgehog and the Fox: An Essay on Tolstoy's View of History* (London: Weidenfeld and Nicolson, 1953).
101. Wachtel, 90.
102. For a useful comparison between Tolstoy and Joyce, see George R. Clay, 'Tolstoy in the Twentieth Century', *Cambridge Companion to Tolstoy*, ed. Orwin, 206–21.
103. Alfred, Lord Tennyson, *Idylls of the King*, ed. J. M. Gray (London: Penguin, 1983).
104. Hallam Tennyson, *Alfred Lord Tennyson: A Memoir* (London: Macmillan, 1897) II, 89–90.
105. John D. Rosenberg, *The Fall of Camelot: A Study of Tennyson's 'Idylls of the King'* (Cambridge, MA: Belknap Press of Harvard University Press, 1973) 33 and Robert Pattison, *Tennyson and Tradition* (Cambridge, MA: Harvard University Press, 1979) 143–4.
106. Pattison, 144.
107. Henry Kozicki, *Tennyson and Clio: History in the Major Poems* (Baltimore, MD: Johns Hopkins Press, 1979) 131.
108. Alastair Thomson, *The Poetry of Tennyson* (London: Routledge, 1986) 167.
109. Tucker, *Tennyson and the Doom of Romanticism* (Cambridge, MA: Harvard University Press, 1988) 322.
110. Browning, *The Ring and the Book*, ed. Richard D. Altick (London: Penguin, 1971).
111. Richard D. Altick and James F. Loucks, *Browning's Roman Murder Story* (Chicago: University of Chicago Press, 1968) 9.
112. Altick and Loucks, 30.
113. Altick and Loucks, 361.

114. William E. Buckler, *Poetry and Truth in Browning's* The Ring and the Book (New York: New York University Press, 1985) 282–8 and Ann P. Brady, *Pompilia: A Feminist Reading of Robert Browning's* The Ring and the Book (Athens: Ohio University Press, 1988).

Chapter 5

1. Malcolm Bradbury and James McFarlane, 'The Name and Nature of Modernism', *Modernism: A Guide to European Literature 1890–1930*, ed. Bradbury and McFarlane (1976; London: Penguin, 1991) 25.
2. Georg Lukács, *The Theory of the Novel: A Historico-Philosophical Essay on the Forms of Great Epic Literature*, trans. Anna Bostock (1920; London: Merlin Press, 1978) 60.
3. Lukács, 71.
4. Mikhail Bakhtin, 'Epic and Novel', *The Dialogic Imagination: Four Essays*, ed. Michael Holquist, trans. Caryl Emerson and Michael Holquist (Austin: University of Texas Press, 1981) 8.
5. C. M. Bowra, *Heroic Poetry* (London: Macmillan, 1952) and E. M. W. Tillyard, *The English Epic and Its Background* (London: Chatto and Windus, 1954).
6. James E. Miller, *The American Quest for a Supreme Fiction* (Chicago: University of Chicago Press, 1979) 31 and Van Kelly, 'Criteria for the Epic: Borders, Diversity, and Expansion', *Epic and Epoch: Essays on the Interpretation and History of a Genre*, eds. Steven M. Oberhelman, Van Kelly, and Richard Golson (Lubbock: Texas Tech University Press, 1994) 1–21.
7. Franco Moretti, *Modern Epic: The World System from Goethe to García Márquez* (London: Verso, 1996) 5.
8. W. B. Stanford, *The Ulysses Theme: A Study in the Adaptability of a Traditional Hero* (New York: Barnes, 1968) 2nd edn, 246ff.
9. David Adams, *Colonial Odysseys: Empire and Epic in the Modernist Novel* (Ithaca, NY: Cornell University Press, 2003).
10. Adams, 13–44.
11. Hardy, *The Dynasts: An Epic-Drama, of the War with Napoleon, in Three Parts, Nineteen Acts, and One Hundred and Thirty Scenes, The Poetical Works of Thomas Hardy in Prose and Verse*, vols II and III (London: Macmillan, 1920); references to the text are to part, act and scene numbers.
12. Hardy, *The Dynasts* II, x.
13. Florence Emily Hardy, *The Life of Thomas Hardy* (London: 1928) 286, qtd. in R. J. White, *Thomas Hardy and History* (London: Macmillan, 1974) 72.
14. Hardy, *The Dynasts* II, viii.
15. White, 103.
16. William R. Rutland, *Thomas Hardy: A Study of his Writings and their Background* (New York: Russell and Russell, 1962) 278.
17. G. Glen Wickens, 'Hardy's Inconsistent Spirits and the Philosophic Form of *The Dynasts*', *The Poetry of Thomas Hardy*, ed. Patricia Clements and Juliet Grindle (London: Vision Press, 1980) 101–18.
18. Hardy, *Tess of the d'Urbervilles* (1891; New York: Bantam, 1971) ch. 19, 123.
19. Herbert Gorman, *James Joyce: A Definitive Biography* (1939; London: John Lane and Bodley Head, 1941) 45.

232 *The History of the Epic*

20. Georges Borach, 'Conversations with James Joyce', trans. Joseph Prescott, *College English* 15 (1954): 325.
21. For the Linati schema, see Richard Ellmann, *Ulysses on the Liffey* (London: Faber, 1974); for the Gilbert schema, see Stuart Gilbert, *James Joyce's 'Ulysses': A Study* (1930; London: Faber, 1952).
22. Letter to Frank Budgen, *Letters of James Joyce*, ed. Stuart Gilbert (New York: Viking, 1957) vol. 1, 139–40.
23. See Ellmann and Gilbert.
24. Bernard Benstock, ed., *Critical Essays on James Joyce's* Ulysses (Boston: G. K. Hall, 1989) 145.
25. A. Walton Litz, *The Art of James Joyce* (London: Oxford University Press, 1961) 15.
26. Litz, 40.
27. Frank Budgen, *James Joyce and the Making of 'Ulysses'* (1934; Bloomington: Indiana University Press, 1960) 15–17.
28. Joyce, *Selected Letters of James Joyce*, ed. Ellmann (New York: Viking, 1975) 271.
29. S. L. Goldberg, *The Classical Temper: A Study of James Joyce's* Ulysses (London: Chatto and Windus, 1960) 32.
30. David Hayman, Ulysses: *The Mechanics of Meaning* (1970; Madison: University of Wisconsin Press, 1982) 20–1.
31. Goldberg, 146.
32. Daniel R. Schwarz, *Reading Joyce's* Ulysses (Basingstoke: Macmillan, 1987) 37.
33. Schwarz, 38.
34. Joyce, *Ulysses*, ed. Jeri Johnson (Oxford: Oxford University Press, 1993); references are to page numbers.
35. Harry Blamires, *The New Bloomsday Book: A Guide Through Ulysses* (London: Routledge, 1996) 3rd edn, 70.
36. Schwarz, 39–40.
37. Carl Jung, '*Ulysses*: A Monologue', *The Collected Works of Carl Jung*, trans. R. F. C. Hull (Princeton, NJ: Princeton University Press, 1966) 120.
38. Eliot, '"Ulysses", Order, and Myth', *Selected Prose of T. S. Eliot*, ed. Frank Kermode (London: Faber, 1975) 175.
39. Eliot, '"Ulysses", Order, and Myth', 177.
40. Eliot, '"Ulysses", Order, and Myth', 177–8.
41. Hugh Kenner, *The Invisible Poet: T. S. Eliot* (1959; London: Methuen, 1965) 129.
42. Eliot, *The Waste Land and Other Poems* (1940; London: Faber, 1972) 42; further references are to line numbers.
43. Jessie L. Weston, *From Ritual to Romance* (1920; Princeton, NJ: Princeton University Press, 1993) 113–36.
44. James Frazer, *The Golden Bough: A Study in Magic and Religion*, ed. George W. Stocking (1890; London: Penguin, 1996), abridged edn, 390–429.
45. Steven Spender, *Eliot* (London: Fontana, 1975) 116.
46. Kenner, *The Invisible Poet*, 150.
47. Pound, *The Cantos of Ezra Pound* (London: Faber and Faber, 1975).
48. Forrest Read, 'Pound, Joyce, and Flaubert', *New Approaches to Ezra Pound: A Co-ordinated Investigation of Pound's Poetry and Ideas*, ed. Eva Hesse (London: Faber, 1969) 135; also see Michael André Bernstein, *The Tale of the Tribe: Ezra Pound and Modern Epic* (Princeton: Princeton University Press, 1980) 1–20.

49. Read, 126.
50. Read, 126.
51. Pound, *Guide to Kulchur* (London: Faber, 1952) 152.
52. Kenner, *The Pound Era* (London: Faber, 1972) 178.
53. Albert Cook, 'Rhythm and Person in the *Cantos*'. *New Approaches to Ezra Pound*, ed. Hesse, 357.
54. Cook, 359.
55. Pound, letter to Felix Schelling, 9 July 1922, *Selected Letters of Ezra Pound, 1907–1941*, ed. D. D. Paige (London: Faber, 1950) 180.
56. Cook, 354.
57. Pound, *Literary Essays of Ezra Pound*, ed. T. S. Eliot (London: Faber, 1954) 506.
58. Jacob Korg, *Winter Love: Ezra Pound and H. D.* (Madison: University of Wisconsin Press, 2003) 172; H. D.'s remarks are from her letter to Norman Pearson, *Between History and Poetry: The Letters of H. D. and Norman Holmes Pearson* (Iowa City: University of Iowa Press, 1997) 180.
59. Korg, 180.
60. Susan Stanford Friedman, 'Creating a Women's Mythology: H. D.'s *Helen in Egypt*', *Signets: Reading H. D.*, ed. Friedman and Rachel Blau DuPlessis (Madison: University of Wisconsin Press, 1990) 373–405.
61. Claire Buck, *H. D. and Freud: Bisexuality and a Feminine Discourse* (New York: Harvester Wheatsheaf, 1991) 164.
62. Friedman, *Psyche Reborn: The Emergence of H. D.* (Bloomington: University of Indiana Press, 1981) 256–7.
63. Friedman, *Psyche Reborn*, 266–7.
64. Friedman, *Psyche Reborn*, 257.
65. H. D., *Helen in Egypt* (New York: New Directions, 1974); references are to book and lyric numbers.
66. Friedman, *Psyche Reborn*, 261
67. Friedman, *Psyche Reborn*, 269.
68. Friedman, *Psyche Reborn*, 269.
69. Korg, 176–7.
70. Friedman, *Psyche Reborn*, 294.
71. Friedman, *Psyche Reborn*, 294.
72. Buck, 164.
73. Adams, 13–44.
74. Walcott, *In a Green Night: Poems 1948–1960* (London: Jonathan Cape, 1962) 18.
75. Joseph Farrell, 'Walcott's *Omeros*: The Classical Epic in a Postmodern World', *Epic Traditions in the Contemporary World: The Poetics of Community*, ed. Margaret Beissinger, Jane Tylus and Susanne Wofford (Berkeley: University of California Press, 1999) 273.
76. D. J. R. Bruckner, 'A Poem in Homage to an Unwanted Man', review of *Omeros*, *New York Times* (9 October 1990) 13.
77. J. P. White, 'An Interview with Derek Walcott', *Green Mountain Review* 4.1 (1990): 14–37.
78. Walcott, 'Leaving School', *London Magazine* 5.6 (1965): 13.
79. Walcott, *Omeros* (London: Faber, 1990); references are to page numbers.
80. See, for example, Isabella Maria Zoppi, '*Omeros*, David Walcott and the Contemporary Epic Poem', *Callaloo* 22.2 (1999): 509–28.

81. Bruckner, 13.
82. Walcott, *The Odyssey: A Stage Version* (London: Farrar, Straus Giroux, 1993).
83. Walcott, 'The Antilles: Fragments of Epic Memory', *New Republic* 207 (28 December 1992) 28.
84. Bruckner, 13.
85. Robert D. Hamner, *Epic of the Dispossessed: Derek Walcott's* Omeros (Columbia: University of Missouri Press, 1997) 163.
86. Gregson Davis, '"With No Homeric Shadow": The Disavowal of Epic in Derek Walcott's *Omeros*', *South Atlantic Quarterly* 96.2 (1997): 321–33.
87. Tom Paulin, *The Invasion Handbook* (London: Faber, 2002).
88. Paulin, *Thomas Hardy: The Poetry of Perception* (London: Macmillan, 1975).
89. Robert Crawford, review of *The Invasion Handbook* by Tom Paulin, *The Independent* (6 April 2002).
90. Nicholas Laird, 'The Poet's Ulcer', *Times Literary Supplement* (5 July 2002); and Crawford.

Chapter 6

1. Steve Neale, *Genre and Hollywood* (London: Routledge, 2000) 9–29; see also Neale, *Genre* (London: British Film Institute, 1980).
2. Tom Ryall, 'Teaching Through Genre', *Screen Education* 17 (1975): 28, qtd. in Neale, *Genre and Hollywood*, 12.
3. Walter Benjamin, 'The Work of Art in the Age of Mechanical Reproduction', *Literary Theory: An Anthology*, ed. Julie Rivkin and Michael Ryan (Malden, MA: Blackwell, 1998) 285, and Theodor Adorno and Max Horkheimer, 'The Culture Industry: Enlightenment as Mass Deception', *Dialectic of Enlightenment* (London: Verso, 1997) 120–67.
4. Neale, *Genre and Hollywood*, 10–11.
5. Neale, *Genre and Hollywood*, 26.
6. Neale, *Genre and Hollywood*, 28.
7. See, for example, Derek Elley, *The Epic Film* (London: Routledge, 1984) and Neale, *Genre and Hollywood*, 85–92.
8. Elley, 9–16.
9. Bruce Babington and Peter William Evans, *Biblical Epics: Sacred Narrative in the Hollywood Cinema* (Manchester: Manchester University Press, 1993) 4. Babington and Evans also identify the 'Christ film', which this chapter will discount from consideration, as these represent from the 1950s onwards a distinct generic trend that ultimately manifests itself in such psychologically-driven studies as Nicholas Ray's *King of Kings* (1961) and Martin Scorsese's *Last Temptation of Christ* (1988).
10. Babington and Evans, 4.
11. Maria Wyke, *Projecting the Past: Ancient Rome, Cinema and History* (New York: Routledge, 1997) 37.
12. Elley, 1.
13. Elley, 16.
14. Elley, 17; Wyke, 18–20.
15. Wyke, 25.

16. Review of *Cabiria*, *Film* (23 April 1914), qtd. in Wyke, 9.
17. Wyke, 25.
18. Wyke, 26.
19. Neale. *Genre and Hollywood*, 86.
20. Martin Williams, *Griffith: First Artist of the Movies* (New York: Oxford University Press, 1980) 55.
21. Williams, 61–2.
22. Griffith, 'How I Made *The Birth of a Nation*', *Focus on D. W. Griffith*, ed. Harry M. Geduld (Englewood Cliffs, NJ: Prentice-Hall, 1971) 39.
23. Griffith, 40.
24. 'D. W. Griffith, Producer of the World's Biggest Picture: Interview with D. W. Griffith', *Focus on D. W. Griffith*, ed. Geduld, 28.
25. A. Nicholas Vardac, *Stage to Screen* (Cambridge, MA: Harvard University Press, 1949) 223; and Everett Carter, 'Cultural History Written with Lightning: The Significance of *The Birth of Nation* (1915)', *Hollywood as Historian: American Film in Cultural Context*, ed. Peter C. Rollins (Lexington: University of Kentucky Press, 1983) 9.
26. Griffith, 'How I Made *The Birth of a Nation*', 41.
27. Carter, 16; see also Williams, 72–3.
28. Williams, 62.
29. Griffith, 42.
30. 'D. W. Griffith, Producer of the World's Biggest Picture', *Focus on Griffith*, ed. Geduld, 29.
31. Eisenstein, 'Dickens, Griffith, and the Film Today', *Film Form: Essays in Film Theory*, ed. and trans. Jay Leyda (1949; San Diego: Harcourt Brace Jovanovich, 1977) 232–3.
32. Neale, *Genre and Hollywood* 86.
33. Sumiko Higashi, *Cecil B. DeMille and American Culture: The Silent Era* (Berkeley: University of California Press, 1994) 117–21.
34. Arthur Friend, telegram to DeMille, 23 November 1916, qtd. in Higashi, 117.
35. Higashi, 117.
36. Higashi, 140.
37. Higashi, 125–32.
38. DeMille, telegram to Adolph Zukor, 10 May 1924, qtd. in Higashi, 187.
39. Higashi, 182.
40. Qtd. in Higashi, 191.
41. Elley, 46.
42. Elley, 46.
43. Babington and Evans, 50.
44. Donald Hayne, ed., *The Autobiography of Cecil B. DeMille* (Englewood Cliffs, NJ: Prentice Hall, 1959) 88.
45. Babington and Evans, 54.
46. Babington and Evans, 55–6.
47. Wyke, 29.
48. Review of *The Robe*, *Time* (28 September 1953), qtd. in Wyke, 29.
49. Michael Wood, *America in the Movies: Or, 'Santa Maria, It had Slipped my Mind'* (London: Secker and Warburg, 1975) 173.

50. Babington and Evans, 14.
51. Monica S. Cyrino, '*Gladiator* and Contemporary American Society', Gladiator: *Film and History*, ed. Martin M. Winkler (Malden, MA: Blackwell, 2004) 134.
52. Review of *The Robe*, *Time* (28 September 1953), qtd. in Wyke, 29–31.
53. *Ben-Hur: The Making of an Epic*, dir. and prod. Scott Benson, Turner Home Entertainment, 1993.
54. Elley, 131.
55. Elley, 131.
56. *Ben-Hur: The Making of an Epic.*
57. *Ben-Hur: The Making of an Epic.*
58. Wyke, 60.
59. Wyke, 61–2.
60. Wyke, 63–4.
61. Wyke, 65.
62. Carl Hoffman, 'The Evolution of a Gladiator: History, Representation, and Revision in *Spartacus*', *Journal of American and Comparative Cultures* 23 (2000): 66.
63. Hoffman, 66.
64. Wyke 65; Hoffman, 68.
65. Wyke, 71.
66. *Variety* (7 October 1960), qtd. in Wyke, 72.
67. Hoffman, 68.
68. Elley, 27.
69. Martin M. Winkler, '*Star Wars* and the Roman Empire', *Classical Myth and Culture in the Cinema*, ed. Winkler (Oxford: Oxford University Press, 2001) 272–90.
70. Geoff King, *Spectacular Narratives: Hollywood in the Age of the Blockbuster* (London: I. B. Tauris, 2000) 1–15.
71. King, 47–53.
72. Cyrino, 129.
73. Cyrino, 129.
74. Diana Landau, ed., *Gladiator: The Making of the Ridley Scott Epic* (New York: Newmarket, 2000) 50.
75. *Ben-Hur: The Making of an Epic* and Cyrino, 130.
76. Winkler, '*Gladiator* and the Traditions of Historical Cinema', Gladiator: *Film and History*, ed. Winkler, 27.
77. Qtd. in Cyrino, 142.
78. Cyrino 127–29.
79. Winkler, '*Gladiator*', 24.
80. Cyrino 127–28, citing Herbert Muschamp, 'Throwing Our Anxieties to the Lions', *New York Times* (30 April 2000) section 2A, 1.
81. Qtd. in Cyrino, 131.
82. Cyrino, 128.
83. Arthur J. Pomeroy, 'The Vision of a Fascist Rome in *Gladiator*', Gladiator: *Film and History*, ed. Winkler, 119.
84. Mark Morris, 'Empire Strikes Back', *The Observer* (23 April 2000).
85. Philip French, 'Rome with a View', *The Observer* (14 May 2000).
86. Grace Bradberry, 'Toga Sagas Conquer the World', *The Observer* (10 August 2003).

87. Leon Hunt, 'What Are Big Boys Made Of? *Spartacus, El Cid* and the Male Epic', *You Tarzan: Masculinity, Movies and Men*, ed. Pat Kirkham and Janet Thurmin (London: Lawrence and Wishart, 1993) 75–6.

88. Peter Green, 'Heroic Hype, New Style: Hollywood Pitted Against Homer', *Arion* 12 (2004): 171–87.

89. Jonathan Romney, review of *Troy, The Independent* (16 May 2004); French, 'Well, the Horse Looks Great . . .', *The Observer* (16 May 2004).

Glossary

Blank verse: unrhymed iambic pentameter, that is, a line of verse that consists of five feet, each foot comprised of two syllables – the first stressed and the second unstressed. It became a standard metrical form for epic in English after it was employed by John Milton in *Paradise Lost*.

Epic: usually defined as a long heroic poem narrating great deeds, sometimes of national or cultural importance. Since the earliest epics, the *Iliad* and the *Odyssey*, were composed in about the eighth century BC, the form has undergone significant changes and has been subject to much experimentation.

Epic theory: the critical writings that surround the epic, sometimes traced to Aristotle's *Poetics*. These became a substantial body of critical precepts in the Renaissance, first in Italy and then in England and France. These precepts were largely undermined and challenged from the end of the eighteenth century onwards.

Formulae: the recurring phrases in Homeric epic, such as epithets or descriptions. Defined by Milman Parry as 'a group of words which is regularly employed under the same metrical conditions to express a given essential idea', the formula is one of the building blocks of Homeric epic.

Genre: literary form – for example, epic, romance, tragedy. Genre is best viewed not as a firm category, but as a set of negotiable rules by which writers and readers are able to make a work intelligible. Genre theory refers to the body of criticism surrounding the concept of genre.

Heroic couplets: iambic pentameter rhymed in pairs. It became one of the standard metrical forms for epic in English from the Renaissance onwards, and was particularly popularised by John Dryden's translation of Virgil's *Aeneid* and Alexander Pope's translations of the Homeric epics.

In medias res: the conventional beginning of epic in the middle of the narrative action, after which chronologically earlier events are filled in by the narrator, or told in flashback. The phrase occurs in Horace's *Ars Poetica* and means literally, 'in the midst of things'.

Invocation to the muse: the conventional opening of the epic, in which one of the muses – or classical guardians of poetry – is invoked in order to inspire the poet to compose his poem.

Katabasis: The epic convention of the hero's descent to the underworld, in which he encounters dead acquaintances and learns of prophecies for the future.

Kleos: a term prominent in Homeric epic, loosely translatable as 'honour'. It refers to the martial deeds performed by the epic hero, as well as the fame that he wins through being the subject of epic.

Primary epic: epic that was originally transmitted orally and usually in a primitive society, such as Homer's *Iliad* and *Odyssey*, the early English *Beowulf* and the Hindu epics, the *Ramayana* and *Mahabharata*.

Romance: also 'chivalric romance', a genre that arose in about the twelfth century and influenced the subsequent development of the epic. It is concerned largely with a courtly or chivalric setting, and is usually defined by a plot trajectory of a knight who quests to defend love and honour of both his lady and his king.

Secondary epic: epic that is literary as opposed to oral, composed in writing in imitation of earlier primitive epics.

Supernatural machinery: the epic convention of gods or divine forces in general, particularly in interaction with mortals.

Chronology

3000–2600 BC	Development of Sumerian writing
ca. 2300 BC	Development of Akkadian writing
2200–2000 BC	Oral *Gilgamesh* poems
1200–1100 BC	Standard Babylonian Text of *Gilgamesh* by Sîn-liqe-uninni
	Invasion of Troy
800–700 BC	The *Iliad* and the *Odyssey* of Homer composed
ca. 700 BC	Development of Greek writing
390–350 BC	Plato's *Republic* composed
335–322 BC	Aristotle's *Poetics* composed
ca. 200 BC	Apollonius' *Argonautica*
	Naevius' *Bellum Poenicum* ('The Punic War')
200–100 BC	Quintus Ennius' *Annales* ('The Annals')
29–19 BC	Virgil's *Aeneid* composed
AD 1–8	Ovid's *Metamorphoses* composed
6–65	Lucan's *Pharsalia* or *Bellum Civile* ('The Civil War') composed
500–600	Fulgentius' commentary on the *Aeneid*
ca. 1000	*Beowulf* composed
1098–1100	*Chanson de Roland* ('The Song of Roland') composed
1100–1200	*Roman d'Eneas* ('The Romance of Aeneas') composed
1307–21	Dante's *La Divina Commedia* ('The Divine Comedy') composed
1370s	Chaucer's *The House of Fame* composed
1487	Matteomaria Boiardo's *Orlando Innamorato* published
1532	Ludovico Ariosto's *Orlando Furioso* published
1536	Alessandro Pazzi's revised Latin translation of Aristotle' *Poetics* published
1561	Julius Caesar Scaliger's *Poetics* published
1580	Torquato Tasso's *Gerusalemme Liberata* ('Jerusalem Delivered') published
1590–96	Edmund Spenser's *The Faerie Queene* published
1605–15	Miguel de Cervantes' *Don Quixote* published
1667	John Milton's *Paradise Lost* published
1674	René Rapin's *Réflexions sur la Poétique d'Aristotle* published
1675	René Le Bossu's *Traité du poëme épique* published
1681	John Dryden's *Absalom and Achitophel* published
1682	Dryden's *Mac Flecknoe* published
1695	Le Bossu's *Traité* translated into English as *A Treatise on the Epick Poem*
1697	Dryden's *Aeneid* published
1711	Madame Dacier's translations of Homer published
1712–14	Alexander Pope's *The Rape of the Lock* published
1715–20	Pope's *Iliad* published

1725–26	Pope's *Odyssey* published
1728–42	Pope's *The Dunciad* published
1742	Henry Fielding's *Joseph Andrews* published
1748–73	Frederich Klopstock's *Der Messias* ('The Messiah') published
1748	Tobias Smollett's *The Adventures of Roderick Random* published
1749	Fielding's *Tom Jones* published
1751	Smollett's *The Adventures of Peregrine Pickle* published
1782	William Hayley's *Essay on Epic Poetry* published
1798–1850	William Wordsworth's *The Prelude* composed
1804	William Blake's *Milton* published
1818	John Keats' *Hyperion* published
1819	Keats' *The Fall of Hyperion* composed
1819–24	Lord Byron's *Don Juan* published
1850	Wordsworth's *The Prelude* published
1857	Elizabeth Barrett Browning's *Aurora Leigh* published
1856	Keats' *Fall of Hyperion* published
1856–74	Alfred, Lord Tennyson's *Idylls of the King* composed
1868	Leo Tolstoy's *War and Peace* published
1868–69	Robert Browning's *The Ring and the Book* published
1891	Tennyson's *Idylls of the King* published in full sequence
1904–8	Thomas Hardy's *The Dynasts* published
1913	Enrico Guazzoni's *Quo Vadis?* released
1914	Giovanni Pastrone's *Cabiria* released
1915	D. W. Griffith's *Birth of a Nation* released
1916	Cecil B. DeMille's *Joan the Woman* released
1917–70	Ezra Pound's *Cantos* published
1922	James Joyce's *Ulysses* published
	T. S. Eliot's *The Waste Land* published
1923	DeMille's *The Ten Commandments* released
1927	DeMille's *The King of Kings* released
1933	DeMille's *The Sign of the Cross* released
1934	DeMille's *Cleopatra* released
1944	DeMille's *Cleopatra* re-released
1953	Henry Koster's *The Robe* released
1956	DeMille's remake of *The Ten Commandments* released
1959	William Wyler's *Ben-Hur* released
1960	Stanley Kubrick's *Spartacus* released
1961	H. D.'s *Helen in Egypt* published
1963	Joseph Mankiewicz's *Cleopatra* released
1964	Anthony Mann's *The Fall of the Roman Empire* released
1966	John Huston's *The Bible* released
1977	George Lucas's *Star Wars* released
1990	Derek Walcott's *Omeros* published
1998	Ridley Scott's *Gladiator* released
2001	Peter Jackson's *The Lord of the Rings* released
2002	Tom Paulin's *The Invasion Handbook* published
2004	Wolfgang Petersen's *Troy* released

Bibliography and Filmography

Epics

Ariosto, Ludovico. *Orlando Furioso*. Trans. Guido Waldman. Oxford: Oxford University Press, 1983.

Beowulf. Trans. Seamus Heaney. New York: Norton, 2002.

Blake, William. *Milton*. Ed. Kay Parkhurst Easson and Roger R. Easson. London: Thames and Hudson, 1978.

Browning, Elizabeth Barrett. *Aurora Leigh*. Ed. Kerry McSweeney. Oxford: Oxford University Press, 1993.

Browning, Robert. *The Ring and the Book*. Ed. Richard D. Altick. London: Penguin, 1971.

Byron, George Gordon. *Don Juan*. Ed. T. G. Steffan, E. Steffan and W. W. Pratt. London: Penguin, 1993. Rev. edn.

Cervantes, Miguel. *Don Quixote*. Trans. John Rutherford. London: Penguin, 2000.

Dante Alighieri. *The Divine Comedy*. Trans. C. H. Sisson. Oxford: Oxford University Press, 1993.

Dryden, John. *The Aeneid*. *The Poems of John Dryden*. Ed. James Kinsley. Oxford: Oxford University Press, 1958.

Eliot, T. S. *The Waste Land and Other Poems*. 1940. London: Faber, 1972.

The Epic of Gilgamesh. Trans and ed. Andrew George. London: Penguin, 1999.

Fénelon, François de. *Telemachus, Son of Ulysses*. Ed. Patrick Riley. Cambridge: Cambridge University Press, 1994.

Fielding, Henry. *Joseph Andrews*. Ed. R. F. Brissenden. London: Penguin, 1985.

Fielding, Henry. *Tom Jones*. Ed. John Bender and Simon Stern. Oxford: Oxford University Press, 1996.

Hardy, Thomas. *The Dynasts: An Epic-Drama, of the War with Napoleon, in Three Parts, Nineteen Acts, and One Hundred and Thirty Scenes*. *The Poetical Works of Thomas Hardy in Prose and Verse*. Vols II and III. London: Macmillan, 1920.

H. D. *Helen in Egypt*. 1961. New York: New Directions, 1974.

Homer. *The Iliad of Homer*. Trans. Richmond Lattimore. Chicago: University of Chicago Press, 1951.

Homer. *The Odyssey of Homer*. Trans. Richmond Lattimore. New York: HarperCollins, 1965.

Joyce, James. *Ulysses*. Ed. Jeri Johnson. Oxford: Oxford University Press, 1993.

Keats, John. 'Hyperion' and 'The Fall of Hyperion'. *John Keats: The Complete Poems*. Ed. John Barnard. London: Penguin, 1988. 3rd edn.

Klopstock, Friedrich. *The Messiah: Attempted from the German of Mr. Klopstock*. Trans. Mary Collyer and Joseph Collyer. London: Dodsley, 1763.

Lucan. *Civil War*. Trans. Susan H. Braund. Oxford: Oxford University Press, 1992.

Milton, John. *Paradise Lost*. Ed. Scott Elledge. New York: Norton, 1975.

Ovid. *Metamorphoses*. Trans. A. D. Melville. Oxford: Oxford University Press, 1986.

Paulin, Tom. *The Invasion Handbook*. London: Faber, 2002.

Pope, Alexander. *The Iliad of Homer*. Ed. Steven Shankman. London: Penguin, 1996.
Pope, Alexander. *The Rape of the Lock*. Ed. Geoffrey Tillotson. London: Routledge, 1971.
Pound, Ezra. *The Cantos of Ezra Pound*. London: Faber and Faber, 1975.
The Song of Roland. Trans. Glyn Burgess. London: Penguin, 1990.
Spenser, Edmund. *The Faerie Queene*. Ed. Thomas P. Roche. London: Penguin, 1978.
Tasso, Torquato. *Jerusalem Delivered*. Trans. Anthony M. Esolen. Baltimore: Johns Hopkins University Press, 2000.
Tennyson, Lord Alfred. *Idylls of the King*. Ed. J. M. Gray. London: Penguin, 1983.
Tolstoy, Leo. *War and Peace*. Ed. Henry Gifford. Trans. Louise and Aylmer Maude. Oxford: Oxford University Press, 1991.
Virgil. *The Aeneid*. Trans. C. Day Lewis. Oxford: Oxford University Press, 1986.
Walcott, Derek. *Omeros*. London: Faber, 1990.
Wordsworth, William. *The Prelude 1799, 1805, 1850*. Ed. Jonathan Wordsworth, M. H. Abrams and Stephen Gill. New York: Norton, 1979.

Epic films

Attack of the Clones. Dir. George Lucas and prod. Rick MacCallum and George Lucas. With Ewan MacGregor and Natalie Portman. Lucasfilm, 2002.
Ben-Hur. Dir. William Wyler and prod. Sam Zimbalist. With Charlton Heston and Jack Hawkins. Paramount, 1959.
The Bible. Dir. John Huston and prod. Dino DeLaurentiis. With George C. Scott and Ava Gardner. Twentieth-Century Fox, 1966.
The Birth of a Nation. Dir. and prod. D. W. Griffith. With Lillian Gish and Henry B. Walthall. David W. Griffith, 1915.
Cabiria. Dir. and prod. Giovanni Pastrone. With Lidia Quaranta. Italia, 1914.
Cleopatra. Dir. and prod. Cecil B. DeMille. With Claudette Colbert and Warren William. Paramount, 1934.
Cleopatra. Dir. Joseph Mankiewicz and prod. Walter Wanger. With Elizabeth Taylor and Richard Burton. Twentieth-Century Fox, 1963.
The Day After Tomorrow. Dir. and prod. Roland Emmerich. With Dennis Quaid and Jake Gyllenhaal. Twentieth-Century Fox, 2004.
The Empire Strikes Back. Dir. Irvin Kershner and prod. Gary Kurtz and George Lucas. With Harrison Ford and Mark Hamill. Lucasfilm, 1980.
The Fall of the Roman Empire. Dir. Anthony Mann and prod. Samuel Bronston. With Christopher Plummer and Sophia Loren. Samuel Bronston Productions, 1964.
Gladiator. Dir. Ridley Scott and prod. David Franzoni. With Russell Crowe and Joaquin Phoenix. Dreamworks, 2000.
Independence Day. Dir. and prod. Roland Emmerich. With Will Smith and Bill Pullman. Twentieth-Century Fox, 1996.
Joan the Woman. Dir. and prod. Cecil B. DeMille. With Geraldine Farrar. Famous Players-Lasky, 1916.
The King of Kings. Dir. and prod. Cecil B. DeMille. With H. B. Warner and Dorothy Cumming. Pathé, 1927.
The Lord of the Rings: The Fellowship of the Ring. Dir. and prod. Peter Jackson. With Ian McKellen and Orlando Bloom. New Line Cinema, 2001.

The Lord of the Rings: The Two Towers. Dir. and prod. Peter Jackson. With Ian McKellen and Elijah Wood. New Line Cinema, 2002.
The Lord of the Rings: The Return of the King. Dir. and prod. Peter Jackson. With Ian McKellen and Elijah Wood. New Line Cinema, 2003.
The Phantom Menace. Dir. George Lucas and prod. Rick MacCallum and George Lucas. With Liam Neeson and Ewan MacGregor. Twentieth-Century Fox, 1999.
Quo Vadis? Dir. Enrico Guazzoni. With Amletto Novelli and Gustavo Serena. Cines, 1913.
Return of the Jedi. Dir. Richard Marquand and prod. Howard Kazanjian and George Lucas. With Harrison Ford and Mark Hamill. Lucasfilm, 1983.
The Robe. Dir. Henry Koster and prod. Frank Ross. With Richard Burton and Jean Simmons. Twentieth-Century Fox, 1953.
Samson and Delilah. Dir. and prod. Cecil B. DeMille. With Hedy Lamarr and Victor Mature. Paramount, 1949.
The Sign of the Cross. Dir. and prod. Cecil B. DeMille. With Claudette Colbert and Charles Laughton. Paramount, 1932.
Spartacus. Dir. Stanley Kubrick and prod. Kirk Douglas and Edward Lewis. With Kirk Douglas and Lawrence Olivier. Bryna, 1960.
Star Wars. Dir. George Lucas and prod. Gary Kurtz and George Lucas. With Harrison Ford and Mark Hamill. Lucasfilm, 1977.
Superman. Dir. Richard Donner and prod. Ilya Salkind. With Christopher Reeve and Marlon Brando. Alexander Salkind, 1978.
Superman II. Dir. Richard Lester and prod. Ilya Salkind. With Christopher Reeve and Gene Hackman. Alexander Salkind, 1980.
Superman III. Dir. Richard Lester and prod. Ilya Salkind. With Christopher Reeve and Richard Pryor. Alexander Salkind, 1983.
The Ten Commandments. Dir. and prod. Cecil B. DeMille. With Theodore Roberts and Estelle Taylor. Famous Players-Lasky, 1923.
The Ten Commandments. Dir. and prod. Cecil B. DeMille. With Charlton Heston and Yul Brynner. Paramount, 1956.
Titanic. Dir. and prod. James Cameron. With Leonardo DiCaprio and Kate Winslett. Twentieth-Century Fox, 1997.
Troy. Dir. and prod. Wolfgang Petersen. With Brad Pitt and Eric Bana. Warner Brothers, 2004.

Genre theory

Bakhtin, Mikhail. 'Epic and Novel'. *The Dialogic Imagination: Four Essays*. Ed. Michael Holquist, trans. Caryl Emerson and Holquist. Austin: University of Texas Press, 1981. 3–21.
Cohen, Ralph. 'History and Genre'. *New Literary History* 17 (1986): 210–18.
Derrida, Jacques. 'The Law of Genre'. *Glyph* 7 (1980): 176–232.
Duff, David, ed. *Modern Genre Theory*. Harlow: Longman, 2000.
Fowler, Alastair. *Kinds of Literature: An Introduction to the Theory of Genres and Modes*. Oxford: Clarendon Press, 1982.
Fowler, Alastair. 'The Life and Death of Literary Forms'. *New Directions in Literary History*. Ed. Ralph Cohen. Baltimore: Johns Hopkins University Press, 1974. 77–94.

Frye, Northrop. *Anatomy of Criticism: Four Essays*. Princeton: Princeton University Press, 1957.

Genette, Gérard. *The Architext: An Introduction*. 1979. Trans. Jane E. Lewin. Berkeley: University of California Press, 1992.

Hirsch, E. D. *Validity in Interpretation*. New Haven: Yale University Press, 1967.

Jauss, Hans Robert. *Toward an Aesthetic of Reception*. Trans. Timothy Bahti. Brighton: Harvester, 1982.

Lukács, Georg. *The Theory of the Novel: A Historico-Philosophical Essay on the Forms of Great Epic Literature*. Trans. Anna Bostock. 1920; London: Merlin Press, 1978.

Neale, Steve. *Genre*. London: British Film Institute, 1980.

Neale, Steve. *Genre and Hollywood*. London: Routledge, 2000.

Rosmarin, Adena. *The Power of Genre*. Minneapolis: University of Minnesota Press, 1985.

Schaeffer, Jean-Marie. 'Literary Genres and Textual Genericity'. *The Future of Literary Theory*. Ed. Ralph Cohen. New York: Routledge, 1989. 167–87.

Todorov, Tzvetan. *Genres in Discourse*. Trans. Catherine Porter. Cambridge: Cambridge University Press, 1990.

General and comparative studies of the epic

Bowra, C. M. *Heroic Poetry*. London: Macmillan, 1952.

Burrow, Colin. *Epic Romance: Homer to Milton*. Oxford: Clarendon Press, 1993.

Dixon, W. Macneile. *English Epic and Heroic Poetry*. London: J. M. Dent, 1912.

Feeney, D. C. 'Epic Hero and Epic Fable'. *Comparative Literature* 38 (1986): 137–58.

Greene, Thomas M. *The Descent from Heaven: A Study in Epic Continuity*. New Haven, CT: Yale University Press, 1963.

Hainsworth, J. B. *The Idea of Epic*. Berkeley: University of California Press, 1991.

Kelly, Van. 'Criteria for the Epic: Borders, Diversity, and Expansion'. *Epic and Epoch: Essays on the Interpretation and History of a Genre*. Eds. Steven M. Oberhelman, Van Kelly, and Richard Golson. Lubbock: Texas Tech University Press, 1994. 1–21.

Lord, George deForest. *Trials of the Self: Heroic Ordeals in the Epic Tradition*. Hamden, CT: Archon Books, 1983.

Merchant, Paul. *The Epic*. London: Methuen, 1971.

Quint, David. *Epic and Empire: Politics and Generic Form from Virgil to Milton*. Princeton, NJ: Princeton University Press, 1993.

Stanford, W. B. *The Ulysses Theme: A Study in the Adaptability of a Traditional Hero*. New York: Barnes, 1968. 2nd edn.

Swedenberg, H. T. *The Theory of the Epic in England 1650–1800*. Berkeley: University of California Press, 1944.

Tillyard, E. M. W. *The English Epic and Its Background*. London: Chatto and Windus, 1954.

Vogler, Thomas A. *Preludes to Vision: The Epic Venture in Blake, Wordsworth, Keats and Hart Crane*. Berkeley: University of California Press, 1971.

The classical age

Aristotle. *Poetics*. Trans. Malcolm Heath. London: Penguin, 1996.

Beye, Charles Rowan. *The* Iliad, *the* Odyssey, *and the Epic Tradition*. London: Macmillan, 1968.

Clarke, Howard. *Homer's Readers: A Historical Introduction to the* Iliad *and the* Odyssey. London: Associated University Presses, 1981.

Conte, Gian Biagio. *The Rhetoric of Imagination: Genre and Poetic Memory in Virgil and Other Latin Poets*. Ed. Charles Segal. Ithaca, NY: Cornell University Press, 1986.

Feeney, D. C. *The Gods in the Epic: Poets and Critics of the Classical Tradition*. New York: Oxford University Press, 1993.

Ford, Andrew. 'Epic as Genre'. *A New Companion to Homer*. Ed. Ian Morris and Barry Powell. Leiden: Brill, 1997. 398–416.

Ford, Andrew. *Homer: The Poetry of the Past*. Ithaca, NY: Cornell University Press, 1992.

Fowler, Don. 'The Virgil Commentary of Servius'. *The Cambridge Companion to Virgil*. Ed. Charles Martindale. Cambridge: Cambridge University Press, 1997. 73–87.

Graziosi, Barbara. *Inventing Homer: The Early Reception of Epic*. Cambridge: Cambridge University Press, 2002.

Haubold, Johannes. 'Greek Epic: A Near Eastern Genre?' *Proceedings of the Cambridge Philological Society* 48 (2002): 1–19.

Heinze, Richard. *Virgil's Epic Technique*. Trans. Hazel and David Harvey. London: Bristol Classical Press, 1993.

Kennedy, Duncan F. 'Virgilian Epic'. *The Cambridge Companion to Virgil*. Ed. Charles Martindale. Cambridge: Cambridge University Press, 1997. 145–54.

Lamberton, Robert. 'Homer in Antiquity'. *A New Companion to Homer*. Ed. Ian Morris and Barry Powell. Leiden: Brill, 1997. 33–54.

Mills, Donald H. *The Hero and the Sea: Patterns of Chaos in Ancient Myth*. Wauconda, IL: Bolchazy-Carducci, 2003.

Morris, Sarah. 'Homer and the Near East'. *A New Companion to Homer*. Ed. Ian Morris and Barry Powell. Leiden: Brill, 1997. 599–623.

Nagy, Gregory. *The Best of the Achaeans: Concepts of the Hero in Archaic Greek Poetry*. 1979. Baltimore: Johns Hopkins University Press, 1999. Rev. edn.

Newman, John Kevin. *The Classical Epic Tradition*. Madison: University of Wisconsin Press, 1986.

Parry, Milman. *The Making of Homeric Verse: The Collected Papers of Milman Parry*. Ed. Adam Parry. Oxford: Clarendon Press, 1971.

Powell, Barry B. 'Homer and Writing'. *A New Companion to Homer*. Ed. Ian Morris and Barry Powell. Leiden: Brill, 1997. 3–32.

Ray, Benjamin Caleb. 'The Gilgamesh Epic: Myth and Meaning'. *Myth and Method*. Ed. Laurie L. Patton and Wendy Doniger. Charlottesville: University Press of Virginia, 1996. 300–26.

Rutherford, Richard. *Homer*. Oxford: Oxford University Press, 1996.

Schein, Seth L. *The Mortal Hero: An Introduction to Homer's* Iliad. Berkeley: University of California Press, 1984.

Seaford, Richard. *Reciprocity and Ritual: Homer and Tragedy in the Developing City-State*. Oxford: Clarendon Press, 1994.

Segal, Charles. *Singers, Heroes, and Gods in the* Odyssey. Ithaca, NY: Cornell University Press, 1994.

Slatkin, Laura M. *The Power of Thetis: Allusion and Interpretation in the* Iliad. Berkeley: University of California Press, 1991.

Tarrant, R. J. 'Aspects of Virgil's Reception in Antiquity'. *The Cambridge Companion to Virgil*. Ed. Charles Martindale. Cambridge: Cambridge University Press, 1997. 56–72.

Thalmann, William G. *Conventions of Form and Thought in Early Greek Epic Poetry.* Baltimore: Johns Hopkins University Press, 1984.

Toohey, Peter. *Reading Epic: An Introduction to the Ancient Narratives.* London: Routledge, 1992.

Wofford, Susanne Lindgren. *The Choice of Achilles: The Ideology of Figure in the Epic.* Stanford, CA: Stanford University Press, 1992.

Zug, Charles G. 'From Sumer to Babylon: The Evolution of the *Gilgamesh* Epic'. *Genre* 5 (1972): 217–34.

The Middle Ages and Renaissance

Baswell, Christopher. *Virgil in Medieval England: Figuring the* Aeneid *from the Twelfth Century to Chaucer.* Cambridge: Cambridge University Press, 1995.

Brownlee, Marina Scordilis. 'Cervantes as Reader of Ariosto'. *Romance: Generic Transformation from Chrétien de Troyes to Cervantes.* Ed. Kevin Brownlee and Marina Scordilis Brownlee. Hanover, NH: University Press of New England, 1985. 220–37.

Burrow, Colin. 'Virgils, from Dante to Milton'. *The Cambridge Companion to Virgil.* Ed. Charles Martindale. Cambridge: Cambridge University Press, 1997. 21–37.

DiBattista, Maria. '*Don Quixote*'. *Homer to Brecht: The European Epic and Dramatic Traditions.* Ed. Michael Seidel and Edward Mendelson. New Haven, CT: Yale University Press, 1977). 105–22.

Fichter, Andrew. *Poets Historical: Dynastic Epic in the Renaissance.* New Haven, CT: Yale University Press, 1982.

Frank, Roberta. 'The *Beowulf* Poet's Sense of History'. *The Wisdom of Poetry: Essays in Early English Literature in Honor of Morton W. Bloomfield.* Ed. Larry D. Benson and Siegfried Wenzel. Kalamazoo: Medieval Institute Publications, 1982. 53–65.

Frye, Northrop. 'Notes for a Commentary on Milton'. *The Divine Vision: Studies in the Poetry and Art of William Blake.* Ed. Vivian de Sola Pinto. London: Victor Gollancz, 1957. 99–137.

Frye, Northrop. *The Return of Eden: Five Essays on Milton's Epics.* Toronto: University of Toronto Press, 1965.

Hill, Thomas D. 'The Christian Language and Theme of *Beowulf*'. *Companion to Old English Poetry.* Ed. Henk Aertsen and Rolf H. Bremmer, Jr. Amsterdam: VU University Press, 1994. 63–77.

Javitch, Daniel. 'The Emergence of Poetic Genre Theory in the Sixteenth Century'. *Modern Language Quarterly* 59 (1998): 139–69.

Lewis, C. S. *A Preface to Paradise Lost.* Oxford: Oxford University Press, 1942.

Martindale, Charles. *John Milton and the Transformation of Ancient Epic.* 1986. London: Bristol Classical Press, 2002.

Martínez-Bonati, Félix. Don Quixote *and the Poetics of the Novel.* Trans. Dian Fox. Ithaca, NY: Cornell University Press, 1992.

McGaha, Michael D. 'Cervantes and Virgil'. *Cervantes and the Renaissance.* Ed. McGaha. Easton, PA: Juan de la Cuesta, 1980. 34–50.

Murillo, L. A. '*Don Quixote* as Renaissance Epic'. *Cervantes and the Renaissance.* Ed. Michael D. McGaha. Easton, PA: Juan de la Cuesta, 1980. 51–70.

Tasso, Torquato. *Discourses on the Heroic Poem*. Trans. Mariella Cavalchini and Irene Samuel. Oxford: Clarendon Press, 1973.

Treip, Mindele Anne. *Allegorical Poetics and the Epic: The Renaissance Tradition to Paradise Lost*. Lexington: University Press of Kentucky, 1994.

The eighteenth century

Addison, Joseph. 'Notes upon the Twelve Books of *Paradise Lost*'. *Spectator* no. 267 (5 January 1712).

Browning, Robert M. *German Poetry in the Age of Enlightenment: From Brockes to Klopstock*. University Park: Pennsylvania State University Press, 1978.

Close, Anthony. *The Romantic Approach to 'Don Quixote': A Critical History of the Romantic Tradition in 'Quixote' Criticism*. Cambridge: Cambridge University Press, 1977.

Connelly, Peter J. 'The Ideology of Pope's *Iliad*'. *Comparative Literature* 40 (1988): 358–83.

Davis, Lennard J. *Factual Fictions: The Origins of the English Novel*. New York: Columbia University Press, 1983.

Hammond, Paul. *Dryden and the Traces of Classical Rome*. Oxford: Oxford University Press, 1999.

Keener, Frederick M. 'Pope, *The Dunciad*, Virgil, and the New Historicism of Le Bossu'. *Eighteenth-Century Life* 15 (1991): 35–57.

Knapp, Lewis M. 'Smollett's Translation of Fenelon's *Télémaque*'. *Philological Quarterly* 44 (1965): 405–7.

Le Bossu, René. *Treatise of the Epick Poem* (1695). Rpt. in *Le Bossu and Voltaire on the Epic*. Ed. Stuart Curran. Gainesville, FL: Scholars' Facsimiles and Reprintings, 1970.

Levine, Joseph M. *The Battle of the Books: History and Literature in the Augustan Age*. Ithaca, NY: Cornell University Press, 1991.

Lynch, Kathryn L. 'Homer's *Iliad* and Pope's Vile Forgery'. *Comparative Literature* 34 (1982): 1–15.

McKeon, Michael. *The Origins of the English Novel 1600–1740*. Baltimore, MD: Johns Hopkins University Press, 1987.

Paulson, Ronald. 'The Pilgrimage and the Family: Structures in the Novels of Fielding and Smollett'. *Tobias Smollett: Bicentennial Essays Presented to Lewis M. Knapp*. Ed. G. S. Rousseau and Paul-Gabriel Boucé. Oxford: Oxford University Press, 1971. 57–78.

Paulson, Ronald. *Don Quixote in England: The Aesthetics of Laughter*. Baltimore, MD: Johns Hopkins University Press, 1998.

Proudfoot, L. *Dryden's* Aeneid *and Its Seventeenth-Century Predecessors*. Manchester: Manchester University Press, 1960.

Richetti, John. 'The Old Order and the New Novel of the Mid-Eighteenth Century: Narrative Authority in Fielding and Smollett'. *Eighteenth-Century Fiction* 2 (1990): 183–96.

Simonsuuri, Kirsti. *Homer's Original Genius: Eighteenth-Century Notions of the Early Greek Epic (1688–1798)*. Cambridge: Cambridge University Press, 1979.

Thomas, Richard. *Virgil and the Augustan Reception*. Cambridge: Cambridge University Press, 2001.

Weinbrot, Howard D. '*The Rape of the Lock* and the Contexts of Warfare'. *The Enduring Legacy: Alexander Pope Tercentenary Essays*. Ed. G. S. Rousseau and Pat Rogers. Cambridge: Cambridge University Press, 1988. 21–48.

The nineteenth century

Altick, Richard D. and James F. Loucks. *Browning's Roman Murder Story*. Chicago: University of Chicago Press, 1968.

Bate, Jonathan. 'Keats's Two *Hyperions* and the Problem of Milton'. *Romantic Revisions*. Ed. Robert Brinkley and Keith Hanley. Cambridge: Cambridge University Press, 1992. 321–38.

Bayley, John. *Tolstoy and the Novel*. London: Chatto and Windus, 1966.

Berlin, Isaiah. *The Hedgehog and the Fox: An Essay on Tolstoy's View of History*. London: Weidenfeld and Nicholson, 1953.

Bernstein, Carol L. 'Subjectivity as Critique and the Critique of Subjectivity in Keats's *Hyperion*'. *After the Future: Postmodern Times and Places*. Ed. Gary Shapiro. Albany, NY: SUNY Press, 1990. 41–52.

Blake, Kathleen. 'Elizabeth Barrett Browning and Wordsworth: The Romantic Poet as a Woman'. *Victorian Poetry* 24.4 (1986): 387–98.

Bode, Christoph. '*Hyperion, The Fall of Hyperion* and Keats's Poetics'. *Wordsworth Circle* 31 (2000): 31–37.

Bourke, Richard. *Romantic Discourses and Political Modernity: Wordsworth, the Intellectual and Cultural Critique*. New York: Harvester Wheatsheaf, 1993.

Brady, Ann P. *Pompilia: A Feminist Reading of Robert Browning's* The Ring and the Book. Athens: Ohio University Press, 1988.

Buckler, William E. *Poetry and Truth in Browning's* The Ring and the Book. New York: New York University Press, 1985.

Christian, R. F. *Tolstoy*. Cambridge: Cambridge University Press, 1969.

Clay, George R. 'Tolstoy in the Twentieth Century'. *The Cambridge Companion to Tolstoy*. Ed. Donna Tussing Orwin. Cambridge: Cambridge University Press, 2002. 206–21.

Curran, Stuart. *Poetic Form and British Romanticism*. Oxford: Oxford University Press, 1986.

Davies, Hugh Sykes. *Wordsworth and the Worth of Words*. Cambridge: Cambridge University Press, 1986.

Foerster, Donald M. *The Fortunes of Epic Poetry*. Washington, DC: Catholic University of America Press, 1965.

Fulford, Tim. *Landscape, Liberty and Authority: Poetry, Criticism and Politics from Thomson to Wordsworth*. Cambridge: Cambridge University Press, 1996.

Garber, Frederick. 'Self and the Language of Satire in *Don Juan*'. *Thalia: Studies in Literary Humor* 5 (1982): 35–44.

Hartman, Geoffrey H. 'A Poet's Progress: Wordsworth and the *Via Naturaliter Negativa*'. *Modern Philology* 59 (1962): 214–24.

Hayley, William. *An Essay on Epick Poetry*. Ed. M. Celeste Williamson. 1782. Gainesville, FL: Scholars' Fascimiles and Reprints, 1968.

Jacobus, Mary. *Romanticism, Writing, and Sexual Difference: Essays on* The Prelude. Oxford: Clarendon Press, 1989.

Kozicki, Henry. *Tennyson and Clio: History in the Major Poems*. Baltimore, MD: Johns Hopkins University Press, 1979.

LaChance, Charles. '*Don Juan*, "a Problem, Like All Things"'. *Papers on Language and Literature* 34 (1998): 273–300.

Laird, Holly A. '*Aurora Leigh*: An Epical *Ars Poetica*'. *Writing the Woman Artist: Essays on Poetics, Politics, and Portraiture*. Ed. Suzanne W. Jones. Philadelphia: University of Pennsylvania Press, 1991. 353–70.

Leighton, Angela. *Elizabeth Barrett Browning*. Brighton: Harvester, 1986.

McGann, Jerome J. Don Juan *in Context*. London: John Murray, 1976.

Mermin, Dorothy. *Elizabeth Barrett Browning: The Origins of a New Poetry*. Chicago: University of Chicago Press, 1989.

Mooney, Harry J. *Tolstoy's Epic Vision: A Study of* War and Peace *and* Anna Karenina. Tulsa: University of Tulsa, 1968.

Morson, Gary Saul. *Hidden in Plain View: Narrative and Creative Potentials in 'War and Peace'*. Stanford, CA: Stanford University Press, 1987.

Morson, Gary Saul. '*War and Peace*'. *The Cambridge Companion to Tolstoy*. Ed. Donna Tussing Orwin. Cambridge: Cambridge University Press, 2002. 65–79.

Newlyn, Lucy. *Paradise Lost and the Romantic Reader*. 1993. Oxford: Oxford University Press, 2004.

O'Neill, Michael. '"When this Warm Scribe My Hand": Writing and History in *Hyperion* and *The Fall of Hyperion*'. *Keats and History*. Ed. Nicholas Roe. Cambridge: Cambridge University Press, 1995. 143–64.

Opul'skaya, L. D. *Roman-èpopoeia L. N. Tolstogo 'Voina i mir'* (*Tolstoy's Epic-Novel, 'War and Peace'*). Moscow: Prosveshchenie, 1987.

Pattison, Robert. *Tennyson and Tradition*. Cambridge, MA: Harvard University Press, 1979.

Rajan, Tilottama. 'The Other Reading: Transactional Epic in Milton, Blake, and Wordsworth'. *Milton, the Metaphysicals, and Romanticism*. Ed. Lisa Low and Anthony John Harding. Cambridge: Cambridge University Press, 1994. 20–46.

Reeve, Clara. *The Progress of Romance and the History of Charoba, Queen of Aegypt*. 1785. New York: Facsimile Text Society, 1930.

Reiman, Donald H. '*Don Juan* in Epic Context'. *Studies in Romanticism* 16 (1977): 587–94.

Riede, David. 'Blake's *Milton*: On Membership of Church Paul'. *Re-membering Milton: Essays on the Texts and Tradition*. Ed. M. Nyquist and M. W. Ferguson. New York: 1988.

Sandy, Mark. '"To See as a God Sees": The Potential *Übermensch* in Keats's *Hyperion* Fragments'. *Romanticism* 4 (1998): 212–23.

Silbajoris, Rimvydas. *War and Peace: Tolstoy's Mirror of the World*. New York: Twayne, 1995.

Simmons, Ernest J. *Tolstoy*. London: Routledge and Kegan Paul, 1973.

Sperry, Stuart M. *Keats the Poet*. Princeton: Princeton University Press, 1973.

Stone, Marjorie. *Elizabeth Barrett Browning*. Basingstoke: Macmillian, 1995.

Taylor, Beverly. '"School-Miss Alfred" and "Materfamilias": Female Sexuality and Poetic Voice in *The Princess* and *Aurora Leigh*'. *Gender and Discourse in Victorian Art and Literature*. Ed. Antony H. Harrison and Beverly Taylor. Dekalb: Northern Illinois University Press, 1992. 5–29.

Thomson, Alastair. *The Poetry of Tennyson*. London: Routledge, 1986.

Tucker, Herbert F. '*Aurora Leigh*: Epic Solutions to Novel Ends'. *Famous Last Words: Changes in Gender and Narrative Closure*. Ed. Alison Booth. Charlottesville: University Press of Virginia, 1993. 62–83.

Tucker, Herbert F. *Tennyson and the Doom of Romanticism*. Cambridge, MA: Harvard University Press, 1988.

Wachtel, Andrew Baruch. *An Obsession with History: Russian Writers Confront the Past*. Stanford, CA: Stanford University Press, 1994.

Rosenberg, John D. *The Fall of Camelot: A Study of Tennyson's 'Idylls of the King'*. Cambridge, MA: Belknap Press, 1973.

Wilkie, Brian. *Romantic Poets and Epic Tradition*. Madison: University of Wisconsin Press, 1965.

Wittreich, Joseph Anthony. *Angel of the Apocalypse: Blake's Idea of Milton*. Madison: University of Wisconsin Press, 1975.

Wittreich, Joseph Anthony. *The Romantics on Milton: Formal Essays and Critical Asides*. Cleveland, OH: The Press of Case Western Reserve University, 1970.

Wordsworth, Jonathan. 'Revision as Making: *The Prelude* and Its Peers'. *Romantic Revisions*. Ed. Robert Brinkley and Keith Hanley. Cambridge: Cambridge University Press, 1992. 18–42.

The twentieth century

Adams, David. *Colonial Odysseys: Empire and Epic in the Modernist Novel*. Ithaca, NY: Cornell University Press, 2003.

Benstock, Bernard, ed. *Critical Essays on James Joyce's* Ulysses. Boston: G. K. Hall, 1989.

Bernstein, Michael André. *The Tale of the Tribe: Ezra Pound and Modern Epic*. Princeton: Princeton University Press, 1980.

Blamires, Harry. *The New Bloomsday Book: A Guide Through* Ulysses. 1966. London: Routledge, 1996. 3rd edn.

Buck, Claire. *H. D. and Freud: Bisexuality and a Feminine Discourse*. New York: Harvester Wheatsheaf, 1991.

Budgen, Frank. *James Joyce and the Making of 'Ulysses'*. 1934. Bloomington: Indiana University Press, 1960.

Cook, Albert. 'Rhythm and Person in the *Cantos*'. *New Approaches to Ezra Pound*. Ed. Eva Hesse. London: Faber, 1969. 349–64.

Davis, Gregson. '"With No Homeric Shadow": The Disavowal of Epic in Derek Walcott's *Omeros*'. *South Atlantic Quarterly* 96.2 (1997): 321–33.

Eliot, T. S. '"Ulysses", Order, and Myth'. *Selected Prose of T. S. Eliot*. Ed. Frank Kermode. London: Faber, 1975. 175–8.

Ellmann, Richard. *Ulysses on the Liffey*. London: Faber, 1974.

Farrell, Joseph. 'Walcott's *Omeros*: The Classical Epic in a Postmodern World'. *Epic Traditions in the Contemporary World: The Poetics of Community*. Ed. Margaret Beissinger, Jane Tylus and Susanne Wofford. Berkeley: University of California Press, 1999) 270–96.

Friedman, Susan Stanford. 'Creating a Women's Mythology: H. D.'s *Helen in Egypt*'. *Signets: Reading H. D.* Ed. Friedman and Rachel Blau DuPlessis. Madison: University of Wisconsin Press, 1990. 373–405.

Friedman, Susan Stanford. *Psyche Reborn: The Emergence of H. D.* Bloomington: University of Indiana Press, 1981.

Gilbert, Stuart. *James Joyce's 'Ulysses': A Study.* 1930. London: Faber, 1952.

Goldberg, S. L. *The Classical Temper: A Study of James Joyce's* Ulysses. London: Chatto and Windus, 1960.

Hamner, Robert D. *Epic of the Dispossessed: Derek Walcott's* Omeros. Columbia: University of Missouri Press, 1997.

Hayman, David. Ulysses: *The Mechanics of Meaning.* 1970. Madison: University of Wisconsin Press, 1982.

Jung, Carl. '*Ulysses*: A Monologue', *The Collected Works of Carl Jung.* Trans. R. F. C. Hull. Princeton, NJ: Princeton University Press, 1966. 109–32.

Kenner, Hugh. *The Invisible Poet: T. S. Eliot.* 1959. London: Methuen, 1965.

Kenner, Hugh. *The Pound Era.* London: Faber, 1972.

Korg, Jacob. *Winter Love: Ezra Pound and H. D.* Madison: University of Wisconsin Press, 2003.

Litz, A. Walton. *The Art of James Joyce.* London: Oxford University Press, 1961.

Moretti, Franco. *Modern Epic: The World System from Goethe to García Márquez.* London: Verso, 1996.

Read, Forrest. 'Pound, Joyce, and Flaubert'. *New Approaches to Ezra Pound: A Co-ordinated Investigation of Pound's Poetry and Ideas.* Ed. Eva Hesse. London: Faber, 1969. 125–44.

Schwarz, Daniel R. *Reading Joyce's* Ulysses. Basingstoke: Macmillan, 1987.

Spender, Steven. *Eliot.* London: Fontana, 1975.

Walcott, Derek. 'The Antilles: Fragments of Epic Memory'. *New Republic* 207 (28 December 1992): 26–32.

Wickens, G. Glen 'Hardy's Inconsistent Spirits and the Philosophic Form of *The Dynasts*'. *The Poetry of Thomas Hardy.* Ed. Patricia Clements and Juliet Grindle. London: Vision Press, 1980. 101–18.

Zoppi, Isabella Maria. '*Omeros*, David Walcott and the Contemporary Epic Poem'. *Callaloo* 22.2 (1999): 509–28.

Epic film

Arenas, Amelia. 'Popcorn and Circus: *Gladiator* and the Spectacle of Virtue'. *Arion* 9 (2001): 1–12.

Babington, Bruce and Peter William Evans. *Biblical Epics: Sacred Narrative in the Hollywood Cinema.* Manchester: Manchester University Press, 1993.

Ben-Hur: The Making of an Epic. Dir. and prod. Scott Benson. Turner Home Entertainment, 1993.

Carter, Everett. 'Cultural History Written with Lightning: The Significance of *The Birth of Nation* (1915)'. *Hollywood as Historian: American Film in Cultural Context.* Ed. Peter C. Rollins. Lexington: University of Kentucky Press, 1983. 9–19.

Cyrino, Monica S. '*Gladiator* and Contemporary American Society'. Gladiator: *Film and History.* Ed. Martin M. Winkler. Malden, MA: Blackwell, 2004. 124–49.

'D. W. Griffith, Producer of the World's Biggest Picture: Interview with D. W. Griffith'. *Focus on D. W. Griffith.* Ed. Harry M. Geduld. Englewood Cliffs, NJ: Prentice-Hall, 1971. 27–9.

Elley, Derek. *The Epic Film*. London: Routledge, 1984.

Green, Peter. 'Heroic Hype, New Style: Hollywood Pitted Against Homer'. *Arion* 12 (2004): 171–87.

Griffith, D. W. 'How I Made *The Birth of a Nation*'. *Focus on D. W. Griffith*. Ed. Harry M. Geduld. Englewood Cliffs, NJ: Prentice-Hall, 1971. 39–45.

Hayne, Donald, ed. *The Autobiography of Cecil B. DeMille*. Englewood Cliffs, NJ: Prentice Hall, 1959.

Higashi, Sumiko. *Cecil B. DeMille and American Culture: The Silent Era*. Berkeley: University of California Press, 1994.

Hoffman, Carl. 'The Evolution of a Gladiator: History, Representation, and Revision in *Spartacus*'. *Journal of American and Comparative Cultures* 23 (2000): 63–70.

Hunt, Leon. 'What Are Big Boys Made Of? *Spartacus, El Cid* and the Male Epic'. *You Tarzan: Masculinity, Movies and Men*. Ed. Pat Kirkham and Janet Thurmin. London: Lawrence and Wishart, 1993. 65–83.

King, Geoff. *Spectacular Narratives: Hollywood in the Age of the Blockbuster*. London: I. B. Tauris, 2000.

Landau, Diana, ed. *Gladiator: The Making of the Ridley Scott Epic*. New York: Newmarket, 2000.

Pomeroy, Arthur J. 'The Vision of a Fascist Rome in *Gladiator*'. Gladiator: *Film and History*. Ed. Martin M. Winkler. Malden, MA: Blackwell, 2004. 111–23.

Williams, Martin. *Griffith: First Artist of the Movies*. New York: Oxford University Press, 1980.

Winkler, Martin M. '*Gladiator* and the Traditions of Historical Cinema'. Gladiator: *Film and History*. Ed. Winkler. Malden, MA: Blackwell, 2004. 16–30.

Winkler, Martin M. '*Star Wars* and the Roman Empire'. *Classical Myth and Culture in the Cinema*. Ed. Winkler. Oxford: Oxford University Press, 2001. 272–90.

Wyke, Maria. *Projecting the Past: Ancient Rome, Cinema and History*. New York: Routledge, 1997.

Index

Printed in the United States
73249LV00001B/266